MIGHTIER THAN THE SWORD

Powerful Writing In The Legal Profession

Blue Jeans Press
A division of LEL Enterprises
P.O. Box 5628
Charlottesville, VA 22905
(804) 293-7360
(800) 662-9673 (orders only)

C. Edward Good

Blue Jeans Press
A division of LEL Enterprises
P.O. Box 5628
Charlottesville, VA 22905
(804) 293-7360
(800) 662-9673 (orders only)

ISBN 0-934961-03-4
MIGHTIER THAN THE SWORD
Powerful Writing in the Legal Profession

TABLE OF CONTENTS

PREFACE xvii

CHAPTER 1 1

THE GRAMMATICAL NATURE OF STYLE

Introduction 3

The Nature of a Bad Writing Style 4

The Nature of a Good Writing Style 5

The Right Kind of Grammar 6

CHAPTER 2 9

THE ENGLISH SENTENCE

Introduction 11

Some Preliminary Rules of Grammar 11

The Difference Between Transitive and Intransitive Verbs 12

The Nature of the Verb "To Be" 13

The Nature of Linking Verbs 13

Four Basic Sentence Structures 13

Average Sentence Length 15

The Not-Too-Many-Thoughts-Per-Sentence Rule 16

The Subject-Predicate = Main Message Rule 21

The Art of Inversion 23

The Art of Subordination 24

Avoiding Gaps 27

Between parts of a complex verb 28

Between a verb and its object 29

Between the parts of an infinitive: the split infinitive rule 30

Between "that" of a clause and the balance of the
clause = the "that-that" problem 31

Parallel Constructions 32

Tabulation 36

Summary 39

The Rules of Good Writing 39

CHAPTER 3 .... **41**

NOUNINESS —WRITE WITH VERBS

Introduction 43

Grammatical and Typographical Sentences 44

Exhibiting a Preference for Nouns 44

Groped-for Verbs and Other Bits of Noun Glue 45

The Wishy-Washy, Groped-for Verbs 46

Derivative Adjectives 47

Consequences of Nouniness 47

The Five Ways Verbs Work in the English Language 49

1. The Main Verb 49

2. The Infinitive Phrase 50

3. The Present Participial Phrase 50

4. The Past Participial Phrase 51

5. One-Word Adjectives 52

Engaging in a Conversion of Nouns to Verbs 53

Piles of Goo—Nouny Expressions of Auxiliary Verbs
and Adverbs 53

Write Like Willie Nelson 55

The Rules of Good Writing 58

CHAPTER 4 .... **59**

"TO BE" OR NOT "TO BE"

Introduction 61

Like and *Go*—The Next *Be's?* 62

The Meaning of the Verb *To Be* 64

The Rule: Use the Verb *To Be* Only When You Mean It 66

Expletive Deleted 68

Summary 69

The Rules of Good Writing 69

CHAPTER 5 .... **71**

COMPOUND PREPOSITIONS —
THE COMPOST OF OUR LANGUAGE

Introduction 73
Preposition and Prepositional Phrase Defined 73
The Importance of Prepositions 75
Compound Preposition Defined 75
Garbage 76
Imprecision 77
A List of Compound Prepositions 78
Some Common Prepositions You Might Have Forgotten 79
The Rules of Good Writing 81

CHAPTER 6 .... **83**

CLAUSINESS —WRITE WITH NOUNS (AND PHRASES)

Introduction 85
Clauses Defined 86
Clause Starters 87
    Subordinating Conjunctions 87
    Relative Pronouns 88
    Other Clause Starters 89
Three Kinds of Clauses 90
    The Noun Clause 90
    The Adjective Clause 93
    That and Which Clauses 93
    The Adverb Clause 98
The Art of Clause-Cutting 99
Cutting Noun Clauses 100
    Noun Clause-Cutting Trick #1 102
    A Special Note on the Gerund Approach 104
    Noun Clause-Cutting Trick #2 105
Writing as Good Writers Write 105
Cutting Adjective and Adverb Clauses 106
    Cut Clause Down to Adjective 107

Cut Clause Down to Adverb 107
Cut Clause Down to Prepositional Phrase 107
Cut Clause Down to Verbal Phrase 107
Cut Clause Down to Adjective Appositive 108
Cut Clause Down to Noun Appositive 109
Cut Clause Down to Absolute 109
Cut Clause Down to Truncated Adverb Clause 109
That-Dropping 110
Summary 111
Three Strange Clause Myths 111
Myth: Do Not Begin a Sentence with "Because" 112
Myth: "Since" Never Means "Because" 112
Myth: "While" Never Means "Although" 113
The Rules of Good Writing 113
CHAPTER 7 115

THE GREAT DEBATE—ACTIVE VS. PASSIVE VOICE

Introduction 117
Verbs: Transitive or Intransitive 118
Voice of Transitive Verbs 121
The Active Voice 121
The Passive Voice 121
Forming the Passive Voice: *To Be* + Past Participle 122
Three Strikes Against the Passive Voice 124
When the Passive Voice *Is Preferred* 126

   1. When you are generalizing and you want to avoid using *one*
     as the subject of too many sentences. 126

   2. When the identity of the actor is the *punch* of the sentence
     and you want to place it at the end. 126

   3. When the identity of the actor is irrelevant and you simply
     want to omit it. 127

   4. When the identity of the actor is unknown. 127

   5. When you want to hide the identity of the actor. 127

   6. When you want to avoid sexist writing but also want to avoid
     those horrible s(he)'s, he/she's, him/her's, and his/her's. 127

7. When the passive voice sounds better. 128

8. When the recipient of the action is the subject matter of the rest of the paragraph. 128

The Rules of Good Writing 128

CHAPTER 8 .... **131**

LOSING WEIGHT—MISCELLANEOUS MATTERS

Introduction 133

Long Words 133

Favoring Concrete Words over Abstract Words 135

Modification 136

The Noun Modifier Proliferation Problem 137

Do Not Tie Yourself Up In *Not's* 137

The Rules of Good Writing 138

CHAPTER 9 .... **139**

HIS/HERMAPHRODISM

Introduction 141

Agreement in Number—Agreement in Gender 141

The Problem 143

The Plural Antecedent Solution 143

The Passive Voice Solution 143

The Second-Person Pronoun Solution 144

The Pick-a-Pronoun Solution 144

The Rules of Good Writing 144

CHAPTER 10 .... **147**

SOME PARTING SHOTS ON MATTERS OF STYLE

The Rules of Good Writing 149

1. Use an average of 25 words per sentence.

2. Avoid putting too many messages in a single sentence.

3. Put most of your messages at the subject-predicate position.

4. For variety or emphasis, invert your sentences.

5. Use the art of subordination to smooth out choppiness.

6. Avoid disrupting your sentences with thought-stopping gaps.

7. Watch out for the rule of parallel construction.

8. Tabulate particularly complex information.

9. Hammer home your point with the powerful, versatile verb.

10. Use the verb *to be* only when you mean it.

11. Get rid of compound prepositions.

12. Cut adjective, adverb, and noun clauses to other structures satisfying the same functions.

13. Prefer the active voice, but use the passive to satisfy certain objectives concerning the identity or placement of the actor or the recipient.

14. Favor short words over long, fancy words.

15. Use concrete words to paint vivid images in your reader's mind.

16. Use modification to trim down the fat in your language.

17. Use phrases to smooth out the choppy noun-noun modifier.

18. Do not use too many negative expressions.

19. Be fair and nonsexist, but don't be stupid.

CHAPTER 11 . . . . **153**
CONTENT OF LEGAL WRITING

Introduction 155

The Purpose of a Memorandum of Law 157

Various Formats 158

The Statement of Facts 160

Sample Fact Pattern 161

Questions Presented 164

The Conclusion 165

The Discussion of Authority 166

Organizational Devices 168

Introduction 174

Paragraphing and Topic Sentences 176

Legislative or Regulatory Presentations 179

Case Discussions 181
Other Legal Presentations 184
Proper Quotations 185
Transitions 190
Application of Law to Facts 192
Legal Comparisons 193
Reaching and Stating the Final Result 194
Conclusion 196

CHAPTER 12 197

A BIG, HEAVY CASEBOOK

Introduction 199
The Statute 199
28 U.S.C. § 1359 (1982) 199
The Cases 199
McSparran v. Weist, 402 F.2d 867 (3d Cir. 1968), *cert.
denied*, 395 U.S. 903 (1969) 199
Bishop v. Hendricks, 495 F.2d 289 (4th Cir.), *cert.
denied*, 419 U.S. 1056 (1974) 208
Hackney v. Newman Memorial Hospital, Inc., 621
F.2d 1069 (10th Cir.), *cert. denied*, 449 U.S. 982 (1980) 211
*Bianca v. Parke-Davis Pharmaceutical Division of
Warner-Lambert Co.*, 723 F.2d 392 (5th Cir. 1984) 213
Joyce v. Siegel, 429 F.2d 128 (3d Cir. 1970) 220

CHAPTER 13 227

SAMPLE MEMORANDUM OF LAW

Introduction 229
Sample Memorandum of Law 229

INDEX 241

Beneath the rule of men entirely great
The pen is mightier than the sword.

—Edward George Bulwer-Lytton

Richelieu, Act II, scene ii

About the Author

C. Edward Good received his law degree from the University of Virginia in 1971. For five years, he taught legal writing to law students at the University of Virginia and to paralegal students at the Georgetown University Legal Assistant Program. Mr. Good was also selected to serve the Supreme Court of the United States and the Federal Judicial Center as a Tom C. Clark Judicial Fellow in 1977-78. Since 1980, he has presented seminars on persuasive writing to hundreds of practicing attorneys in major cities across the country. Other than writing this book, his most ambitious and professionally rewarding project has been creating and conducting training programs in effective writing for 400 attorneys in the Associate Chief Counsel's Office of the Internal Revenue Service in Washington, D.C.—a project currently underway as this book goes to press.

Other legal departments sponsoring Mr. Good's seminars include the General Counsel's Office of the Washington Gas Light Company, the Judge Advocate General of the Department of the Navy, the Department of Justice, the New York Regional Office of the Securities & Exchange Commission, the General Counsel's Office of the Securities & Exchange Commission in Washington, D.C., the Commodity Futures Trading Commission, and many others.

To all the participants in these courses, Mr. Good expresses his gratitude, for they were the ones who taught the teacher most everything he knows.

Dedication

For my junior high school English teachers,
Mary Frances Hazelman and Helen V. Hamrick,
whose dedication to our language
and strict insistence on correct expression
enriched the lives of thousands of children
in Greensboro, North Carolina.

Preface

Omne tulit punctum qui miscuit utile dulci,
Lectorem delectando pariterque monendo.

He has gained every point who has mixed practicality with pleasure, by delighting the reader at the same time as instructing him.

—Horace

Latina Sententia in libri capite elegantissima est.

A Latin quotation at the chapter's front is cool.

—Good

Preface

Must we be so stuffy?

The New York Court of Appeals doesn't think so and blasted an attorney who was too big in his brief:

> [T]his case presents an appropriate opportunity to comment on a matter that concerns us greatly, namely, the quality, length and content of briefs presented to this court. Although this is an extreme example, unfortunately it is not always the rare case in which we receive poorly written and excessively long briefs, replete with burdensome, irrelevant, and immaterial matter. Although counsel candidly admits that his 284-page brief is "unusually long", his claim that it is "meticulously structured, thoroughly documented, exhaustively researched, carefully analyzed and comprehensively presented" seems too self-congratulatory. His argument wanders aimlessly through myriad irrelevant matters . . . pausing only briefly to discuss the issues raised by this appeal. The brief pursues, in seemingly endless fashion, matters not properly before this court for the simple reason that they were not raised below.

Slater v. Gallman, 38 N.Y.2d 1, 4, 339 N.E. 863, 864, 377 N.Y.S.2d 448, 450 (1975). Do you suppose the attorney in *Slater* gave a copy of the opinion to the client? Stapled, perhaps, to the invoice "for services rendered"? In a frame suitable for hanging? Somehow I doubt it.

Why is it, in our profession, that many practitioners think that more is better, that fancy words have more force than simple words, and that long-winded sentences impress? In law school, our professors taught us to "think like a lawyer." They taught us to delve into the mysteries of case law. They taught us to analogize the favorable authority and to "distinguish away" the unfavorable. They taught us the importance of "policy" in judicial decision-making. They instilled in us the knack of unraveling a statute or a regulation. They, and their memorable exams, tested our ability to "spot the issues."

But did they teach us to write like lawyers? Did any law professor ever sit down with us to encourage or teach or beg or force us to say:

> The characterization of this amount as ordinary income is to effectuate the principle that, with respect to the characterization of income attributable to a discharge of indebtedness, a taxpayer filing the consent pursuant to section 108 to adjust basis pursuant to section 1017 should be in no better or worse position having filed the consent than it would have been had it actually recognized the income in the year such discharge occurred.

Law professors did a lot to us, no doubt. But they emphatically did not teach us to write that way. At least they didn't mean to. At least I hope they didn't mean to.

Where did we learn such stuff?

Easy. We learned it from judges, legislators, regulators, headnote writers, treatise writers, and editors for *C.J.S., A.L.R.,* and *Am. Jur. 2d.* We learned to spew out poorly written judicial fluff, endless legislative goo, brow-wrinkling regulatory ooze, and mounds of words posing as sentences. We learned to build those weighty sentences, stretching on forever, with stuffy abstractions, piles of pillowy nouns, and imprecise compound prepositions. We learned to prefer the passive voice. We learned to proliferate clauses. We learned to write like the stuff we read. We learned, in short, to break every rule of style in the book.

There is a much better way.

The style of traditional legal writing is fairly predictable. Review some legal writing in a law firm in Charlotte, and it likely will resemble that found in a trial brief in Butte. Study an opinion of a state intermediate appellate court in Wichita, and you will find the same grammatical structures used by an administrative law judge in Washington. Quite naturally, when lawyers tackle the same subject matter—highly abstract rules of law—they produce written material that looks and sounds pretty much the same.

Many people in the profession believe this typical style cries out for change. Others, no doubt, will cling to traditional ways of expression. Those fearful of change might feel threatened. Writing simply, they think, is the same as thinking simply. Legal subject matter is complex, they point out. Legal thinking is abstract. Legal doctrines are multifaceted. Therefore, writing about the stuff of the law must be complex, abstract, multifaceted—in short, *hard*. If the message is tough, so too must be its medium.

Exactly the reverse is true. As information becomes more complex, writers should take greater care to present it in a simple way. If readers must strain to figure out highly complex sentences, replete with clauses and clauses within clauses, they will have little mental energy left over to deal with the message itself. Many of the great legal writers of our time knew this to be true. The Blacks, Jacksons, Traynors, and Cardozos all favored simple styles. As a result, they were able to grab their readers' attention and lead them through the most difficult legal analysis. If at all, their readers would pause only to think about substance, not to fight their way through the fog of legalistic style.

The grammatical causes of this fog are easy to identify. Certain grammatical constructions actually hinder communication. Certain types of words get in the way of the message. Much professional jargon seeks to exclude the outsider. Styles handed down from hundreds of years ago cloud comprehension. Once legal writers understand these constructions and see how they do indeed cloud communication—and ultimately lose arguments—they can, with practice, cut through the fog and develop instead a style that wins.

Some features of legal style are empirical. The number of words a writer uses, for example, is empirical. The number of sentences a writer uses is empirical. Dividing words by sentences yields an average sentence length, which is empirical. Study after study has shown that as average sentence length goes up, reader comprehension goes down. Perhaps that's why Justice Black used sentences averaging only 26 words.

Other features are also empirical. Stylists like Henry Fowler, William Strunk, and E.B. White knew the power of the short word. Fowler analyzed the writing in *Paradise Lost*, *The Idylls of the King*, and *The Bible* by calculating the percentage of monosyllabic words and finding in various passages 52 out of 56 and 89 out of 101. H. Fowler, *Modern English Usage* 344 (2d ed. 1965). Never one to mince his own words, Fowler took aim at the pedant and blasted away: "Those who run to long words are mainly the unskillful and tasteless; they confuse pomposity with dignity, flaccidity with ease, and bulk with force." *Id.* at 342. In a similar vein, Strunk & White advised: "Avoid the elaborate, the pretentious, the coy, and the cute. Do not be tempted by a twenty-dollar word when there is a ten-center handy, ready and able. Anglo-Saxon is a livelier tongue than Latin, so use Anglo-Saxon words." W. Strunk & E. White, *The Elements of Style* 76-77 (3d ed. 1979). Perhaps that's why 66 percent of the words used by Justices Black and Cardozo are monosyllabic.

Other features of a legalistic style can be identified and analyzed. The main problems include writing with gaps, putting crucial information at subordinate parts of sentences, failing to use parallelism as a strategy (as I am now doing), using derivative nouns and adjectives to convey the meaning of verbs, preferring clauses over phrases, confusing restrictive and nonrestrictive clauses, misusing the verb *to be*, overusing the passive voice, and succumbing to his/hermaphrodism. His/her what? Nonsexist writing. More about that later.

Working in classes and in individual sessions with hundreds of attorneys, law students, and paralegals, I have seen first hand the vast improvements writers can make in their writing styles. Initially my students, especially the practicing attorneys, are skeptical. They write like everyone else. How can there be a better way, they wonder. We've done it like this for hundreds of years, they explain with satisfaction. Besides, they think, style is just a matter of opinion. No one can prove that one way of writing is necessarily better than another.

But then the light turns on. They begin to look at their writing in a new way. They learn to identify the predictable features of legal styles. They begin to learn the grammatical names of those features. They start to think, believe it or not, about phrasing information with present participles and infinitives instead of derivative nouns. They slowly begin to see the connection between long-forgotten rules of grammar and the very real and current problem of winning a case.

All you need to improve your style dramatically is a clear understanding of some grammatical tricks that heighten the clarity of expression. Learning these tricks will not be easy. At times you will be frustrated, thinking you could forget about grammar after escaping from high school. Making the new way of writing a part of you—a part of your professional trademark—will require dedication and plain hard work. Daily practice and careful thought will mark your effort. But once you realize you can jump all over and trounce the competition by writing clearly, simply, and forcefully, you will gladly abandon the traditional way of writing about the law and adopt instead a style that is simple, direct, forceful, and, as a result, effective.

Way back when, way back when you were young, your parents taught you that you are what you eat. Now you're big. Now you're in the legal profession. Now, as you read this book, you'll learn a completely different but equally important truth:

As a lawyer, you are what you write.

Chapter 1

The Grammatical Nature of Style

Mediocribus esse poetis
Non homines, non di, non concessere columnae.

Not gods, nor men, nor even booksellers have put up with poets' being second-rate.

—Horace

Chapter 1

The Grammatical Nature of Style

Introduction

What's so good about good writing? Put the other way: what's so bad about bad writing? Is it really possible to analyze a person's writing, give it an *A*, and explain why it's superior to another person's writing? Can one review a paper, give it a *C*, and rationally describe its deficiencies?

These questions nagged at me when I took over the legal writing program at the University of Virginia School of Law in 1975. I knew that law students would not sit back, smile, and accept their *B's* and *C's* equably. Not without a fight. Not without some explanation showing them why their writing came up short of the standard set by their colleagues.

I tried at first using those conclusory labels we were all familiar with in college. I could always put little helpful messages in the margins of the students' papers. I could point out that passages were "awkward." Or, more helpfully, I could conclude that a particular sentence was "wordy." Maybe I could even guide them away from "legalese." Predictably, these efforts failed.

I was faced with the task of figuring out exactly what was bad about bad legal writing and good about good legal writing. While at Virginia, I slowly developed a list of attributes that characterized the good and the bad. After five years at Virginia, I began my own consulting firm to provide training programs for lawyers and legal support staff in the art of writing clearly and persuasively. I felt I knew why lawyers write the way they do and how to help them change.

After I taught persuasive writing by lecturing to attorneys in various parts of the country, several federal agencies commissioned me to present in-house training programs and to work individually with members of their legal staffs. The most ambitious of these efforts was launched by the Associate Chief Counsel's Office of the Internal Revenue Service. The IRS commissioned a series of 12 courses over three years to train nearly 400 attorneys in the art of persuasive writing. The program required me to review writing samples, write analyses of any problems detected, and meet with each person for a one-on-one feedback conference.

Needless to say, the labels of "wordy" or "awkward" wouldn't help these attorneys. Instead, I had to figure out exactly what, if anything, was wrong with each paper submitted, articulate those problems, and attempt to rewrite the criticized passages. The experience gave me the chance to test my own theories of clear expression as well as those of Fowler, Strunk, White, and other experts. Also, the experience allowed me to see whether attorneys who had written in a particular way for years could change or, indeed, would want to change the way they write. Of most importance, the experience enabled me to find out if a grammatical analysis of traditional legal style might be the most effective way of teaching clear expression.

The positive response by the IRS attorneys convinced me that grammatical theories of style do work. I learned that lawyers are open to change. They do want to write clearly. They emphatically want to win cases and arguments. I found that most attorneys, like most professionals everywhere, have forgotten rules of grammar, probably because those rules as taught to us in school were eminently forgettable. The attorneys did not *break* grammatical rules. They were not *un*grammatical. Instead, like most people, they never realized the close connection between rules of grammar and rules of style.

That's what you can expect in this book—a careful and, I hope, informative and, I hope, entertaining discussion of the *grammar* that makes good writing good and bad writing bad.

The Nature of a Bad Writing Style

What does bad legal writing look like? Here's some:

> The original, duplicate and triplicate copies of the enclosed agreement should be signed and dated, as indicated, with the corporate name, followed by the signature of an authorized corporate officer or an authorized representative. After it has been executed in triplicate, the original and copies of this agreement must be returned to this office within thirty days. If the signed original and copies of the agreement are not received by this office within thirty days, it will be assumed that you no

longer desire to enter into a closing agreement and our files with respect to this matter will be closed without further action.

Now look at this:

Please sign and date the original and the two copies of the enclosed agreement. You should use the corporate name and follow it with the signature of an authorized corporate officer or authorized representative. After signing the agreement and the copies, please return them to this office within thirty days. If we do not receive them within that time, we will assume that you no longer want to enter into a closing agreement and, accordingly, will close our files on this matter without further action.

What's the difference? Did the writer just rewrite the passage to make it sound simpler and more direct? Yes, but how? The writer recognized immediately that the original passage appeared exclusively in the passive voice. In the rewritten passage, the writer used the active voice. The writer also wanted to avoid words like *triplicate* and *execute* and to use instead simpler words like *two copies* and *sign*. The writer reduced the passage from 104 words to 85 words. The average sentence length dropped from 35 to 21. The number of polysyllabic words dropped from 44 to 31. Finally, the writer trashed the compound preposition *with respect to* and substituted the simple preposition *on*.

The Nature of a Good Writing Style

Here's what Mr. Justice Black had to say about the First Amendment:

Since the earliest days philosophers have dreamed of a country where the mind and spirit of man would be free; where there would be no limits to inquiry; where men would be free to explore the unknown and to challenge the most deeply rooted beliefs and principles. Our First Amendment was a bold effort to adopt this principle—to establish a country with no legal restrictions of any kind upon the subjects people could investigate, discuss and deny. The Framers knew, better perhaps than we do today, the risks they were taking. They knew that free speech might be the friend of change and revolution. But they also knew that it is always the deadliest enemy of tyranny. With this knowledge they still believed that the ultimate happiness and security of a nation lies in its ability to explore, to

> change, to grow and ceaselessly to adapt itself to a new
> knowledge born of inquiry free from any kind of governmental
> control over the mind and spirit of man. Loyalty comes from
> love of good government, not fear of a bad one.

Black, *The Bill of Rights*, 35 N.Y.U. L. Rev. 865, 880-81 (1960).

Let's give Mr. Justice Black an *A* for the following reasons: (1) he used 182 words in seven sentences, which yields an average sentence length of 26 words per sentence; (2) he used 126 monosyllabic words, a ratio of 66 percent; (3) he used zero compound prepositions; (4) he used zero passive voice constructions; (5) he used only three *-ion* words; (6) he used zero *which* clauses; (7) he used only three *that* clauses; (8) he separated the subject from the verb in only two of the seven sentences; and (9) he used 14 parallel constructions.

By grammatically analyzing Mr. Justice Black's style, we can explain our decision to award an *A*. Grammar, therefore, is not some set of obscure rules leering over your shoulder, like your grammar teacher of yore, poised to pounce when you make the slightest mistake. Grammar is not a source of dread. Instead, the vast array of grammatical structures is your arsenal of weapons. Learn them—as you will in this book—and you can make grammar work for you. You can use grammar to spot the weaknesses in your current style and figure out ways to improve it.

The Right Kind of Grammar

At this stage in my *Mightier than the Sword Seminar*, I usually warn the lawyer-students:

> Get ready. We are about to take a trip down bad-memory lane.
> You are about to be bombarded with long-forgotten rules of
> grammar. Fear not, however, for I will assume your knowledge
> of grammar is not broad and deep, but thin and shallow.

My assumption is usually correct. Though the vast majority of attorneys and other professionals write grammatically, they do not *think* in grammatical terms. By that I mean this: lawyers and others who write for a living have a natural feel for the language. They have grown up in grammatical households or overcome their ungrammatical upbringings by dedicated hard work. They do not make many grammatical mistakes. If they hear or see a grammatical mistake, they can identify it as such.

But they might have a little trouble explaining the precise nature of the mistake.

The question naturally arises: must lawyers become expert grammarians before they can possibly be excellent writers? The answer is an emphatic "no." Next question: can lawyers identify their problems without referring to grammar at all? A more emphatic "no." We seek, instead, a middle ground. To become a better legal writer, you must know enough grammar and the right kind of grammar.

"The right kind of grammar?" you ask.

For the past 17 years, I have studied legal writing from a unique perspective. I have been asked by hundreds of law students, paralegal students, and lawyers to explain what is wrong with their writing. I have tried to explain style in terms of style and found such an approach totally fruitless. When I shifted my focus and explained style in terms of grammar, I saw the students respond. Rules of grammar, after all, are like rules of law. Cite authority, analyze it, apply it to the given situation, and reach a conclusion.

Sound familiar? Sure. It's what you do every day.

"But what grammar?" you ask. "I know all about subject-verb agreement. I never confuse the case of pronouns. And never would I split an infinitive. Just exactly what do you mean 'the right kind of grammar'?"

As mentioned in the Preface to this book, the style of legal writing is predictable. Certain structures characterize legal writing as typical legal writing. When those structures are analyzed grammatically, the writer can begin to see why they do not do the job as effectively as others. These structures of typical legal writing involve certain basic but often complicated rules of grammar.

The *right kind of grammar* includes those rules that keep popping up when one analyzes typical legal writing. For example, because legal writers tend to prefer the passive voice, the *right kind of grammar* includes an extensive discussion of transitive and intransitive verbs and the differences between the active voice and the passive voice. Because legal writers favor tangles of clauses, the *right kind of grammar* includes a careful study of adjective, adverb, and noun clauses. Because legal writers adore stuffy noun forms—a condition known as *nouniness*—the *right kind of grammar* will explore derivative nouns and derivative adjectives and instruct you in the proper use of verb forms.

Looked at the other way, plenty of rules of grammar just don't even come up when analyzing typical legal writing. For example, legal writing rarely displays problems of subject-verb agreement. Thus, noticeably absent from the *right kind of grammar* is any discussion whatsoever of plural subjects and plural verbs.

This book seeks to teach you the grammatical principles that make good writing good and bad writing bad. By learning to recognize these grammatical attributes of clear writing, you will learn to use them to increase your power as a writer, to influence other people through the written word, and perhaps even to think in a different and clearer way.

At a minimum you will learn why some writers get an *A* and most writers don't.

Chapter 2

The English Sentence

Dixeris egregie notum si callida verbum
Reddiderit iunctura novum.

You will have written exceptionally well if, by skillful
arrangement of your words, you have made an ordinary
one seem original.

—Horace

Chapter 2

The English Sentence

Introduction

We begin our search for clarity in style by looking carefully at the English sentence. Not surprisingly, if you have trouble writing, chances are good you are breaking some very basic rules on constructing effective sentences. Understanding these basic rules and seeing what happens when you break them in legal writing are indispensable first steps along the road to clarity.

That road begins by backing up to grade school and studying the four basic structures of English sentences. With those structures firmly in mind, you will then see the important relationship between sentence structure and *sentence length*. The *not-too-many-thoughts-per-sentence rule*, the most frequently violated in all of legal writing, will make a great deal of sense. A basic rule—*the subject-predicate = main message rule*—will guide the ordinary structure of your sentences. For variety and emphasis, you will learn the *art of inversion*. To avoid choppiness, you will learn the *art of subordination*. You will appreciate the *rule against gaps* and see how and why traditional legal writers routinely ignore it. You will recall the *grammatical rule of parallelism* and see how the best writers use the rule to their advantage. You will see how to use *tabulation* to handle particularly complex information.

Having mastered the intricacies of effective sentence-building, you will then be ready to learn the ways of choosing the right word, working powerfully with verbs, using nouns effectively, and paring it all down into a nice, tight package.

Some Preliminary Rules of Grammar

Before we get to the four basic ways you can build the English sentence, you must first recall three bits of grammar: (1) the difference between *transitive* and *intransitive verbs*, (2) the nature of the verb *to be*, and (3) the nature of *linking verbs*. Though we'll return to the effective use of verbs throughout this book, for now you should ponder their nature and the basic ways they work in our language.

The Difference Between Transitive and Intransitive Verbs

> <u>Transitive Verb</u>: A transitive verb is an action verb that has a direct object. An action verb is transitive if it can be followed immediately by a noun that receives the action from the verb. Thus: *The court decided the case.* The verb *decided* is transitive because it is capable of having a noun immediately follow it. The noun, the direct object, is *the case*, which receives the action of the verb *decided*.

> <u>Intransitive Verb</u>: An intransitive verb, on the other hand, is not followed immediately by a noun. Indeed, an intransitive verb yearns not for a noun but for an adverb. Thus: *The employee complied with the personnel policy.* The verb *complied* is intransitive because it cannot be followed immediately by a noun. It can have no direct object at all.

You can test the *transitiveness* of a verb by answering this question: *Can I [verb] something or somebody?* Plug in the verb and answer the question. If the answer is "yes," the verb is transitive. If the answer is "no," the verb is intransitive. Apply the test to the two verbs above. Can I *decide* something? Yes, I can decide a case or decide an issue. *Decide* is transitive. Can I *comply* something? No. I can only comply *with* something. *Comply* is intransitive.

Many people incorrectly think that all action verbs are transitive verbs. Well, some are and some aren't. Some action verbs have dual meanings, a transitive one and an intransitive one. Take the action verb *to walk*, for example. Test it. Can I *walk* something or somebody? Ordinarily not. I don't walk *something* [noun]. Instead, I walk *where* [adverb], *how* [adverb], *why* [adverb], or *when* [adverb]. Thus, I walk *to the store* [adverbial prepositional phrase]. I walk *quickly* [adverb]. I walk *for exercise* [adverbial prepositional phrase]. Or I walk *during the evening* [adverbial prepositional phrase]. As a rule, I do not walk *something* or *somebody*. The verb *to walk*, therefore, is intransitive. If I take my dog along, however, the verb becomes transitive. Thus, I walk *my dog* to the store. Now I've got the direct object *dog* receiving the action of the transitive verb *walk*.

Later, we will return to study transitive verbs at some length when we examine the crucial rules governing the active and passive voice.

The Nature of the Verb "To Be"

Though there are a few exceptions, as a rule the verb *to be* will be followed either by an adjective (predicate adjective) or a noun (predicate nominative or subject complement). Thus: *The issues are pertinent to our case. Pertinent* is the predicate adjective following the verb *are* and describing the subject of the sentence *issues*. Or: *The decision was a landmark case in the area of civil rights. Case* is the predicate nominative (also called the *subject complement*) following the verb *was* and restating or defining the subject of the sentence *decision.*

The Nature of Linking Verbs

In addition to transitive verbs, intransitive verbs, and the verb *to be*, the English language includes another verb form, the linking verb. A linking verb is really a surrogate for the verb *to be*. It "links" the subject of the sentence to an *adjective* in the predicate position, that is, following the verb.

The most common linking verbs include the following: *seem, appear, feel,* and *look*. Thus: *He seems ill. He appears quick. He feels bad. He looks defeated.*

Please note that these verbs link the subjects of sentences to adjectives, not adverbs. Indeed, if you follow a linking verb with an adverb, you will say some rather weird things because the adverb must modify the verb: *He feels badly* means his tactile ability is deficient. Also, a linking verb, particularly in England, might link the subject to a noun: *He seems an honest man.*

Four Basic Sentence Structures

Every English sentence must have a grammatical subject (a noun or noun form) and a conjugated verb. The conjugated verb might also be called the *predicate verb*. A conjugated verb can form a sentence—an independent clause. It can also form a dependent clause. (For simplicity, I am going to refer to the conjugated verb as the *main verb*, whether it appears in an independent clause or a dependent clause.) Each sentence will have, at least, one grammatical subject and one main verb.

Thus, right off the bat, you can see two "biggies" in the typical sentence: the subject and the main verb. Sentences have a third "biggie," however. The third part will be determined by the main verb. If the main verb is transitive, the third part of the sentence will be the direct object—if the sentence appears in the active voice. However, if the sentence appears in the passive voice, the third part might be a prepositional phrase revealing the actor. (We'll study the *voice* of transitive verbs in great detail in Chapter 7.) If the main verb is intransitive, the third part typically will be an adverb or adverbial phrase. If the main verb is the verb *to be*, the third part will be a predicate adjective or a predicate nominative. And, finally, if the main verb is a linking verb, the third part will be a predicate adjective. Thus, the four basic structures of the English sentence look like this:

1. Subject (actor) + Transitive Verb (active) + Direct Object (recipient)
   Example: The school board punished the student.

   Subject (recipient) + Transitive Verb (passive) + Phrase (actor)
   Example: The student was punished by the school board.

2. Subject + Intransitive Verb + Adverb
   Example: Thereafter, the student complied with the policy.

3. Subject + To Be + Predicate Adjective
   Example: At first, the student was arrogant.

   Subject + To Be + Predicate Nominative
   Example: The student was the first offender of the new regulations.

4. Subject + Linking Verb + Predicate Adjective
   Example: When caught, the student felt terrible.

The English sentence, therefore, has three milestones: the subject, the main verb, and the other stuff. Readers, even legal readers, anticipate this three-part structure. They expect to find these three parts of the sentence. They know to look for them. They want them to be the most important parts of the sentence. They know that other parts of the sentence are less important or *subordinate*. Your readers expect these messages:

interrogative pronouns that describe grammatical places in a sentence

1. Who or What (subject) Does What (transitive verb)
   To What or To Whom (direct object)

   Who or What (subject) *Was Done To* (transitive verb in passive voice) By What or By Whom (actor)

2. Who or What (subject) Does What (intransitive verb) How or Where or
   When or Why (adverb)

3. Who or What (subject) *Is* (verb *to be*) Who or What (predicate nominative)

   Who or What (subject) *Is* (verb *to be*) What Kind or What Character
   or What Size, etc. (predicate adjective)

4. Who or What (subject) *Seems* or *Feels* (linking verb) What Kind or What
   Character or What Size, etc. (predicate adjective)

One-Two-Three. That's the basic, three-part structure of the
English sentence. One-Two-Three. That's the message your readers
expect to hear. And, as we'll soon see, this basic, three-part structure
dictates many rules of style and provides several tests you may use to
measure the quality of your writing.

Average Sentence Length

If stylists agree on one thing, they agree on a rather basic rule: the
average sentence length of effective writing will not exceed 30 words
per sentence. The ideal average, for some unknown reason, is 25 words
per sentence.

Recall the passage by Mr. Justice Black in Chapter 1 exploring the
nature of the First Amendment. For your convenience, here it is again:

> Since the earliest days philosophers have dreamed of a
> country where the mind and spirit of man would be free; where
> there would be no limits to inquiry; where men would be free
> to explore the unknown and to challenge the most deeply rooted
> beliefs and principles. Our First Amendment was a bold effort
> to adopt this principle—to establish a country with no legal
> restrictions of any kind upon the subjects people could inves-
> tigate, discuss and deny. The Framers knew, better perhaps
> than we do today, the risks they were taking. They knew that
> free speech might be the friend of change and revolution. But
> they also knew that it is always the deadliest enemy of tyranny.
> With this knowledge they still believed that the ultimate happi-
> ness and security of a nation lies in its ability to explore, to
> change, to grow and ceaselessly to adapt itself to a new
> knowledge born of inquiry free from any kind of governmental
> control over the mind and spirit of man. Loyalty comes from
> love of good government, not fear of a bad one.

[handwritten annotations: "no gap between subject + verb"; "○ is parallelism"; "first gap but okay, b/c 1 adverb"; "universal 2. of how and why are discussed here"]

The passage contains seven sentences having the following number of words: 47, 31, 14, 13, 13, 51, and 13. The total is 182. The average is 26. Did Mr. Justice Black know what he was doing? Or did he just write that way? Believe me. He knew exactly what he was doing. He knew the power of variety and varied his sentence length from a low of 13 to a high of 51. He knew the emphasis of isolation and surrounded his long sentences with short ones. He knew the value of repetition and willingly used the same verb (*knew*) as the main verb of three consecutive sentences. (I just copied him and used the same verb in four consecutive sentences.) When building long sentences, the first and the sixth, he understood the need for an easily recognized structure and chose repetitive parallel forms to help the reader stay on track.

In short, he broke his information down into digestible bites, spoon-feeding his reader one bite at a time. He avoided the traditional legalistic style of cramming the whole loaf down the reader's throat all at once.

You too should break down your information. You too should go right now to your files and fish out a sample of your writing. You too should get out your abacus or solar-powered calculator and tally the total of your words. You too should count the total number of your sentences. Then divide words by sentences to produce an average sentence length. If it's over thirty, you're in big trouble. You suffer from Long-Winded Sentence Syndrome, a malady afflicting 94.62 percent of the entire legal profession.

The causes are two. Either you cram too many messages into one sentence or you cram too many words into one message. The first cause is easy to cure. The second—wordiness—signifies a host of problems, which will occupy us for much of the remainder of this book.

Let's deal with the easily curable problem: trying to stuff a two-week vacation in an overnight bag. I'll abandon that metaphor now—or I'll never get out of it—and state the rule another way.

✱ → The Not-Too-Many-Thoughts-Per-Sentence Rule

Everyone reading this book has written, at one time in their lives, a never-ending sentence. You know the kind. Somehow you get started with an idea, but suddenly that idea has all sorts of qualifications, which seem to fit only within the same sentence. So, what the heck, why not

can't answer too many questions in one sentence; remember that each sentence may have more than one when, more than one who, etc. Simple sentences only have one of each just continue. The reader can read it several times and figure it out. Besides, we think, expressing ourselves with these long sentences is cool. At least they'll demand a higher fee. Or impress our date. Or our professor.

What they demand is our collective scorn. Our profession should be rid of such fluff. The Long-Winded Sentence Syndrome has been stuffing up our professional language for hundreds of years. We haven't won many friends. And, truth be known, we haven't won any Pulitzer Prizes either.

I can best demonstrate the rule by showing its flagrant violation. Here's the California legislature writing down the instructions to California judges telling them when, where, how, and why to bifurcate a jury trial. It has 86 words in one sentence. It crams a three-week cruise in a rowboat:

> In a trial by jury, the court may, when the convenience of witnesses or the ends of justice would be promoted thereby, on motion of a party, after notice and hearing, make an order, no later than the close of the pretrial conference in cases in which such pretrial conference is to be held, or, in other cases, no later than ten days before the trial date, that the trial of the issue of liability shall precede the trial of any other issue in the case.

[handwritten annotations: "prepositional phrase to state a circumstance"; "huge gap"; "The whole phrase is the verb; to avoid rowhiness / say the court may order"; "gap between verb + object"]

The sentence breaks the *not-too-many-thoughts-per-sentence rule.* Of course, if a sentence should avoid having too many thoughts, two questions inevitably arise: (1) what's a thought? and (2) how many are too many? *(6 is not too many)*

Good questions.

I'm not sure anyone has ever defined a thought as some quantifiable measurement. Now's as good a time as any, I suppose. Alert the philosophers. Here's the definition of a Thought (I thought the upper case added a nice touch):

> Thought = a sufficient number of words enabling a reader to answer one of the six universal questions.

As we all know, the six universal questions are: *who, what, where, when, how,* and *why.* These, and a few variations, are the only questions in the universe that one person can ask another person. It's a well-known, documented, anthropological fact that Thoughts and Language arose around these six universal questions.

When our forebears were grunting at one another in caves, one rushed in with the news that he had killed an animal. "What kind?" grunted the clan. Out came enough grunts to identify a "moose." "Where'd you get him?" continued the clan. Out came enough grunts to say "over by the river in the pine forest." The interrogatories would continue until all questions had elicited all the Thoughts from the successful hunter.

Reversing the process illustrates the definition of a Thought. If I write just enough words to allow you to answer one of the six universal questions, then I can define the information transmitted to your brain as One Thought. We then have the handy device of being able to classify information into six broad categories. Classifying our Thoughts as *what* information, *where* information, *when* information, *who* information, *why* information, and *how* information helps us organize our Thoughts and follow the *not-too-many-thoughts-per-sentence rule*.

Here's how it works. Let's classify the information in the above statute. But first, some definitions. *When* information is temporal and has three dimensions: past, present, and future. *Where* information is not only geographical but circumstantial as well. *How* information is limited to information describing the means by which something is done or takes place. *What* information includes persons, places, things, and ideas [nouns], actions [verbs], and qualities [adjectives]. *Who* information is limited to people. And *why* information describes the reasons certain activities or events take place.

Grammatically, you can see that *what* information includes nouns and verbs. *What* also includes adjective meanings such as *what kind, how many*, or *how big. Who* information necessarily is limited to nouns. Four of the questions—*where, when, why*, and *how*—are all adverbial.

Here is an inventory of the above statute:

Words	Thought
In a trial by jury	where
the court	who
may make an order that the trial of the issue of liability shall precede the trial of any other issue in the case	does what

Words	Thought
when the convenience of witnesses would be promoted thereby	why
when the ends of justice would be promoted thereby	why
on motion of a party	when
after notice and hearing	when
no later than the close of the pretrial conference in cases in which such pretrial conference is to be held	when
or, in other cases, no later than 10 days before the trial date	when

Nine Thoughts: one *who*, one *what*, one *where*, two *whys*, and four *whens*. Because the above sentence is clearly too long, we can only conclude that Nine Thoughts is *too many* for one sentence to handle.

At the other extreme, we could write nine sentences with only one thought per sentence and produce *Dick and Jane* sentences like this: *The court is the subject matter of this statute.* Or like this: *The court may do this in a trial by jury.* Obviously, if nine is too many, one is too few. Somewhere between these two extremes our prose should lie.

The Six Universal Question device of classifying information helps us detect the major error of the statute's structure. The reader does not get a full picture of the *does what* information until the final breath. The statute reveals the *does what* a little bit at a time: *the court may* [23 words] *make an order* [33 words] *that the trial of the issue of liability shall precede the trial of any other issue in the case.*

The Six Universal Question device also helps us reorganize the information and rewrite the statute. We can immediately see that the *who* and the *what* information are the most crucial bits of information. Indeed, the other bits of information are circumscribing the court's power. The court may make this order in a jury trial and not in a nonjury trial [one *where*]. The order must promote justice and serve the convenience of witnesses [two *whys*]. Then the statute says *when* the judge may make the order, specifying two events in time that must occur before the order may be made, and two precise time periods for making the order in pretrial-conference cases and non-pretrial-conference cases [four *whens*].

Thinking about the information in this way serves as a guide in reducing the size of the bites we feed to our reader. As a first try, *using the original words*, we produce this:

> In a trial by jury, when the convenience of witnesses or the ends of justice would be promoted thereby, the court may make an order that the trial of the issue of liability shall precede the trial of any other issue in the case. The court may make the order on motion of a party, after notice and hearing. The order must be made no later than the close of the pretrial conference in cases in which such pretrial conference is to be held, or, in other cases, no later than 10 days before the trial date.

At least we've followed the *not-too-many-thoughts-per-sentence rule*. At least we've reduced our average sentence length from 86 to 32. At least our reader doesn't choke.

Recall, however, that the Long-Winded Sentence Syndrome has two causes: breaking the *not-too-many-thoughts-per-sentence rule* and wordiness. Though our rewritten statute follows the first rule, it ignores the rule against wordiness. As mentioned above, the causes of wordiness are many and are explored in detail in later chapters in this book. But to give you a flavor of things to come, here's a rewritten version of the statute that follows both rules and uses only 65 words to say the same thing:

> In a jury trial, to promote the convenience of witnesses or the ends of justice, the court may order the issue of liability tried first. The court may so order on motion of a party, after notice and hearing. The order must be made before the close of the pretrial conference if held, or, if not held, at least 10 days before the trial date.

In addition to the Six Universal Question device, another trick can help you follow the *not-too-many-thoughts-per-sentence rule*. For lack of a better name, I call this the Stop-Start approach to writing. Often legal writers get started in a sentence and, for some reason, refuse to stop. They keep on going, adding message upon message on the back of a single sentence. Sooner, not later, the sentence collapses of its own weight, as does the patience of the reader.

The trick is to Stop at the end of one main message and Start at the beginning of the next. Simply Stop the sentence with a period. Then Start the next with a capital letter. It's often that simple. Here's an example:

> The basis of the depreciable property consisting of selected assets as described in the schedule of selected assets contained in the Assistant Commissioner's letter dated 20 November 1979, from the machinery and equipment operated by the companies that are on hand as of December 31, 1979, shall be reduced by 100 percent of the income realized from the purchase of such debentures.

The writer of this passage fails to identify the three main messages: (1) the assets are described in the letter; (2) the assets include certain property; and (3) the basis of the assets shall be reduced. Instead, the writer continues and continues and continues, heaping thought upon thought upon thought. The better approach is to Stop. Then Start. Stop. Start. Stop. Here's how:

> The depreciable property includes property described in the schedule of selected assets in the Commissioner's letter of November 20, 1979. Specifically, this property includes the companies' machinery and equipment on hand as of December 31, 1979. The basis of this property shall be reduced by 100 percent of the income realized from the purchase of such debentures.

In sum, break your information down into digestible bites. Each bite should be a main message, which should appear in a single sentence. Use the Six Universal Question Device to classify information and to organize information in a logical sequence. Finally, use the Stop-Start device to kick the habit of cramming all your information down your reader's throat in a single, long-winded sentence. Your reader will appreciate the effort. Your reader won't choke.

The Subject-Predicate = Main Message Rule

Recall the four basic sentence structures. Here they are again:

1. Subject (actor) + Transitive Verb (active) + Direct Object (recipient)
   Example: The school board punished the student.

   Subject (recipient) + Transitive Verb (passive) + Phrase (actor)
   Example: The student was punished by the school board.

2. Subject + Intransitive Verb + Adverb
   Example: Thereafter, the student complied with the policy.

3. Subject + To Be + Predicate Adjective
   Example: At first, the student was arrogant.

   Subject + To Be + Predicate Nominative
   Example: The student was the first offender of the new regulations.

4. Subject + Linking Verb + Predicate Adjective
   Example: When caught, the student felt terrible.

As a rule, you should identify your main message and position it at the subject-predicate position in the sentence. When reviewing your writing, you should pick out your subjects, your main verbs, and the other stuff (direct object, adverb, predicate adjective, or predicate nominative). You should then read this three-part structure aloud. Listen to your message and be sure it's the main thing you want to say. These three parts in most of your sentences should carry most of your messages. They should inform. If, when you read these three vital parts of your sentences, you find very little information, you are probably suffering from the Thomas Paine Syndrome. You remember him from History 101. He was that famous American revolutionary who wrote:

These are the times that try men's souls.

Let's test the sentence against the *subject-predicate = main message rule*. The subject is *These*. The main verb is *are*. The predicate nominative is *times*. *These are times.* Not much there, huh? No, Paine *subordinated* his main message in the dependent clause: *that try men's souls.* Had he followed the rule, here's what he would have written:

These times try men's souls.

In these times, men's souls are tried.

Neither of those would have stirred the hearts of the colonists. Paine knew what he was doing. For emphasis he intentionally broke the *subject-predicate = main message rule*. By forcing his main message to

the end of his sentence, by delaying his main message, he created tension
in his reader. He created an exclamation point. He used the spice of our
language.

Many legal writers, perhaps fancying themselves to be modern-day
Thomas Paines, put very little information at the subject-verb-other-
stuff structure of the sentence. Instead, they subordinate everything to
dependent clauses and phrases. They dump way too much spice on their
words, try to emphasize everything, and end up emphasizing nothing.
They write like this:

> There are several procedures involved, which, if there is to be
> an increase in corporate income, must be carefully followed.

The subject? *There*. The main verb? *Are*. The predicate nominative? *Procedures*. Folks, I can now announce for the first time in history
(a drum roll please):

THERE ARE PROCEDURES!

What a letdown. Here the writer is using the crucial, drum-rolling
part of a sentence for naught. Instead, identify the message: (1) What,
(2) Must what, (3) Why. (1) What [procedures], (2) Must what [must
be followed], (3) Why [to increase corporate income]. One-two-three.
That's the way most messages break down in the English language. We
should therefore use the English language to say precisely what we
mean:

> Several procedures must be carefully followed to increase
> corporate income.

To write powerfully, look at your subjects, look at your main verbs,
and look at the other stuff. Read those three parts aloud. If you say very
little, your writing is breaking the *subject-predicate = main message rule*.
You are abandoning the most important parts of the English sentence.
Use those parts for most of your messages. When it's time to drive a
point home or vary your style, then play Thomas Paine or use other
well-recognized ways to break the pattern.

The Art of Inversion

If your writing becomes predictable, your reader will become
bored. Every now and then you need to change the rules on your reader,
to mix things up a bit, to break the pattern of the way you say things.

One way to achieve highly desirable variety in your language is to invert the ordinary order of a sentence.

Here's the way *inversion* can work for you.

The grammatical subject is at the front of the English sentence. (Or should I say: *At the front of the English sentence is the grammatical subject.*) The main verb is after the subject in the English sentence. (Or should I say: *After the subject in the English sentence is the main verb.*) The other stuff comes at the end. (Or should I say: *At the end comes the other stuff.*) You have just witnessed the art of inversion. I began each of the three parenthetical sentences above with the *other stuff.* I then stated the main verb. Finally, at the end of the sentence, I positioned the subject.

In formal writing, the inverted sentence works well with the verb *to be.* Especially when describing factual events or settings, you should consider inversion as a particularly effective tool. Thus, instead of saying, *A large bush was to the plaintiff's right and partially obstructed the view*, try inverting the sentence like this: *To the plaintiff's right was a large bush, partially obstructing the view.* Changing the ordinary order of sentences grabs your reader's attention. Without knowing why, your reader becomes glued to your words.

Although you may invert sentences having verbs other than the verb *to be,* you should be very careful. You might succumb to the Grandmother's House Syndrome.

> Over the river and through the woods, to Grandmother's house
> we go.

Or worse, if you invert too many sentences, you might fall prey to the Real Estate Classified Ad Syndrome:

> Nestled in this wooded lot is this three-bedroom charmer.
> Happy will be the day . . . .

Later in this book, you'll learn how to play around with positioning the actor of your sentences by switching the voice of your transitive verbs from active to passive.

The Art of Subordination

I have taught persuasive writing to scores of practicing attorneys. Invariably, when they begin to adapt their styles to the rules of clear writing, they tend to overdo it a bit and produce sentences that are too short and choppy. To help them find a balance between the short, choppy style and the long-winded style, I always suggest the art of subordination as the cure.

Each English sentence has one of the four basic structures we discussed above. For convenience, here they are again:

1. Subject (actor) + Transitive Verb (active) + Direct Object (recipient)
   Example: The school board punished the student.

   Subject (recipient) + Transitive Verb (passive) + Phrase (actor)
   Example: The student was punished by the school board.

2. Subject + Intransitive Verb + Adverb
   Example: Thereafter, the student complied with the policy.

3. Subject + To Be + Predicate Adjective
   Example: At first, the student was arrogant.

   Subject + To Be + Predicate Nominative
   Example: The student was the first offender of the new regulations.

4. Subject + Linking Verb + Predicate Adjective
   Example: When caught, the student felt terrible.

Although I oversimplify somewhat, to these basic structures you may add only two things: adjectives and adverbs. These adjectives and adverbs might come in single-word form or multi-word form. If they come in multi-word form, they are either phrases or clauses. Phrases, you might recall, are defined as follows: *a bunch of words without a main verb in it.* Clauses, of course, are defined as follows: *a bunch of words with a main verb in it.* This book will deal at some length with phrases and clauses when we tackle problems of wordiness.

The four structures above are the strategic parts of the English sentence. All other parts—those containing adjectives, adverbs, adjective phrases, adverb phrases, adjective clauses, and adverb clauses—are *subordinate* parts of the sentence. Above we saw the general rule of placing your main message at the strategic part of the sentence. By the same token, a general rule requires that you place subordinate information in subordinate parts of the sentence.

The art of subordination requires you to recognize subordinate information in separate sentences and put it in a nearby sentence containing more important information. Let's see how the art of subordination might smooth out the short, choppy sentences of a child:

> I like my teacher.

> My teacher is handsome.

> My teacher's name is Mr. Jones.

Using *handsome* as a subordinate, one-word adjective and *Mr. Jones* as a subordinate appositive (a noun restating another noun), the subordinated sentence looks like this:

[handwritten left margin: imbedding + subordinating]

[handwritten right margin: imbedding + subordinating are the same process (different names)]

> I like my handsome teacher, Mr. Jones.

Leaving grade school behind and moving up the scale of complexity, let's look at two other sentences crying out for subordination:

> Smith's employment was terminated by the Board. The Board relied on its conflict of interest policy in reaching this decision.

If you have trouble distinguishing the subordinate message from the strategic message, ask Smith. He'll tell you. The subordinate message is the Board's *relying on its conflict of interest policy*. The strategic message is Smith's getting the boot. Using the art of subordination, we produce this:

> Relying on its conflict of interest policy, the Board terminated Smith's employment.

The subordinate message appeared as an introductory present participial phrase. It acted as an adjective. It modified *Board*. Or should I say: The subordinate message appeared as an introductory present participial phrase acting as an adjective and modifying *Board*. Somehow I like the second, *subordinated* way better.

When you overdo it in your efforts to be brief, consider subordination as the ideal cure to choppiness. Of course, you might overdo it in your efforts to subordinate. You might put *strategic* information in subordinate positions. Or you might break the *not-too-many-thoughts-per-sentence rule* and try to cram too much information into subordinate parts of your sentences. If you do, the inevitable result is *gaps*, the great thought-stoppers in legal writing.

Avoiding Gaps

Recall the sample passage by Mr. Justice Black in Chapter 1. The passage had seven sentences. In only two of those sentences was the subject separated from the verb by other words. Only two sentences had *gaps*. And if you'll go back and study the passage, you'll see that the gaps between subject and verb were one-word adverbs.

Here's another well-known jurist writing the statement of facts in a well-known case, *Palsgraf v. Long Island Railroad*, 248 N.Y. 339, 162 N.E. 99, 99 (1928):

> Plaintiff was standing on a platform of defendant's railroad after buying a ticket to go to Rockaway Beach. A train stopped at the station, bound for another place. Two men ran forward to catch it. One of the men reached the platform of the car without mishap, though the train was already moving. The other man, carrying a package, jumped aboard the car, but seemed unsteady as if about to fall. A guard on the car, who had held the door open, reached forward to help him in, and another guard on the platform pushed him from behind. In this act, the package was dislodged and fell upon the rails. It was a package of small size, about fifteen inches long, and was covered by a newspaper. In fact, it contained fireworks, but there was nothing in its appearance to give notice of its contents. The fireworks when they fell exploded. The shock of the explosion threw down some scales at the other end of the platform many feet away. The scales struck the plaintiff, causing injuries for which she sues.

In those twelve sentences, Mr. Justice Cardozo kept subject close to main verb. Let's test the twelve sentences for gaps: (1) plaintiff was standing (no gap); (2) train stopped (no gap); (3) men ran (no gap); (4) one of the men reached (three-word prepositional phrase); (5) man, carrying a package, jumped (three-word present participial phrase); (6) guard on the car, who had held the door open, reached (three-word prepositional phrase and six-word nonrestrictive clause); (7) package was dislodged (no gap); (8) it was (no gap); (9) it contained (no gap); (10) fireworks when they fell exploded (three-word adverb clause); (11) shock of the explosion threw (three-word prepositional phrase); and (12) scales struck (no gap).

Cardozo strictly limited those situations where strategic parts of sentences were pulled apart to allow other words to come in between. That's a gap. In only five sentences did he permit gaps. Four of those five were mere three-word gaps. The longest stretched only to nine words. Good writers avoid gaps. You should too.

The English sentence prefers strategic parts to remain close together. Your reader is looking for these milestones in your sentences. By disrupting ordinary patterns with thought-stopping gaps, you only baffle and irritate your reader.

Above we saw how Mr. Justice Cardozo limited gaps between subject and verb. Here's what a subject-verb gap looks and sounds like:

> This *office*, after a thorough review of its policies and proce-dures, a complete consideration of the ramifications of this decision, and an assessment of the performance which you have made from the commencement of your employment to the present time, *has made* the determination that your services will no longer be needed.

Gaps disrupt other strategic sentence parts as well. You will likely encounter gaps between parts of a complex verb, between a verb and its object, between the parts of an infinitive, and between *that* and the balance of a dependent clause.

Between parts of a complex verb

Before I show an example of the complex verb gap, perhaps a quick review of grammar is in order. Remember verb conjugation? You conjugate verbs to show tense or time. A conjugated verb is a *predicate verb* used in an independent or dependent clause. As mentioned above, to make things simple, I call these conjugated verbs *main verbs*. The 12 major tenses of main verbs include: present, past, future, present perfect, past perfect, future perfect and six progressive tenses. Only two tenses—present and past—can be shown with one-word verbs. Thus: *he writes* (present) and *he wrote* (past). All other tenses require *helping verbs*, also known as *auxiliary verbs*, to show the precise time when something happens. Thus: *he will write* (future), *he has written* (present perfect), *he had written* (past perfect), and *he will have written* (future perfect). Six additional tenses, the progressive tenses, allow us to show ongoing actions. All progressive tenses require the use of *to be* as an auxiliary verb: *he is writing* (present progressive), *he was writing* (past progressive), *he will be writing* (future progressive), *he has been writing* (present perfect progressive), *he had been writing* (past perfect progressive), and *he will have been writing* (future perfect progressive). Though these are the 12 major tenses, other auxiliary verbs help us show certain conditions (might, may, can), obligations (must), or other meanings (should). Thus: *he can write, he must write*, or *he should have written.*

Adding these auxiliary verbs to show tense or other meanings produces a complex verb. And, as a general rule of style, you should, in order to make your writing clear, avoid gaps between the parts of a complex verb. Naturally, I meant:

> To make your writing clear, you should avoid gaps between the parts of a complex verb.

In the olden days, a popular rule discouraged any words from intruding between the parts of a complex verb. A big No-No: I *have definitely decided* to go to the beach. These days, however, modern stylists recognize the desirability of permitting such small gaps between the auxiliary *have* and the base verb *decided*. The large gaps, however, remain *verboten*.

Between a verb and its object

Remember that a transitive verb is one that carries an object—a noun following the verb. In a conjugated state, a main verb forms an independent or dependent clause. If that main verb is transitive, its object usually will come somewhere after the verb. In an unconjugated state, a verb forms a verbal phrase, such as an infinitive phrase (*to enact the statute*) or a present participial phrase (*enacting the statute*). If the verb forming a phrase is transitive, its object must come somewhere after the verb. If you're scratching your head trying to remember all these grammatical terms, you won't scratch much longer. Later in this book, you will learn everything you need to know about verbal phrases. For now, just remember to keep the object of a verb close to the verb. In the negative, do not let a gap disrupt the natural relationship a transitive verb has with its object. Avoid this:

> The Board of Directors has decided *to surrender*, without admitting any responsibility in this matter and with no intent to establish this decision as any kind of precedent for the future, its *rights* under the insurance policy.

The transitive verb *surrender* in its infinitive form *to surrender* yearns for its object *rights*. When you hit your reader with the transitive verb *to surrender*, the reader's mind immediately asks "surrender what?" The faster you answer that question, the tighter your writing will be. Thus, avoid gaps. Keep transitive verbs close to their objects.

Between the parts of an infinitive: the split infinitive rule

As you might remember, each verb in the English language has an infinitive form. Add the word *to* before any base verb in the language and you get what we think of as the infinitive: *to have, to hold, to love, to honor, to cherish*, to recite part of the wedding vows. As shown above, and as discussed later, these infinitives form phrases, which act as nouns, adjectives, or adverbs. More about that later.

Whenever you use an infinitive, you should try to avoid splitting the *to* from the base verb. Usually, you'll be tempted to put an adverb between the two words, as in *to quickly consider*. Old rules of style would require you to say *quickly to consider* or *to consider quickly*. But inflexible rules of style should not get in the way of clear expression.

Good style, and many stuck-up grammarians, used to forbid splitting infinitives under any circumstances. Good style today, and more realistic grammarians, recognize that rules of style should not get in the way of clarity or grace. If following the no-split-infinitive rule produces an ambiguous statement or grates the ear, you definitely should break the rule in the interest of clarity. You should also ignore the rule in the interest of a graceful style. If the unsplit infinitive is bizarre, go ahead and split. Let's look at an example. Here's my sentence:

We have decided to consider hiring you.

Suppose I want to modify *to consider* with the adverb *quickly*. Following the no-split rule would produce this:

We have decided *quickly to consider* hiring you.

Quickly what? Quickly decided? Or quickly consider? No rule of grammar or style nails my precise meaning. An adverb can come before or after the verb it modifies. Here I've got two verbs: *decided* and *to consider*. Thus, I've produced an ambiguity. Let's try it the other way and still follow the no-split rule:

We have decided *to consider quickly* hiring you.

Again, my reader doesn't have the foggiest idea of my meaning. Am I *quickly considering* or *quickly hiring*? The *only* way to nail my meaning precisely is to split the infinitive as follows:

> We have decided *to quickly consider* hiring you.

Hence the rule: split an infinitive to avoid an ambiguity.

Let's consider some more examples. Fowler provided the following as sentences written by (in his words) "a non-split die-hard." Also, in his words, the sentences are "disasters":

> What alternative can be found which the Pope has not condemned, and which will make it possible *to organize legally* public worship?

> It will, when better understood, tend *firmly to establish* relations between Capital and Labour.

> Both Germany and England have done ill in not combining *to forbid flatly* hostilities.

> Every effort must be made *to increase adequately* professional knowledge and attainments.

> We have had *to shorten somewhat* Lord D 's letter.

> The kind of sincerity which enables an author *to move powerfully* the heart would . . . .

> Safeguards should be provided *to prevent effectually* cosmopolitan financiers from manipulating these reserves.

H. Fowler, *Modern English Usage* 580-81 (2d ed. 1965).

Hence another rule: split an infinitive when your ear demands it. After all, what could be worse than going through life as a "non-split die-hard"?

Between "that" of a clause and the balance of the clause = the "that-that" problem

Sometime this week you will hear or see this common mistake. A writer or speaker begins a dependent clause with *that*. He then throws in a gap. He forgets he already has the *that* setting up the clause. He throws in another *that*. He ends up with the *that-that* problem. Here's what it looks like:

> This agency has decided *that* regardless of the position taken by your firm in the petition for application for review *that* the petition will be denied.

Remove the gap and read what's left over: This agency has decided *that that* the petition will be denied. Instead, you should keep the *that* close to and part of the clause it introduces:

> Regardless of your firm's position in its petition for review, this agency has decided that the petition will be denied.

What causes these thought-stopping gaps? Usually the writer is breaking the *not-too-many-thoughts-per-sentence rule*. When you find inordinately long sentences in your writing, the chances are good you'll find gaps as well. Look carefully at your main messages and your subordinate messages. You can and should subordinate your subordinate messages. But if those subordinate messages are not truly subordinate or if you are putting too many in one sentence, the inevitable result is gaps.

Set about solving the gap problem and you'll often solve other problems as well. Your reader, for sure, will appreciate the effort.

Parallel Constructions

Time out for another 10-minute grammar review.

Whenever you say a series of things in a sentence, each part of the series must appear in the same grammatical structure. If the first part of the series is a noun acting as the object of a preposition, each succeeding part must be a noun acting as the object of the same preposition. If the first part of the series is a main verb of a dependent clause, each succeeding part must be a main verb of the same dependent clause. The list of possible parallel constructions, of course, is virtually endless, limited only by the number of grammatical structures in the English language. Perhaps an example will make the rule clear.

You would break the rule if you said: *Yesterday I went hiking, biking, and took a boat ride.* The first part of the series *hiking* is a present participial verb form—an unconjugated *verbal*; the last part *took* is a main verb—a conjugated verb form. You would follow the rule if you said: *Yesterday I went hiking, biking, and boating.*

Here's another nonparallel construction. Can you spot the problem?

> The Service also will not follow the rationale of the decision of the United States Court of Appeals for the Second Circuit in Bongiovanni v. Commissioner, 470 F.2d 921 (2d Cir. 1972), involving a similar transaction and which held that the term "liabilities," as used in section 357(c) of the Code, did not include all liabilities which are included for accounting purposes, but was meant to apply only to what might be called "tax" liabilities, that is, liens in excess of tax costs, particularly mortgages encumbering property transferred in an exchange within the meaning of section 351.

The nonparallel construction occurred when the writer began a series with a present participial phrase *involving a similar transaction* and continued the series with a dependent clause *and which held . . . .* Either the first part should read *which involved* or the second part should read *holding.*

Where does this rule of parallel construction come from? It is not a rule of style. Rather, it is one of the cardinal rules of grammar. It derives from the definition of *coordinating* and *correlative conjunctions.*

The English language has only three types of conjunctions: *coordinating, correlative*, and *subordinating.* Here we're only concerned with coordinating and correlative conjunctions, but to satisfy your curiosity, let's get subordinating conjunctions out of the way. Subordinating conjunctions join subordinate clauses (or dependent clauses). Subordinating conjunctions are *clause starters.* Samples of subordinating conjunctions include: *when, if, as, because, while, though, although, as long as*, and others. These conjunctions join dependent clauses to independent clauses and play no part in the rule of parallel construction.

The rule of parallelism instead derives from the coordinating and correlative conjunctions. English has seven coordinating conjunctions: *and, or, but, for, so, yet*, and *nor.* English has only three correlative conjunctions: *not only . . . but also, neither . . . nor*, and *either . . . or.* Each of these joining words must link equal grammatical units. That's what they mean. That's their definition. Hence the rule of parallel construction. The rule comes directly from the meaning of coordinating and correlative conjunctions. To break the rule violates the very definition of these vital words.

Though many legal writers are unfamiliar with the niceties of parallel construction, few actually break the rule with a vengeance. Nonparallel constructions do crop up, even in court opinions. But most legal writers have a firm enough *feel* for the language that they avoid the nonparallel construction most of the time.

Why bring it up, you might reasonably ask.

I bring it up for a very good reason. You can use the notion of parallel construction in two ways: (1) you can look at your own writing to see whether you use many parallel constructions at all (the good writers do), and (2) you can search your writing for parallel constructions to determine which structures you favor and which structures you fail to use at all.

We can use the notion of parallel construction to analyze the passage of Mr. Justice Black quoted above. Here it is again. The bracketed numerals precede each parallel construction appearing in the passage:

> Since the earliest days philosophers have dreamed of a country where the mind and [1] spirit of man would be free; [2] where there would be no limits to inquiry; [3] where men would be free to explore the unknown and [4] to challenge the most deeply rooted beliefs and [5] principles. Our First Amendment was a bold effort to adopt this principle — to establish a country with no legal restrictions of any kind upon the subjects people could investigate, [6] discuss and [7] deny. The Framers knew, better perhaps than we do today, the risks they were taking. They knew that free speech might be the friend of change and [8] revolution. But they also knew that it is always the deadliest enemy of tyranny. With this knowledge they still believed that the ultimate happiness and [9] security of a nation lies in its ability to explore, [10] to change, [11] to grow and ceaselessly [12] to adapt itself to a new knowledge born of inquiry free from any kind of governmental control over the mind and [13] spirit of man. Loyalty comes from love of good government, not [14] fear of a bad one.

To open your eyes, you might take a passage of your own writing, find a paragraph of 180 words or so, and count the number of times you use parallel constructions. Do you have sentences with three main verbs like the one beginning this paragraph? Do you use a variety of parallel constructions as Mr. Justice Black did in the above passage? His structures ranged from three dependent clauses in the first sentence to four consecutive infinitive phrases in the penultimate one.

The notion of parallel construction can also help you analyze habitual structures you favor. Scour your writing for parallel constructions and figure our which structures you tend to repeat in parallel. If you write on a word processor, then have your machine search for the words *and* and *or*. As the cursor lands on each *and* and *or*, look around and identify those structures you are connecting. By looking at those you use, you can identify those you never use. Here's a partial list, along with examples, of some structures that should appear in clear and persuasive writing:

Structure	Parallel Construction
infinitive phrases	To increase the power of your writing, attract the reader's attention, and impress your professor, you should use some infinitive phrases.
present participial phrases	Careful writers pay attention to putting their thoughts in phrases and avoiding too many clauses.
prepositional phrases	The effective writer argues not only with force but also with style.
objects of a prepositional phrase	To write well, pay attention to sentence length, parallel construction, and the rules of tabulation.
main verbs in dependent clauses	Though dependent clauses sometimes cloud your messages and confuse your readers, you can use clauses to condense considerable information into one sentence.
independent clauses	I came, I saw, I conquered.

I came, I saw, I conquered. See? Even the good writers use parallel constructions. So should you.

Tabulation

Sometimes the writer is not long-winded. The information is. Especially in the law we often find information that seemingly never stops. The main idea of a sentence is qualified in so many ways that a sentence expressing that idea necessarily becomes long and burdensome.

Somehow the *United States Code* springs to mind.

In these situations, it is often desirable to present information in a list form. The technique is called tabulation, and nine separate qualifications govern its proper use. In fact, the rules of tabulation are so complex that I figured the best way to present them was by tabulation. Here are the rules of tabulation tabulated.

You can present complicated material in a single sentence by:

1. listing each element of the idea;
2. making each part of the list grammatically and generically the same;
3. indenting the list;
4. numbering the list;
5. introducing the list with a colon;
6. beginning each item on the list with a lowercase letter;
7. ending each item on the list with a semicolon;
8. placing *and* or *or* after the next-to-last item on the list; and
9. ending the list with a period.

Most of these rules are simple and easy to follow. Numbers 2 and 8, however, might cause some trouble. Rule 2 requires the items on the list to be in the same genus or class and to appear in parallel structure. Often, you will find that the rule of parallel construction dictates the genus or class. Some items in your chosen class just will not fit grammatically with the other items on the list. The cure? Change the grammatical construction or narrow the scope of the class.

Rule 8 involves boolean logic. Placing *and* after the penultimate item produces what lawyers like to call a *conjunctive test*. All items on the list are logically necessary. Placing *or* after the penultimate item, however, produces the *disjunctive test*. Only one item is logically necessary. The world, and reality, of course, are rarely so neat. It is this trick of logic, no doubt, that prompts the need for subparagraphs and sub-subparagraphs in legislative drafting.

As an exercise, let's tabulate the statute we saw above—the one that violated so many rules of style. Here it is again:

> In a trial by jury, the court may, when the convenience of witnesses or the ends of justice would be promoted thereby, on motion of a party, after notice and hearing, make an order, no later than the close of the pretrial conference in cases in which such pretrial conference is to be held, or, in other cases, no later than ten days before the trial date, that the trial of the issue of liability shall precede the trial of any other issue in the case.

To create a list, we must first decide what goes on the list, what is our genus or class. The Six Universal Question device can help identify or classify information by type. Here is the inventory we created:

In a trial by jury	where
the court	who
may make an order that the trial of the issue of liability shall precede the trial of any other issue in the case	does what
when the convenience of witnesses would be promoted thereby	why
when the ends of justice would be promoted thereby	why
on motion of a party	when
after notice and hearing	when
no later than the close of the pretrial conference in cases in which such pretrial conference is to be held	when

or, in other cases, no later
than 10 days before the trial
date   when

Of the nine units of information, the *whens* are the most prevalent. We could, therefore, define our class as the temporal limitations on the court's power. Or we could recognize that the legislature gave the power to bifurcate a trial to a trial judge and then limited that power to a jury trial, to situations where justice and witness convenience would be promoted, and to four distinct time factors. Thus, we could broaden our genus to include all limitations on the court's power (the *where*, the two *whys*, and the four *whens*).

Taking a stab at tabulation, we first try the broader class containing all limitations on the court's power. Here we go:

The court may order the issue of liability tried first if:

1. the convenience of witnesses would be promoted;

2. the ends of justice would be promoted;

3. in a jury trial;

4. on motion of a party . . . .

Whoops. What happened to our parallel structure? It broke down. The first two items wanted a main verb (promoted). The next items, however, definitely wanted to appear in prepositional phrases. Either we express the first two items as prepositional phrases or the remaining items as clauses. Let's give each a try:

The court may order the issue of liability tried first:

1. for the convenience of witnesses;

2. for the ends of justice;

Wait a minute. I've changed the meaning. I've lost that idea of *promoting justice*. Let's give it another go:

The court may order the issue of liability tried first:

1. for the promotion of the convenience of witnesses;

2. for the promotion of the ends of justice . . . .

Ugh. Now I sound like the winner of the Prepositional Phrase-Maker of the Year Award. Thus, I abandon the grammatical-shift approach and try limiting the scope of my class. Instead of putting all limits of court power on the list, I'll try just the temporal conditions:

In a jury trial, to promote the convenience of witness or the ends of justice, the court may order the issue of liability tried first:

1. on motion of a party;

2. after notice and hearing; and

3. before the close of the pretrial conference if held, or, if not held, at least ten days before the trial date.

Bingo.

Summary

In this chapter, we have looked at the English sentence from a variety of different angles. We saw how all sentences break down into four broad categories, which are primarily determined by the verb of the sentence. In those four categories, we saw the three recurring structures of subject, verb, and the other stuff (adverb, predicate nominative, or predicate adjective). We then studied the vital relationship between sentence length and clarity and saw how, as sentence length goes up, comprehension goes down. We learned to keep sentences short by limiting the number of messages each sentence conveys. We looked at the *subject-predicate = main message rule* and learned to place most of our messages at the subject-verb-object, subject-verb-adverb, subject-verb-adjective, or subject-verb-noun position of the sentence. To give the reader some relief from these structures, we pondered the art of inversion and learned to write backwards. We then ended with techniques of subordination, problems of gaps, the rule of parallel construction, and the device of tabulation.

The Rules of Good Writing

Your beginning list of the rules of good writing looks like this:

1. Use an average of 25 words per sentence. *— Larue says, this is a check; alone is not a good rule,*

2. Avoid putting too many messages in a single sentence.

rather, should try to follow the other rules; longer sentences are okay

3. Put most of your messages at the subject-predicate position.

4. For variety or emphasis, invert your sentences.

5. Use the art of subordination to smooth out choppiness.

6. Avoid disrupting your sentences with thought-stopping gaps.

7. Watch out for the rule of parallel construction.

8. Tabulate particularly complex information.

Now let's add to the list by narrowing our focus to a host of habits that prompt professors, bosses, and other powerful people to write this nasty little message in the margins of our papers:

WORDY!

Or: *AWKWARD!*

Or worse: *WHAT DO YOU MEAN?*

Chapter 3

Nouniness — Write with Verbs

Le mot, c'est le Verbe, c'est Dieu.

The word is the Verb, and the verb is God.

—Hugo

A verb has a hard time enough of it in this world when it's all together. It's downright inhuman to split it up. But that's just what those Germans do. They take part of a verb and put it down here, like a stake, and they take the other part of it and put it away over yonder, like another stake, and between these two limits they just shovel in German.

—Twain

Chapter 3

Nouniness - Write with Verbs

Introduction

This chapter begins our study of the causes and cures of those twin diseases of American, English, Canadian, Australian, and all other legal writing: wordiness and awkwardness. All readers of this book have found this invective glaring at them from the margins of their papers: WORDY! Or perhaps you have found this equally embarrassing tag hanging on your paper: AWKWARD! Is legal writing wordy? Sure it is. Is legal writing awkward? You betcha. But these are diagnoses. They fail to reveal the root causes of these dread diseases. They certainly suggest no cure.

In this and succeeding chapters, I hope to convince you of the link between grammar and style. I intend to show you a grammatical analysis of wordy writing and to teach you fairly easy grammatical solutions to the problems. When you understand the grammar of *nouniness* (in this chapter) and *clausiness* (in Chapter 6), you'll begin to see some easy ways out of these professional bad habits. When you learn and begin to use grammatical cures to the problems of wordiness and awkwardness, you will watch needless words disappear before your very eyes. And when you read your finished product and see how it clips along compelling your readers to pay attention, you too will become a believer. You will join the Plain English Movement and vow never again to say:

> The characterization of this amount as ordinary income is to effectuate the principle that, with respect to the characterization of income attributable to a discharge of indebtedness, a taxpayer filing the consent pursuant to section 108 to adjust basis pursuant to section 1017 should be in no better or worse position having filed the consent than it would have been had it actually recognized the income in the year such discharge occurred.

Here, in this chapter, we'll tackle the problem of nouniness and learn to write with verbs. Then, in Chapter 6, we'll study the problem of clausiness and learn, ironically, to write with nouns (and other forms). Other chapters will treat a host of other structures that cause us to use too many words to say what we want to say. But first, the big one. Nouniness.

Grammatical and Typographical Sentences

In writing, there are two kinds of sentences: grammatical and typographical. A grammatical sentence has all the elements we remember from grade school: a subject and a predicate. Grammatical sentences have a subject, a main verb, and, depending on the kind of verb used, a direct object or predicate adjective or predicate nominative or adverb. Typographical sentences, on the other hand, are just a series of words beginning with a capital letter and ending with a period, question mark, or exclamation point. *See* J. Walpole, *The Writer's Grammar Guide* 30 (1984). When writing this and other books, I use typographical sentences all the time. Just look above: *But first, the big one. Nouniness.* Those are two typographical sentences. Though typographical sentences might play some role in formal legal writing, you primarily will write with grammatical sentences. Typographical sentences might come across as too breezy or, worse, as a mistake.

To produce a grammatical sentence, you need only one word—a verb. You cannot produce a grammatical sentence with a noun, an adjective, an adverb, or any part of speech other than the verb. The one indispensable word we need is the verb. *Stop. Look. Listen.* Three words. Three verbs. Three grammatical sentences. All else revolves around this crucial word.

Yet, for some strange reason, formal legal writing has all but forsaken the powerful verb. The legal profession, priding itself in its ability to argue persuasively, ironically has abandoned the potent verb and chosen in its place the wimpy derivative noun.

Exhibiting a Preference for Nouns

Instead of *preferring verbs,* the legal profession exhibits *a preference for* nouns. Don't get me wrong. We can't live, or write, or think without nouns. But there's a special kind of noun that should attract not our favor but our scorn: *the derivative noun.*

A derivative noun derives directly from a base verb. Examples include: *conclusion, preference,* and *statement.* You can spot these derivative nouns by their suffixes: *-ent, -ant, -ence, -ance, -ency, -ancy,*

-ment, and the all-time favorites *-tion* or *-sion.* Other noun-words have identical verb-words. Examples include: *change, resort,* and *use.*

Suppose a writer wants to express the meaning of the verb *to prefer.* Ordinarily, one would think she would go ahead and use the good old verb *prefer* to say *prefer.* But being a nouny writer, she prefers—whoops, excuse me—she has the preference of using nouns—whoops, pardon me again—she has the preference of noun utilization. There. The nouns won. I mean the nouns experienced a victory.

Undoubtedly, you're getting my drift. Let me continue.

When nouny writers choose the derivative noun to express the meaning of a verb, they face the stark reality of having to write a grammatical sentence. They are left with the dreaded chore of finding a verb on which to hang the noun. They grope around and find the wishy-washiest verbs in these United States of America. And in England. And even in Canada. And probably in Australia. That's right, they find and use the *groped-for verbs.*

Groped-for Verbs and Other Bits of Noun Glue

Think for a minute.

Finished?

Good. Now back to the book.

It's probably been a few years since you thought for a minute about nouns. But let me guide you through the process. It'll do you a world of good.

There are only two major ways to attach nouns to sentences: (1) with verbs and (2) with prepositions. (Another way, the appositive, will come up later.) Nouns relate directly to verbs as subjects, direct objects, predicate nominatives, objects in verbal phrases, or indirect objects. If you find a noun in a sentence and don't find a verb to which it relates directly, then you'll probably find the second bit of noun glue, the preposition. Indeed, that is what a preposition does. That is the definition of a preposition: *a preposition links a noun to a sentence and shows the relationship of that noun to the rest of the sentence.*

To show you that nouns attach to sentences by sticking to verbs or prepositions, here's an explanation of the noun functions in the sentence you just finished reading:

That is the *definition* [predicate nominative after the verb *is*] of a *preposition* [object of the preposition *of*]: a *preposition* [subject of the main verb *links*] links a *noun* [direct object of the main verb *links*] to a *sentence* [object of the preposition *to*] and shows the *relationship* [direct object of the main verb *shows*] of that *noun* [object of the preposition *of*] to the *rest* [object of the preposition *to*] of the *sentence* [object of the preposition *of*].

The nouny writers must find verbs or prepositions as hooks for the nouns they use. The verbs they find are the *groped-for verbs*. Often, the prepositions they find are mushy *compound prepositions*, the topic of a later chapter.

As I stated above, groped-for verbs don't do much for us. They carry very little information. All they do is sit there and hold up nouny constructions. Ironically, these nouny constructions are trying awfully hard to express the meaning of verbs. Here's a partial list of wishy-washy, groped-for verbs along with illustrations of the harm they do.

The Wishy-Washy, Groped-for Verbs

Groped-for Verb	Example of Nouniness
has (and make)	The Freedom of Information Act has pertinence to our agency's duty to make a complete disclosure of personnel information.
	Translation: The Freedom of Information Act governs our agency's duty to completely disclose personnel information.
take	The Board will take these matters under serious consideration.
	Translation: The Board will seriously consider these matters.
drew (and reach)	The Supreme Court drew an inference as to the applicability of the statute in reaching its decision.
	Translation: When deciding the case, the Supreme Court inferred that the statute applied.

[Handwritten margin notes:] Structure of sentence depends on verb — use stronger verb, change noun to verb — result is converted to an act — noun converted to verb — when do this, lose a lot of prepositions: this makes sentence look tighter.; verbs are shorter than nouns

*make grammatical structure of the sentence fit what is
most important to us: make that the main verb

reached (and is)

here went from act to
result and then first
vice versa

> The court reached a conclusion which is
> favorable to our client's position.
>
> *Translation*: The court's conclusion
> favors our client's position.

make

> The President should make a statement
> as to the history of this procedure.
>
> *Translation*: The President should
> describe the history of this procedure.

was (and find)

Changed passive to
active

> The leader was of the belief that his
> policies would find vindication in the
> upcoming economic statistics.
>
> *Translation*: The leader believed that
> the upcoming economic statistics would
> vindicate his policies.

Derivative Adjectives

A first cousin of the derivative noun is the derivative adjective. Adding the suffixes -*ent*, -*ant*, -*ful*, and -*able* often will convert verbs into adjectives. Thus, *hesitant, hopeful*, and *preventable* are adjective substitutes for *hesitate, hope*, and *prevent*. These words have the same effect on your writing as derivative nouns: they are the main cause of wordiness.

Consequences of Nouniness

The main cause of wordiness is nouniness. If you bury the meaning of verbs in derivative nouns or derivative adjectives, you must come up with other words on which to hang the derivative nouns and derivative adjectives. You must grope around for groped-for verbs to hold up these mushy constructions.

Henry Fowler, in his classic *Modern English Usage*, took aim at the nouny writer and blasted away. If you're a nouny writer, duck:

> Turgid flabby English is full of abstract nouns; the commonest ending of abstract nouns is -*ion*, and to count the -*ion* words in what one has written, or, better, to cultivate an ear that without special orders challenges them as they come, is one of the simplest and most effective means of making oneself less unreadable. It is as an unfailing sign of a nouny abstract style

that a cluster of *-ion* words is chiefly to be dreaded. But some
nouny writers are so far from being awake to that aspect of it
that they fall into a still more obvious danger, and so stud their
sentences with *-ions* that the mere sound becomes an offence
. . . .

H. Fowler, *Modern English Usage* 640 (2d ed. 1965).

The sound of it does indeed become an offense. But there is
another drawback to nouniness worthy of even more dread. The nouny
passage is mushy and weak and wimpy. The verb form is powerful and
direct. Noun forms avoid issues. Verb forms hit them head on. Noun
forms lack any sense of motion or action. Verb forms paint vivid pictures
of activity in the reader's mind.

Nothing seems ever to happen in the writing of the nouny writer.
It just sort of sits there, like a couch potato, totally passive and docile.
It always takes matters under consideration. It never considers a thing.
It always places great emphasis upon the fact that . . . . It never stresses
anything. It always has pertinence to many other things, never once
pertaining to anything at all. It always finds things hesitant. Nothing ever
hesitates.

Because I am dealing with a mature audience, I feel safe in using
my favorite example of nouniness. The noun form wants to avoid issues.
The noun form shies away from telling it like it is. The noun form plays
it safe and shies away. You don't believe me? Then find a socially
acceptable verb describing the sex act. Not out loud, please. The verb
form is much too graphic, clinical, or nasty. Instead of [verb]ing, people
make love. Instead of [verb]ing, people *have relations* or *have sex* or
engage in intercourse. Never do they [verb]. The closest we've come in
the language to [verbing], I guess, is the verb *do.* But to tone it down,
we follow *do* with the indefinite pronoun *it.*

Obviously, you'll have plenty of occasions to soften your messages,
to avoid issues, to tone it down. The way to do it is with nouns. When
you want to push your opponent gently to the ground, put on your soft
noun gloves. But when you want to hit your opponent with a Mike Tyson
uppercut, bare your fists with verbs.

You must learn the device of (brace yourself) *denounification.*
This well-tested trick will take some of the wimpiest writing around and
make it downright Olympian. To learn the trick, you must first learn the
magic of verbs.

The Five Ways Verbs Work in the English Language

The trick of doing away with nouniness involves converting derivative nouns and derivative adjectives back to verb forms. Before you see the trick in action, you should review the five ways verbs work in the English language. Knowing how verbs act will help you convert derivative nouns and derivative adjectives back into verb forms. When you do convert, you'll produce five different structures.

1) The Main Verb

To show tense or time, verbs are conjugated into one of the six major tenses: *he shows* (present), *he showed* (past), *he will show* (future), *he has shown* (present perfect), *he had shown* (past perfect), and *he will have shown* (future perfect). To show ongoing acts, verbs are conjugated into the progressive tenses, which are formed with the verb *to be* plus the present participle: *he is showing* (present progressive), *he was showing* (past progressive), *he will be showing* (future progressive), *he has been showing* (present perfect progressive), *he had been showing* (past perfect progressive), and *he will have been showing* (future perfect progressive). Other conjugated verbs are formed by using one of the auxiliary verbs plus the base infinitive: *can, must, may, ought, might, shall, should, would, could, be,* and others. Thus: He *must show* the movie.

A main verb forms an independent clause (a sentence) or a dependent clause. Indeed, a clause is defined as *a bunch of words with a main verb in it.* This use, of course, is the primary use of verbs and forms the basic structure of our sentences. The big deal in the English sentence is the conjugated verb—the predicate verb—the *main verb.* Readers know they can expect to find main verbs pinpointing time and serving as the fulcrums of sentences. Indeed, readers search for the main verb in the independent clause fully expecting to find a whole lot of information dwelling there.

The other four verb structures, however, are equally important. These other structures are unconjugated verb forms called *verbals.* They do not pinpoint tense or time but allow us to express the meaning of verbs without setting up the big deal of a clause. Let's look at each in turn.

2) The Infinitive Phrase

Every verb has a base, unconjugated form. Identifying the base verb is easy. It's the one you'd look up in the dictionary. We think of the infinitive as the base verb preceded by the word *to*. We use these infinitives in our language all by themselves (he wanted *to win*) or with other words to form infinitive phrases (he wanted *to win the race decisively*). Those other words include a noun acting as the object of the infinitive (if the verb is transitive), adverbs modifying the infinitive, and adjectives modifying the noun. Thus: *to win the race decisively*. *To win* is the infinitive, *the race* is the object of the transitive verb *win,* and *decisively* is the adverb modifying the verb form *to win.*

Infinitive phrases can act in three ways—as nouns, adjectives, and adverbs. First, an infinitive can operate as a noun and satisfy many noun functions in the English language. (We'll discuss those functions in Chapter 6.) Here's a direct object: He wanted *to win the race decisively.* Here's a subject: *To win the race decisively* was his goal in life. Second, infinitives can act as adjectives: The man *to beat* is the Democratic candidate for the Senate. Or: The best way *to go* avoids rush-hour traffic. Third, infinitives can act as adverbs: *To win the race decisively,* he trained four hours each day. Or: The homeowner wildly brandished his gun *to scare away the intruder.*

3) The Present Participial Phrase

Every verb has a present participle, formed by adding *-ing* to the base verb. As discussed above, present participles do show up in conjugated form in the progressive tenses. But they can also act as unconjugated verbals in participial phrases. The present participial phrase has the present participle of the verb and some other words. Again, if the verb is transitive, the phrase will have a noun acting as the object of that verb. The verb might have adverbs and the noun might have adjectives. All the words collectively form the present participial phrase.

Present participles act as nouns, adjectives, or adverbs. When they act as nouns, they are called *gerunds* and can serve many noun functions. Here's a direct object: He enjoyed *swimming.* Here's a subject: *Winning the race decisively* was his goal in life.

When you use present participial phrases as adjectives, you must be careful about their placement. When a present participial phrase acts as an adjective and begins a sentence, it must modify the subject of the sentence—or the first noun it finds in the independent clause, which is usually the subject. Ever heard of a dangling participle? Here's one: *Marshalling his forces,* the candidacy of Mr. Smith sailed successfully toward election day. Here the present participial phrase *marshalling his forces* needs a subject. The verb *marshalling* seeks an actor, a *marshaller.* The obvious *marshaller* is Mr. Smith. But the first noun encountered in the independent clause is *candidacy.* The participle is unhooked. It just dangles. Revise the sentence and make Mr. Smith the subject: Marshalling his forces, *Mr. Smith* successfully guided his candidacy toward election day.

Other present participial phrases acting as adjectives will *follow* the nouns they modify. In the preceding sentence, the present participial phrase—*acting as adjectives*—followed the noun it modified—*phrases.* Or: The regulations *governing the issues in our case* include sections 202.132 and 202.135. (In a later chapter, we'll review the correct punctuation of restrictive and nonrestrictive phrases.)

Also, some very effective present participial phrases come at the tail end of sentences and are usually separated from the rest of the sentence by a comma. Thus: The court excluded the evidence, *ruling that it was obtained in an illegal search and seizure.*

Finally, present participles can sometimes act as adverbs. The adverbial structure does exist but is rarely encountered. Thus: He died *laughing.*

4) The Past Participial Phrase

Every verb also has a past participle. The past participles of regular verbs are formed by adding *-ed.* Thus, the past participle of *exclude* is *excluded.* The past participle of *decide* is *decided.* Other verbs are irregular, having their own unique past participle, usually ending in the letter *n.* Thus, the past participle of *see* is *seen.* The past participle of *show* is *shown.*

Past participles also show up in a conjugated form. With the auxiliary verb *have,* the past participle forms the perfect tenses: *I have shown, I had shown, I will have shown.* Indeed, if you have trouble remembering the past participle of any given verb, simply complete this sentence: *I have _____.* Add the correct verb form. It'll be the past participle of that verb. Also, in a conjugated state, past participles form the passive voice, a topic we'll address in great detail in Chapter 7.

In their unconjugated state, past participles form phrases. These phrases can act only as adjectives and precede or follow the nouns they modify. In a later chapter, we'll see that these participial phrases are the product of discarded passive voice clauses. Thus, don't use a passive voice clause like this: The statute, *which was enacted in 1964,* protected our civil rights. Instead, try a past participial phrase like this: The statute, *enacted in 1964,* protected our civil rights. Or: *Enacted in 1964,* the statute protected our civil rights.

5) One-Word Adjectives

The final use of verbs is the one-word participial adjective. These participial adjectives can be present participles or past participles. They are among the most vivid words in the language, describing nouns with verb-like images: *the decided case, the cocked gun, the depreciated property.* All three—*decided, cocked,* and *depreciated*—are past participles. Or: *the winning argument, the limiting factor, the losing team.* All three—*winning, limiting,* and *losing*—are present participles.

How's that for versatility. A verb serves as the pivotal point of the English sentence. The main verb forms that vital fulcrum in our sentence, the independent clause, as well as the dependent clause. The unconjugated verb—the verbal—can function as a noun, as an adjective, and even as an adverb to modify other verbs. The verb does it all. Indeed, one can write a sentence consisting entirely of verbs: *To win is exciting.* No other word in the English language can accomplish as much. In Hugo's words, "the verb is God." Yet, as a profession, we have all but abandoned this highly potent word. Instead, we bury the meaning of verbs in piles of nouns like this:

> Amendment of our request is one of our possible courses of action, but if we make a change in our position as of this late date, we might find the FOIA officer hesitant to place reliance on our exemption arguments.

Adapted from R. Wydick, *Plain English for Lawyers* 38-39 (Carolina Academic Press 1979).

There is a much better way.

Engaging in a Conversion of Nouns to Verbs

Instead of *engaging in a conversion* of nouns to verbs, let's learn *to convert* nouns to verbs. The trick is really quite easy. First identify derivative nouns, primarily those ending in *-tion, -sion, -ence, -ance, -ency, -ancy,* and *-ment.* Second, be on the lookout for noun-words that can operate as verbs, e.g., *change.* Third, look for nouns you can convert to verbs. *Emphasis,* for example, can convert to *emphasize* or *stress.* (Please, under no circumstances should you change perfectly good nouns like *priority* to perfectly terrible verb forms like *prioritize.* Fowler, no doubt, would go nuclear.)

Once you've identified these mushy noun forms, try converting them to verbs or verbals. Not surprisingly, here's what you'll get: (1) main verbs, (2) infinitive phrases acting as nouns, adjectives, or adverbs, (3) present participial phrases acting primarily as nouns or adjectives, (4) past participial phrases acting as adjectives, and perhaps (5) one-word verb-adjectives.

Let's take the passage above and *engage in a conversion.* Here it is again:

> Amendment of our request is one of our possible courses of action, but if we make a change in our position as of this late date, we might find the FOIA officer hesitant to place reliance on our exemption arguments.

Here's the same passage after *denounification*:

> We could amend our request, but if we change our position at this late date, the FOIA officer might hesitate to rely on our exemption arguments.

The first passage has 40 words. The revised passage has 26. Write a 400-page nouny report. I can rewrite the same report in 260 pages. And the only trick I use is *denounification.*

Piles of Goo—Nouny Expressions of Auxiliary Verbs and Adverbs

Nouns are like rabbits. They breed other nouns. Use one noun structure and it's likely to require other noun structures. Here's why.

Suppose a writer buries the meaning of a verb in a noun form. The writer wishes to say *stop,* but, preferring the longer, fancier-sounding word, uses *termination* instead. Further suppose the writer wishes to say *must stop.* The writer needs the auxiliary verb *must* to say what he wants to say. But by choosing the noun form *termination,* the writer has deprived himself of using some of the most forceful words in the entire language—auxiliary verbs. These wonderful little words pack a real punch in a small amount of space. Think about their meanings, especially their meanings in the law: *can, may, must, ought, should, would, might, will,* and others. How does the nouny writer say *must* (other than *a must*)? Here's one way:

> The effectuation of improvement in our relations with the executive branch has as a requirement our termination of the taking of positions inconsistent with stated executive policy.

The noun *termination,* struggling to convey the meaning of the verb *stop,* bred other nouns when it needed to convey the meaning of the auxiliary verb *must.* Thus: *has as a requirement.*

How does the nouny writer say *can?* Here's a way:

> Amendment of our request is one of our possible courses of action, but if we make a change in our position as of this late date, we might find the FOIA officer hesitant to place reliance on our exemption arguments.

The noun *amendment,* struggling to say *amend,* multiplied other piles of goo when it wanted to say *could amend.* The noun form required the mushy expression *possible courses of action.*

How does the nouny writer express crucial adverbial meaning? Recall in our discussion of the Six Universal Questions that adverbs answer some rather important questions: *where, when, how,* and *why.* If writers bury the meaning of a verb in a noun form, they're in big trouble when they need to modify that idea with an adverb. How does the nouny writer say the adverb *sometimes?* Here's a way:

> There are instances in which consumer abuse and exploitation result from advertising which is false, misleading, or irrelevant.

Wydick, *supra* p. 52, at 69.

By using the nouns *abuse* and *exploitation* to bury the meaning of the verbs *abuse* and *exploit,* the nouny writer then buried the meaning of the adverb *sometimes* in the pile of goo *there are instances in which.*

Using the verb form, the writer has the true adverb *sometimes* at hand and ready to go:

> Consumers are sometimes abused and exploited by false, misleading, or irrelevant advertising.

Nouns will breed other nouns in other ways as well. As we saw above, we connect nouns to our sentences with verbs or prepositions. In a later chapter, we'll see that a prepositional form favored by the nouny writer is the *compound preposition,* e.g., *in the event of.* Thus, watch what happens when the nouny writer chooses the noun form *use* over the verb form *use*:

> In the event of the employee's use of intoxicating beverages, the employment will terminate.

Converting to verb, of course, changes the wordy compound preposition *in the event of* into a two-letter subordinating conjunction *if*:

> If the employee uses intoxicating beverages, the employment will terminate.

Write Like Willie Nelson

Though I don't endorse his grammar, I do endorse his style. Willie Nelson, other great writers, and the great legal writers of our day all share a secret: they prefer verb forms over noun forms. By using verbs and verbals, they evoke a sense of motion and activity in their writing. With the verb form, they certainly compact information into fewer words—favoring as they do quick, hard-hitting main verbs; succinct, to-the-point infinitives; and tight, action-packed participles. Need proof? Here's Willie singing 39 words. Eighteen of those words are *verb-words.*

> Them that *don't know* him *won't like* him, and them that *do* sometimes *won't know* how *to take* him. He *ain't* wrong, he's just different, and his pride *won't let* him *do* things *to make* you *think* he's right. (*Mama, Don't Let Your Babies Grow Up To Be Cowboys.*)

Need more proof? Here's Mr. Justice Robert H. Jackson describing the role of the United States Tax Court. He uses plain old verbs like *deals, staffed, bring, clouded, call forth,* and even *fan out.*

The court is independent, and its neutrality is not clouded by prosecuting duties. Its procedures assure fair hearings. Its deliberations are evidenced by careful opinions. All guides to judgment available to judges are habitually consulted and respected. It has established a tradition of freedom from bias and pressures. It deals with a subject that is highly specialized and so complex as to be the despair of judges. It is relatively better staffed for its task than is the judiciary. Its members not infrequently bring to their task long legislative or administrative experience in their subject. The volume of tax matters flowing through the Tax Court keeps its members abreast of changing statutes, regulations, and Bureau practices, informed as to the background of controversies and aware of the impact of their decisions on both Treasury and taxpayer. Individual cases are disposed of wholly on records publicly made, in adversary proceedings, and the court has no responsibility for previous handling. Tested by every theoretical and practical reason for administrative finality, no administrative decisions are entitled to higher credit in the courts. Consideration of uniform and expeditious tax administrations require that they be given all credit to which they are entitled under the law.

Tax Court decisions are characterized by substantial uniformity. Appeals fan out into the courts of appeal of ten circuits and the District of Columbia. This diversification of appellate authority inevitably produces conflict of decision, even if review is limited to questions of law. But conflicts are multiplied by treating as questions of law what really are disputes over proper accounting. The mere number of such questions and the mass of decisions they call forth become a menace to the certainty and good administration of the law.

Dobson v. Commissioner, 320 U.S. 489, 498-99 (1943) (footnotes omitted).

Want to produce an aura of vigor and force? Use verbs. Circuit Judge Frank H. Easterbrook of the Seventh Circuit knows the trick. Listen to his put-down of an attorney who appealed an unappealable order in *Cleaver v. Elias*, 852 F.2d 266, 266, 267-68 (7th Cir. 1988):

A premature notice of appeal *disrupts* proceedings in the district court. That court *must put* the case aside and *wait* for this one *to send* the record back. Such a notice also *imposes unjustified* costs on the adversary, whose lawyers *must monitor* the case and *file* papers in two courts at once, and on the judges who *must set* things straight. [The attorney] *has filed* such a notice of appeal, after the district judge *told* [him] that there *was* no judgment *to appeal*. *Having sanctioned* [the attorney] under Fed.R.Civ.P. 11 earlier in the case for *filing* an obtuse motion, the district judge *warned* counsel: "I don't think I entered a final judgment order. Now, if you have appealed that, sir, you'll probably get sanctioned up there." [The attorney] *replied*: "I doubt it very much, your Honor." Counsel *should have accepted* this free advice. Our views *are* neither advisory nor free. We *dismiss* the appeal for want of jurisdiction and *impose* a sanction of $1,500 under Fed.R.App.P. 38 *to be paid* by counsel personally.

. . . .

[The attorney] *removed* this case to federal court. It *was* his responsibility *to learn* the fundamentals of federal practice whether the forum *was* of his *choosing* or not. Instead he *filed* and stubbornly *clung* to a silly appeal. Lawyers who *invoke* our jurisdiction without *doing* the necessary groundwork *must expect to pay* for the costs they *impose* on their adversaries and the judicial system. [Citations omitted.] [The attorney's] appeal *caused* the district court *to abort* the hearing on June 13 that *had been called to fix* the amount due on the loan. He *was warned* by the district court and by our order *to show* cause; instead of *dismissing* the appeal he obstinately *pressed forward*. He *is penalized* $1,500 under Rule 38, of which $1,000 is *to be paid* to the plaintiffs as rough compensation for the costs of the *wasted* hearing of June 13 and the need *to monitor* this appeal, and $500 to the Treasury.

Zap! Forty-seven verb constructions. Look at some: *put aside, wait, imposes, monitor, set things straight, caused, pressed forward, doing* and ... *clung*. If you want to write the same way—powerfully—then the single most important trick in this entire book requires you to use verbs, frequently and effectively.

Baring Your Knuckles—Using Forgotten Verbs

As I have reviewed many samples of legal writing, I have come to believe that one of the most important keys to powerful prose is the effective use of verbs. Inevitably, when reviewing a paper and getting a sense of flab, I can circle main verbs and find lots of *makes, takes, has, is,* and worse *was the result of.* Spotting what's there prompts me to look for what's not there. Looking high and low, inevitably I come up empty in the tally of infinitive phrases, present participial phrases, past participial phrases, and one-word verb-adjectives.

As a profession, we have forgotten or refused to use the most powerful word in the English language—the verb. In the interest of reviving this lost art form, I urge you to search your memory and find and use hard-hitting verb forms. Try to remember words like *deem, prompt, stress, pinpoint, single out,* Mr. Justice Jackson's *fan out,* and Judge Easterbrook's *cling.* Perhaps we can launch (there's a good one) a campaign to remove the verb from the list of endangered species. Willie and Mr. Justice Jackson would like that. And so would Judge Easterbrook.

The Rules of Good Writing

Your list of the rules of good writing now looks like this:

1 Use an average of 25 words per sentence.

2. Avoid putting too many messages in a single sentence.

3. Put most of your messages at the subject-predicate position.

4. For variety or emphasis, invert your sentences.

5. Use the art of subordination to smooth out choppiness.

6. Avoid disrupting your sentences with thought-stopping gaps.

7. Watch out for the rule of parallel construction.

8. Tabulate particularly complex information.

9. Hammer home your point with the powerful, versatile verb.

Chapter 4

"To Be" or Not "To Be"

To be, or not to be: that is the question . . . .

—Shakespeare

Not "to be": that is the answer.

—Good

Chapter 4

"To Be" or Not "To Be"

Introduction

I learned the answer to this ancient question, as I learn most things about writing, by teaching writing to lawyers. In 1984, I taught a series of persuasive writing courses to attorneys at the Securities & Exchange Commission in Washington and New York. One course, designed for supervising attorneys, stressed the ways to distinguish good writing from bad and methods the supervising attorneys could use to give feedback to the supervised attorneys. To one of these sessions an attorney brought a sample of a brief she was reviewing. She said, "I know this writing needs help, but I don't know what kind."

I looked at it. And looked. And looked.

"You're right," I replied. "And I don't know what kind, either."

Then it jumped right off the page at me. I grabbed my pen and began to circle main verbs. The vast majority of the verbs on a single page were various forms of the verb *to be*. The attorney and I agreed that there simply could not be so much *be-ness* running around. The subject matter simply could not involve so much *being*. There just had to be some *doing* somewhere. Some subject matter in the writing had to involve, not *being*, but *happening*. There just had to be some action. Even in abstract legal writing.

As an experiment, I asked her to return the paper to the writer and instruct him to rewrite the offending page without using the verb *to be* at all, or at least to reduce the number of *be's* on the page. The next week, at the next class session, the attorney showed me the repaired passage. The difference was remarkable. The writing now had flair, vim, and vigor.

Naturally, I hastily repaired to my word processor, called up my course materials, and constructed a giant insert on the verb *to be*. Since that time, I've devoted significant class time to answer the question: *to be* or not *to be*.

My suspicions about the verb *to be* were confirmed when I was teaching a writing workshop to some managers at the Health Care Financing Administration. One of the class members came to me during the break following the segment on the verb *to be*. Before working for the government, he said, he had served as a Jesuit priest, teaching English at a school in Pittsburgh. He had noticed that high school students tended to favor the verb *to be* in their speech and their writing. They, too, had forgotten, or never learned, the potency of action verbs. To repair the damage, this clever teacher cooked up an assignment required of all students: write a paper, on any topic, and do not use the verb *to be* at all. The results, he said, were amazing. The exercise forced considerable thought and demanded creative use of the language.

Like and Go—The Next Be's?

Today's high school, college, and even law student could benefit from such an assignment. Today, not only have many students forgotten the power of verbs, they've invented incredible crutch-words that pepper their spoken language. Sooner, rather than later, these words or similar weak expressions will show up in their written language. These crutch-words come, I think, from Saturday morning cartoons and "Valley Speak" in California. One day, I hope, they'll leave as quickly as they came. If they don't, they threaten to diminish our language significantly.

Though I'm no etymologist, I firmly believe that *like* and *go* came directly from television. Think about the two primary ways young people use *go*. First, it serves as a catchall verb substituting for *said, stated, asked, replied, responded,* or other verb meaning *to speak.* Thus, students might go:

> My teacher asked the hardest question in class today. She went, "How does the Bill of Rights affect the 50 states?"
>
> Did she call on you?
>
> Sure did, and I went, "Don't the states have to provide the same rights?"
>
> And she went, "I'm asking you."
>
> So I went, "Yes, they have to provide the same rights."
>
> Next time I'll go like . . . .

The second use of *go* proves its origins in television. Today's elocutionist, when describing an event, might go like:

> He was running long for the pass. He went [speaker extends arms indicating a reaching motion desperately seeking to connect with the spiraling pigskin]. When he jumped, he went [speaker then whistles from a high *C* down the chromatic scale and immediately follows this noise with an explosive, guttural sound-effect roughly equivalent to a Madden-like "whap."]

The only words used?

> He was running long for the pass. He went .... When he jumped, he went "whap."

One can readily see the connection between television and speech. Just conjure up the image of the typical cartoon character running off the side of a cliff. He continues running in air, realizes the disappearance of ground beneath his feet, panics, begins plummeting wildly to earth to the tune of a whistle down the chromatic scale, and meets his Maker in an ear-splitting collision with Mother Earth—all of which is brought to life by the sound-effect guy in the back room dropping on a concrete slab an overly ripe watermelon from a 10-foot ladder. When asked what happened, the child describes, not what happened, but *what he saw*:

> He went [arms flail wildly in air, whistle down the chromatic scale, terror-stricken expression on face] "whap."

He went "whap." That's it. That's the extent of the language. No other thoughts or expressions of thought are possible. Nor allowed. Nor, worse, understood. When I talked about this problem with my own two sons, the elder, tongue firmly in cheek, went, "Dad, I wonder who was the first person who went 'go'?" I don't know who first *went "go"* but if we continue *to go "go"* and convey our meaning with special visual and sound effects, we can forget about verbs forever.

Go has mutated into an even worse expression: *was-like*. One day, we'll close this compound and have a new word *waslike* or *islike* or even *wasgoinglike*. Listen to the speech around you:

> He waslike, "I just couldn't get out of bed this morning."

> Did he like have a bad night?

> Like, he waslike uhhhhh. He had a six-pack in like an hour.

Do *golikers* really threaten our language? You'd better believe they do. The national press even provides direct quotations of this scourge. While I was putting the finishing touches on this book in the fall of 1988, the valiant Eskimos, marine biologists, and Russian sailors were trying to save the two ice-bound whales off Barrow, Alaska. Quoting the rescue coordinator, the *Washington Post* put the following in one of those boxes designed to catch the reader's attention. It certainly caught mine.

> These guys [the Russians] were all business. We got on board
> and they were like, "Let's go break ice."

Washington Post at A3 (October 26, 1988).

The Valley Girls and their bubble gum have like messed up our like language. Spit it out, folks, or your writing will suffer as well. The *go-like* talk will probably show up in legal writing in the form of too many *be's*. "To be or not to be, that is the question." Not *to be*. Not *go*. Not *like*. Not *waslike*. Those are the answers.

The Meaning of the Verb *To Be*

Before studying the rule on the proper use of the verb *to be*, we would do well to explore its meaning and use in the English language. When used as the main verb of a sentence or clause, the verb *to be* shows a state of being, the existence of something, or a condition. The verb follows a subject and shows the existence of that subject or some condition of that subject. These meanings become plainer when you contemplate grammatical constructions of the verb *to be*.

Rarely, but sometimes, the verb *to be* can appear by itself. Ask Neal Diamond. "I am, I said," he sang. Most of the time, the verb *to be* will be followed by a noun (predicate nominative) or an adjective (predicate adjective). And in some cases, the verb *to be* can be followed by an adverb. Let's look at each construction to see what it means.

When the verb *to be* is followed by a noun (predicate nominative or subject complement), that noun restates or defines the subject of the sentence. Thus: *The decision of the court was a landmark in the development of civil rights law.* Decision was landmark. The predicate nominative *landmark* defines *decision*; it tells what the decision *was*.

When the verb *to be* is followed by an adjective (predicate adjective), that adjective describes the subject of the sentence. This structure is one of the few ways in the English language to get an adjective to follow the word it modifies. Thus: *The decision of the court was instrumental in increasing competition in the telecommunications industry.* Decision was instrumental. The predicate adjective *instrumental* describes *decision*; it states the condition of the decision.

The verb *to be* might be followed by a prepositional phrase. Thus: *He was from the north.* Or: *He was for Bush.* Or: *He is like a child.*

In some situations, the verb *to be* might be followed by an adverb. Recall that adverbs answer four questions: *when, where, how,* and *why.* Though adverbs cannot say *how* or *why* someone *is*, they can say *where* or *when* someone *is.* Thus: *He is here.* Or: *He is late.* But not: *He is "quickly."*

Finally, I should point out that *to be* also acts as an auxiliary verb. Coupled with a present participle, it forms the progressive tenses:

he is showing

he was showing

he will be showing

he has been showing

he had been showing

he will have been showing

Also, when used with a past participle, the verb *to be* forms the passive voice of that verb:

the movie is shown

the movie was shown

the movie will be shown

the movie has been shown

the movie had been shown

the movie will have been shown

We will return to the passive voice for extensive discussion in a later chapter. For now we are interested in *to be* not as an auxiliary, but as the main verb of an independent or dependent clause.

The Rule: Use the Verb *To Be* Only When You Mean It

The verb *to be* properly defines or describes. When you truly want to say what something *is* or what something *is like*, use the verb *to be*. However, if you want to say what something *does*, but use the verb *to be* as a means of showing *doing*, you will end up with inordinately flabby writing.

Not surprisingly, writers that overuse the verb *to be* tend to be nouny writers as well. Recall that the verb *to be* is an ideal *groped-for* verb on which to hang derivative nouns and derivative adjectives. Thus, watch out for this:

> The court was of the belief that a precondition of dismissal is a finding that the evidence is inadmissible.

Getting rid of *be's* and engaging in denounification produce this:

> The court believed that dismissing the case hinged on finding the evidence inadmissible.

As another example, check out the abundance of *be's* in this passage, which is describing the nature of a Senate resolution that confirms a President's judicial nominee:

> This definition leads us to conclude that the nature of a resolution is that it is a formal expression of opinion that has only a temporary effect or no effect at all as a legal matter. The Senate's confirmation vote is an expression of the opinion of the Senate as to whether the Senate will advise and consent to the nomination. This expression of opinion by formal vote is, in substance, virtually identical to the meaning of a resolution. However, it is not clear that the Senate's confirmation vote merely expresses an opinion and has only a temporary effect on a particular matter or thing. While the advice and consent offered by the Senate is an expression of opinion, it is not merely an expression of opinion because it has consequences that ordinarily do not result from the mere expression of an opinion. In short, although the Senate itself labels its confirmation vote a resolution, that vote is in substance not a resolution, but is placed somewhere in the spectrum between Acts and bills, on the one side, and resolutions, on the other side.

Now look at the same passage written without any *be's* instead of the nine used above:

This definition helps us understand the nature of a resolution. A resolution formally expresses the Senate's opinion and has only a temporary effect or no effect at all as a legal matter. The Senate's confirmation vote also expresses the Senate's opinion on whether it will advise and consent to the nomination. Expressing this opinion by formal confirmation vote closely resembles a Senate resolution. However, the Senate's confirmation vote does more than merely express an opinion. It has a lasting, not a temporary, effect on a particular matter or thing. While the advice and consent of the Senate in the confirmation vote does express its opinion, the vote has consequences that go beyond the mere expression of an opinion. In short, although the Senate itself labels its confirmation vote a resolution, that vote differs from a resolution. The vote falls somewhere between Acts and bills, on the one side, and resolutions, on the other side.

As a final example, let's look at Henry Steele Commager's writing in *The American Mind* and see how he uses the verb *to be* when he means it and avoids it when he doesn't:

The American's attitude toward authority, rules and regulations was the despair of bureaucrats and disciplinarians. Nowhere did he differ more sharply from his English cousins than in his attitude toward rules, for where the Englishman regarded the observance of a rule as a positive pleasure, to the American a rule was at once an affront and a challenge. His schools were almost without discipline, yet they were not on the whole disorderly, and the young girls and spinsters who taught them were rarely embarrassed. This absence of discipline in the schools reflected absence of discipline in the home. Parents were notoriously indulgent of their children and children notoriously disrespectful of parents, yet family life was on the whole happy, and most children grew up to be good parents and good citizens.

Notice, in describing what a rule *was* and how the teachers *were* and how the schools *were*, Mr. Commager appropriately used the verb *to be*. But also notice his sentence:

This absence of discipline in the schools reflected absence of discipline in the home.

Notice what he didn't say:

> This absence of discipline in the schools *was the result of* absence of discipline in the home.

Good writers use *to be* only when they mean it.

Expletive Deleted

Before moving on to another first cousin of nouniness—compound prepositions—we should glance quickly at a special construction of the verb *to be*, the expletive. These expletives are not the notorious *expletives deleted* of Watergate-tape-transcript fame. Those expletives were President Nixon's gutter language.

The expletive we discuss here is a surrogate noun expression like *there are, these are, it is,* and *this is.* In these expressions (called expletives), *there, these, it,* or *this* serves as a substitute noun for the true subject of the sentence. Look at the following sentence:

> There are numerous cases of child abuse in the state of Massachusetts.

The grammatical subject is *there*. The verb is *are*. The grammatical predicate nominative is *cases*. The true subject of the sentence, however, is *cases*. The word *there* just stands in the place of *cases*.

Ordinarily, there is nothing wrong with this structure. I just used it. *There is nothing wrong with this structure.* However, if the expletive is followed by a *that* or *which* clause, and if you use lots of these expressions, chances are good your sentences beg for revision. Here are some examples:

> It was the belief of the court that the plaintiff's contributory negligence would be a bar to recovery.

> There are several factors that the court must take into consideration when it decides on the violation of the statute.

> This is one important factor that all courts place great emphasis upon.

No, no, no. When you spot this kind of writing, delete the expletive and make the true subject of the sentence the grammatical subject as well:

The court believed that the plaintiff's contributory negligence barred recovery.

The court must consider several factors when it decides if the statute has been violated.

All courts emphasize this one important factor.

Summary

In this chapter, we've looked carefully, and somewhat harshly, at the verb *to be*. My harsh look is not meant to suggest the abolition of the verb. Indeed, by definition, we just could not be without it.

What I suggest is careful thought. When you truly want to show being, use *to be*. But whenever you can, choose a vigorous action verb to carry your thought. Without any doubt, the powerful writer uses heavy doses of verbs other than the verb *to be*. Give it a try. Your writing will be better. I mean, your writing will improve.

The Rules of Good Writing

Your list of the rules of good writing now looks like this:

1. Use an average of 25 words per sentence.
2. Avoid putting too many messages in a single sentence.
3. Put most of your messages at the subject-predicate position.
4. For variety or emphasis, invert your sentences.
5. Use the art of subordination to smooth out choppiness.
6. Avoid disrupting your sentences with thought-stopping gaps.
7. Watch out for the rule of parallel construction.
8. Tabulate particularly complex information.
9. Hammer home your point with the powerful, versatile verb.
10. Use the verb *to be* only when you mean it.

Chapter 5

Compound Prepositions
The Compost of our Language

[He] is as brisk as a bee in conversation; but no sooner does he take a pen in his hand, than it . . . benumbs all his faculties.

—Samuel Johnson

Chapter 5

Compound Prepositions

The Compost of our Language

Introduction

Lawyers love *with respect to, in reference to, in connection with, for the purposes of,* and similar expressions. In this chapter, I hope to convince you to avoid these *compound prepositions* altogether. If you're hooked, however, perhaps I can get you to reduce your use of these expressions in the interest of vastly improving your writing.

This chapter first will define the preposition, the prepositional phrase, and the compound preposition. Our discussion will then provide an all-out scathing attack on the compound preposition by one of the greatest stylists of our time. Then you'll find examples of the compound-preposition style and see just how vague these expressions are. At the end, I'll provide a list of compound prepositions and their simpler substitutes.

Preposition and Prepositional Phrase Defined

In the chapter on nouniness, you learned that nouns must be glued to sentences by verbs or prepositions. If glued by verbs, nouns serve as subjects or objects of main verbs or verbals. The other major way to glue nouns onto sentences is by the preposition. Looked at in this way—as one of the primary noun-attachers—the preposition readily finds its own definition:

> A preposition is a word used to link a noun or noun form to a sentence and to show the relationship the noun bears to another noun or to a verb.

From the definition of a preposition, we can glean the definition of a prepositional phrase:

> A prepositional phrase consists of a preposition and a noun or noun form acting as the object of the preposition.

A preposition links a noun or noun form to a sentence. Coupled with that noun or noun form, it produces a prepositional phrase. Note that the preposition links a noun and shows the relationship of that noun to another noun in the sentence or to a verb in the sentence. Thus, the prepositional phrase primarily serves two roles in the English sentence. First, by showing the relationship of a noun to another noun, the prepositional phrase acts as an *adjective*. For example: The man *in the front row* paid a hefty price for his ticket. The prepositional phrase *in the front row* modifies the noun *man*. And the prepositional phrase *for his ticket* modifies the noun *price*. Thus, the prepositional phrase serves its first function, that of an adjective. Second, by showing the relationship of a noun to a verb, the prepositional phrase acts as an *adverb*. For example: He ran *down the street* to see the approaching parade. The prepositional phrase *down the street* modifies the verb *ran* by telling *where* he ran. (Please note in this example that *to see the approaching parade* is an infinitive phrase, not a prepositional phrase.) The prepositional phrase thus serves its second function, that of an adverb. (I should note that a prepositional phrase might act as a noun: *After six* is a good time to call.)

A preposition connects a noun to a sentence and, with that noun, forms a phrase acting primarily as an adjective or adverb. The key is the noun—the object of the preposition. Without that noun, the preposition cannot even be in a sentence. At least it cannot serve as a preposition. Without the noun, a word that otherwise would be a preposition must act in some other way.

Take the word *down* as an example. If used in a sentence in some way other than to link a noun to the sentence, the word cannot be a preposition. Consider this sentence: He looked *down the hill* to see the sporting event. Here *down* is used as a preposition in the adverbial prepositional phrase *down the hill* to modify *looked*. Now try this: He looked *down* to hunt for coins. The sentence is almost identical. But the word *down* lacks a noun to link to the rest of the sentence. Therefore, the word *down* is not and cannot be a preposition. It functions as a simple adverb modifying *looked*.

Notice in the above definitions that a noun *or noun form* must join with a preposition to form a prepositional phrase. These *noun forms* include present participles and noun clauses. We've already dealt with present participles acting as nouns. When they do, they're called *gerunds.* Here's one acting as the object of a preposition: He became adept in *coaching his witnesses.* In that sentence, the present participial phrase *coaching his witnesses* acts as the object of the preposition *in.*

The other noun form that can serve as the object of a preposition is the *noun clause.* We will deal extensively with noun clauses in a later chapter. Here, I'll only provide an example of a noun clause used as the object of a preposition and postpone any analysis of noun clauses and the damage they often do to our language:

> Your supervisor was aware of *the fact that you bought this book.*

The noun clause *the fact that you bought this book* serves as the object of the preposition *of.*

The Importance of Prepositions

Why does a book on persuasive writing for lawyers include a discussion of prepositions? For this very good reason. Legal writing not only has abandoned the hard-hitting verb but has lost touch with the simple, but forceful, preposition. Indeed, the legal writer might have asked the above question this way: "Why does a book with regard to persuasive writing for lawyers include a discussion with respect to prepositions?"

Legal writing ignores simple, powerful prepositions like *on* and *of.* It prefers instead fluffy prepositions like *with regard to* and *with respect to.* Learning to discard these *compound prepositions* requires an understanding of the grammatical role of prepositions. That's why this book contains a discussion with respect to prepositions.

Compound Preposition Defined

A *compound preposition* is a series of prepositional phrases that combine to act as a single preposition. Examples include:

> with respect to
> with regard to
> in connection with
> for the purposes of

The beginning of a compound preposition is an apparently complete prepositional phrase. In the above examples, note these apparently complete prepositional phrases:

with respect
with regard
in connection
for the purposes

Yet these apparently complete prepositional phrases could not function in sentences alone. They need to combine forces with another preposition so that together they can link a noun to a sentence.

with respect to your <u>request</u>
with regard to the <u>issue</u> of damages
in connection with the <u>sale</u> of securities
for the purposes of <u>determining</u> total tax owed

In the above list, the italicized compound prepositions serve to link the underlined nouns. The compound preposition needs the apparently complete prepositional phrase *with respect* and the additional preposition *to* to form a single expression acting as a single preposition—*with respect to.*

That's what compound prepositions are. That's what compound prepositions do. That's what compound prepositions look like. Now let's go after them with a vengeance.

Garbage

I hope that heading attracts attention. I didn't make it up. The thought belongs to Henry Fowler. Here's what he has to say about compound prepositions:

> [T]aken as a whole, they are almost the worst element in modern English, stuffing up what is written with a compost of nouny abstractions. To young writers the discovery of these forms of speech, which are used very little in talk and very much in print, brings an expansive sense of increased power; they think they have acquired with far less trouble than they expected the trick of dressing up what they may have to say in the right costume for public exhibition. Later they know better, and realize that it is feebleness instead of power that they have been developing; but by that time the fatal ease that the compound-preposition style gives (to the writer, that is) has become too dear to be sacrificed.

H. Fowler, *Modern English Usage* 102 (2d ed. 1965).

If you are hooked on compound prepositions, you will dramatically improve your writing by sacrificing the compound-preposition style. They clutter up our language and fail to convey our precise meaning. Nouny writers necessarily favor the compound-preposition style, needing as they do lots of prepositions on which to hook their nouns. Thus, the nouny writer is likely to say:

> In the event of the employee's use of intoxicating beverages, the employment will terminate.

Obliterating the noun *use* and changing it to the verb *uses* also erases the need for the compound preposition. Its meaning shifts to the subordinating conjunction *if*:

> If the employee uses intoxicating beverages on the job, the employment will terminate.

Imprecision

Compound prepositions do more than clutter. They prevent or at least hinder precision in our writing. These expressions often are so imprecise that they should be abolished from our language. Consider one of the all-time favorites, *with respect to*. In the following passage, watch what happens to its meaning:

> The problem *with respect to* the compound preposition is its ability to experience a shift *with respect to* meaning. *With respect to* some sentences, it can mean one thing, while *with respect to* other sentences it might have something else to say *with respect to* some other topic.

Need a translation? Watch the meaning of *with respect to* shift from one preposition to an entirely different one.

> *Translation*: The problem *with* the compound preposition is its ability to experience a shift *in* meaning. *In* some sentences, it can mean one thing, while *in* other sentences it might have something else to say *about* some other topic.

Just think how strange it would be, back in your first year of law school, to have your Torts professor give a reading assignment in *Prosser With Respect To Torts*.

Now consider *for the purposes of*. It really means nothing more than *for* or *under*. Compare: *A trust for the purposes of section 101 shall mean a legal entity . . . .* Or: *A trust solely for the purposes of section 101 shall mean a legal entity . . . .* How does either of these sentences differ at all from the following: *Under section 101 a trust shall mean a legal entity . . . .*

Next, think about the expression *for the purposes of* plus an *-ing* verb, a gerund. You can and should convert all these prepositional phrases to infinitive phrases using the infinitive of the *-ing* verb. For example:

for the purposes of ascertaining intent	to ascertain intent
for the purposes of determining income	to determine income
for the purposes of inspecting the property	to inspect the property

Try declaring war on compound prepositions. At first the change will sound strange. Once you get used to it, however, you'll definitely prefer the clearer, more direct style.

A List of Compound Prepositions

To assist you in converting compound prepositions to simpler prepositions or to other grammatical forms, here's a partial list showing compound prepositions and the simpler expressions that should replace them:

Compound Preposition	Simple Expression
at that point in time	then
at this point in time	now
by means of	by
by reason of	because of
by virtue of	by, under
during the course of	during
for the purposes of [+ noun]	for, under
for the purposes of [+ gerund]	infinitive phrase
from the point of view of	from, for
in accordance with	by, under

in a manner similar to	like
in excess of	more than, over
in favor of	for
in receipt of	having received
in relation to	about, concerning
in terms of	in
in the event of	if
in the nature of	like
in the immediate vicinity of	near
in close proximity with	near
on the basis of	by, from
to the extent of	insofar as
with a view to	to
with reference to	about, concerning
with regard to	about, concerning
with respect to	on, about, for, in, concerning, with, to

Some Common Prepositions You Might Have Forgotten

aboard	as against
about	as between
above	as for
according to	aside from
across	as to
after	at
against	barring
along	because of
alongside of (or alongside)	before
along with	behind
amid or amidst	below
among or amongst	beneath
apart from	beside
around	besides

between
beyond
by
concerning
considering
despite
down
during
excepting (or except)
exclusive of
for
from above
from among
from behind
from beneath
from between
from over
from under
in
including
inclusive of
independently of
in front of
in lieu of
inside of (or inside)
in spite of
instead of
into
like
notwithstanding
of
off
on
on account of

on behalf of
onto
opposite to (or opposite)
out of
outside of (or outside)
over
owing to
past
pending
regarding
regardless of
relating to
relative to
respecting
round
saving
short of
since
through
throughout
to
touching
toward (or towards)
under
underneath
until (or till)
unto
up
upon
via
with
within
without

The Rules of Good Writing

Your list of the rules of good writing now looks like this:

1. Use an average of 25 words per sentence.
2. Avoid putting too many messages in a single sentence.
3. Put most of your messages at the subject-predicate position.
4. For variety or emphasis, invert your sentences.
5. Use the art of subordination to smooth out choppiness.
6. Avoid disrupting your sentences with thought-stopping gaps.
7. Watch out for the rule of parallel construction.
8. Tabulate particularly complex information.
9. Hammer home your point with the powerful, versatile verb.
10. Use the verb *to be* only when you mean it.
11. Get rid of compound prepositions.

Chapter 6

Clausiness — Write with Nouns
(And Phrases)

. . . let thy words be few.

—Ecclesiastes 5:2

Chapter 6

Clausiness — Write with Nouns

(And Phrases)

Introduction

In Chapter 3, you learned to remember the forgotten verb. Nouniness, you discovered, is one of the main features of the legalistic style. Converting derivative nouns and derivative adjectives to base verbs, infinitive phrases, present participial phrases, past participial phrases, or one-word verb-adjectives always tightens up your writing and produces a more powerful style. The verb, you learned, is one of the more versatile words in the English language. It can act as verb, noun, adjective, or adverb. No other word, in fact, can serve all these grammatical needs as easily as the verb. We learned in Chapter 3, therefore, to prefer verbs. We learned to forego *groped-for* verbs and place our messages in straightforward verbs and verbal phrases. We learned, in short, a basic truth about our language: *When a sentence goes begging for a verb, give it a verb.*

Now let's learn the opposite. Let's learn to avoid too many verb structures. Let's learn all about clauses. Let's learn that a clause is a *big deal*, which, when sparingly used, drives home our arguments. Let's learn that too many *big deals* diminish our points. Let's learn to cut clauses and write with nouns, adjectives and adverbs, prepositional phrases, verbal phrases, and other structures called appositives. Write with nouns? Am I kidding? No, I'm not. Am I preaching two contradictory messages? Again, no, I'm not. In this chapter, you'll learn another basic truth about our language: *When a sentence goes begging for a noun, give it a noun.*

Simple. When a sentence wants a verb, give it a verb, not a noun. When a sentence wants a noun, give it a noun, not a verb. Seems clear to me. Let me make it clear to you.

Clauses Defined

Recall our discussion of verbs. To show when something takes place, we conjugate verbs to indicate time or tense. The six major tenses include present, past, future, present perfect, past perfect, and future perfect. We can show only two—present and past—with one *verb-word*. Thus: *I write* (present) and *I wrote* (past). All the others require helping verbs, also called auxiliary verbs. Thus: *I will write* (future), *I have written* (present perfect), *I had written* (past perfect), and *I will have written* (future perfect).

Other major tenses include the progressive tenses, formed by conjugating the verb *to be* and adding the present participle. Thus: *I am writing* (present progressive), *I was writing* (past progressive), *I will be writing* (future progressive), *I have been writing* (present perfect progressive), *I had been writing* (past perfect progressive), and *I will have been writing* (future perfect progressive).

With these twelve tenses, you can mix all sorts of auxiliary verbs to achieve any meaning you need: *I might have been writing. He should have written. The court could have written the opinion.*

Using any of these conjugated-verb or *main-verb* forms will create a clause. Hence the definition of a clause:

A clause is a bunch of words with a main verb in it.

Clauses break down into two large categories: independent and dependent. An independent clause is simply a complete sentence. It needs nothing else to express a complete thought that has all the elements of an English sentence. Here are two independent clauses:

The court could have decided the case.

I should have been writing.

A dependent clause, on the other hand, also has a main verb but cannot stand by itself as a complete sentence. To form a sentence, it must connect to an independent clause. Here are two dependent clauses:

Though the court could have decided the case

although I should have been writing

Neither of those two statements qualifies as an independent clause. They are not complete sentences. Our English teachers of yore would have screamed: "Fragments!"

Clause Starters

Subordinating Conjunctions

To form complete sentences, these dependent clauses must be joined to independent clauses. One word that does the *joining* and makes certain clauses dependent is the *subordinating conjunction*. We previously discussed the three kinds of conjunctions in the English language—the *coordinating conjunction*, the *correlative conjunction*, and the *subordinating conjunction*. The first two—*coordinating* and *correlative*—are used to join equal grammatical units (remember the rule of *parallel construction?*) and to join independent clauses. The last—the *subordinating conjunction*—joins a dependent clause to an independent clause.

Below we'll discuss the three functions of dependent clauses and learn that they may serve as nouns, adjectives, or adverbs. The subordinating conjunction typically introduces an adverb clause—one that modifies the verb of the independent clause. Remember that adverbs answer these four questions: *where, when, how,* and *why.*

Thus, here's a dependent adverb clause modifying the verb of the independent clause. Notice that the clause tells *why* the Court *decided* to grant certiorari:

> Because these decisions in the circuits conflicted dramatically
> with each other, the Court decided to grant certiorari.

Here's a list of the most frequently used subordinating conjunctions. As you review the list, think about the adverbial questions such clauses would answer about the verbs they modify. For example, *because* answers the question *why. As* answers the question *when* or *why.*

Subordinating Conjunctions

after	as well as
although	because
as	before
as long as	if
as soon as	insofar as

like	where
since	whereas
though	whether
when	while

Please notice that some of these subordinating conjunctions can serve dual roles. Some can act not only as a conjunction but also as a preposition. For example, here are some samples of these words used as subordinating conjunctions and as prepositions:

Subordinating Conjunction	Preposition
He warmed up *before* he lifted weights.	He warmed up *before* exercise.
He was still hungry *after* he ate lunch.	He was still hungry *after* lunch.
He hasn't played *since* he was injured.	He hasn't played *since* his injury.

Although subordinating conjunctions do begin adverb clauses, I don't want to leave you with the notion that those are the only clauses they introduce. They can also start adjective clauses: I walked on the street *where you live.*

Relative Pronouns

Subordinating conjunctions are not the only *clause starters*. Adjective clauses are joined to independent clauses by *relative pronouns*. Here are the most common:

Relative Pronouns

that	whom
which	whose
who	

Here are two adjective clauses. Each modifies the noun *court*.

The court, *which insisted on using common law principles,* thoroughly researched case law dating back to colonial times.

We know all about the court *that decided the* McSparran *case.*

Most people, especially lawyers, routinely confuse the relative pronouns *that* and *which*. For that reason, I've discussed below the differences between these relative pronouns and the vital differences between restrictive and nonrestrictive clauses.

Other Clause Starters

The final clause starters are those that begin noun clauses, clauses acting as nouns. These words don't really have a name like *subordinating conjunction* or *relative pronoun*. Instead, each might serve a different function within the clause itself. For example: We'll never know *how he writes so many books*. Here the noun clause *how he writes so many books* acts as the direct object of the transitive verb *know*. The word *how* starts the noun clause. It serves as an adverb within the clause, modifying the verb *writes*. Whatever their names, here's a partial list of these *noun clause starters*:

<u>Noun Clause Starters</u>

how	why
that	where
the fact that	whether
what	whoever

Here's a typical noun clause, one that might show up in legal writing:

> The court was aware of *the fact that contributory negligence would be a bar to recovery.*

The clause—*the fact that contributory negligence would be a bar to recovery*—acts as a noun. It serves as the object of the preposition *of*.

Those are the three *clause starters*: the *subordinating conjunctions* (primarily for adverb clauses), the *relative pronouns* (for adjective clauses), and *a special group of clause starters* (for noun clauses).

Let's first study the three kinds of dependent clauses: noun clauses, adjective clauses, and adverb clauses. We'll learn how crucial these clauses are to our language. Then, however, we'll see that legal writing usually relies too heavily on the clause to express our thoughts. Hence, we'll conclude with a review of the ways you can successfully cut clauses down to nouns, prepositional phrases, adjectives and adverbs, verbal phrases, and appositives. And when you cut a clause, what do you get rid of? Those wonderful words we learned to love in Chapter 3: the main verbs.

Three Kinds of Clauses

Dependent clauses serve three roles in the English language. They can act as nouns, adjectives, or adverbs. If they act as nouns, they're called *noun clauses*. If they act as adjectives, they're called *adjective clauses*. Finally, if they act as adverbs, they're called *adverb clauses*. Because we are moving toward a rule favoring the cutting of clauses, you must first understand the nature and function of all three.

The Noun Clause

The noun clause is *a bunch of words with a main verb in it* that acts just as any noun would act in the English language. So that you can see how noun clauses act in English, when you use them, and when you cut them out, a 10-minute review of grammar is in order—a review of the role of nouns.

Recall your English teacher's definition? A noun is a person, place, thing, or idea. Good definition. It covers the bases. Do you remember all eight functions of the noun in the English language? If not, you should know them and know them cold. Here they are with italicized examples of each.

Eight Noun Functions	Italicized Example
1. Subject	Overruling the trial judge, Judge William Womble, the *court* in the <u>Jones</u> case gave the issue its immediate attention.
2. Direct Object	Overruling the trial judge, Judge William Womble, the court in the <u>Jones</u> case gave the issue its immediate *attention.*
3. Indirect Object	Overruling the trial judge, Judge William Womble, the court in the <u>Jones</u> case gave the *issue* its immediate attention.

4. Object of a Preposition	Overruling the trial judge, Judge William Womble, the court in the *Jones* *case* gave the issue its immediate attention.
5. Object in a Verbal Phrase	Overruling the *trial judge*, Judge William Womble, the court in the <u>Jones</u> case gave the issue its immediate attention.
6. Appositive	Overruling the trial judge, *Judge William Womble*, the court in the <u>Jones</u> case gave the issue its immediate attention.
7. Subject Complement (Predicate Nominative)	He will be the next corporate *president.*
8. Object Complement	We elected him *president.*

In the above sentences, I used true nouns or proper nouns to serve the eight noun functions. We've already seen how unconjugated verbals (infinitives and present participles) can satisfy noun functions. Now let's see how main verbs can do the same thing.

A noun clause—*a bunch of words with a main verb in it*—can serve all eight noun functions. As my example, I'll choose a *the fact that* clause, one of the worse constructions in the English language. I'm not alone. My opinion is shared by Mr. Strunk and Mr. White. Here's what they have to say:

> An expression that is especially debilitating is *the fact that*. It should be revised out of every sentence in which it occurs.

W. Strunk & E. White, *The Elements of Style* 24 (3d ed. 1979).

Right now let's see how a *the fact that* noun clause works. Later we'll see exactly how to revise it out of every sentence in which it occurs. Here's my noun clause: *the fact that you came to this course.* Here's the same clause serving all eight noun functions.

<u>Eight Noun Functions</u>	<u>Italicized Example</u>
1. Subject	*The fact that you came to this course* shows your interest in clear writing.
2. Direct Object	Your boss applauded *the fact that you came to this course.*
3. Indirect Object	Your boss gave *the fact that you came to this course* her undivided attention.
4. Object of a Preposition	The reason for your success is found in *the fact that you came to this course.*
5. Object of a Verbal Phrase	Emphasizing *the fact that you came to this course*, your boss gave you a raise.
6. Appositive	In authorizing your Christmas bonus, your boss stressed one thing, *the fact that you came to this course.*
7. Subject Complement	The reason you succeeded was *the fact that you came to this course.*
8. Object Complement	We pronounced the worse clause in the English language *the fact that you came to this course.* [This is the only example of an object complement I've been able to discover. It doesn't really work, functioning instead more like an appositive.]

There. The same noun clause can run through the language in eight ways just like any noun. And what made that bunch of words a clause? The two words: *you came.* The main verb *came* formed a dependent clause. And how might we *un*form a clause? By taking away its verb.

We'll come back to the art of clause-cutting. But first, a visit with the other two kinds of dependent clauses: adjective and adverb clauses.

The Adjective Clause

The adjective clause is one of the most frequently used clauses in legal writing or in any kind of formal writing. Despite its prevalence, the clause invariably confuses many writers and forces them into unnecessary mistakes. The mistakes become not only grammatical embarrassments but also disasters in logic and meaning. For here we discuss the most notorious of all clauses:

That and Which Clauses

Let's begin with some definitions. An adjective clause is *a bunch of words with a main verb in it* that modifies a noun. It functions just like a single-word adjective. It shows the character, kind, shape, size, quantity, uniqueness, or other trait of the modified noun.

Though it functions just like a single-word adjective, the adjective clause does have one unique feature distinguishing it from a single-word adjective. A single-word adjective typically precedes the word it modifies. (The only exceptions are the predicate adjective or adjective appositive, which can follow the words they modify.) An adjective clause, on the other hand, always must follow the word it modifies.

Keep in mind that an adjective clause is modifying a noun in your sentence. Also keep in mind that nouns are persons, places, things, or ideas. Your readers often want to know more about the nouns you include in your sentences. Often they'll want to know *which one* you're talking about. If your noun is a *case*, they might want to know *which case*. If your noun is a *statute*, they might want to know *which statute*. If your noun is a *factor*, they might want to know *which factor*. Or if your noun is a *red Porsche*, they might want to know *which red Porsche*. Keep the *which one* question in mind. The notion of it becomes crucial as we proceed.

An adjective clause, therefore, is describing a particular noun in your sentence. The clause will usually begin with one of these words:

that	whom
which	whose
who	

Here are some examples of adjective clauses:

I always buy his books *that receive rave reviews*.

I always buy his books, *which receive rave reviews*.

The candidate *who runs the best race* usually wins.

Mr. Keyes, *whom we all admire*, will address the convention.

The case, *whose decision started a revolution in products liability law*, prompted radical changes in the doctrine of privity of contract.

Other words, it should be noted, also may introduce an adjective clause. The subordinating conjunctions *where* and *when* often fit quite nicely: At the time *when Columbus discovered America*, the art of navigation was quite primitive. Or: In New York, *where Mayor Koch rules with an iron glove*, the press often has a field day. The clauses that typically cause the trouble, however, are the *that* and *which* clauses.

What causes all the trouble with adjective clauses? Two things: (1) choosing the correct relative pronoun and (2) deciding on the correct punctuation. Understanding these two issues requires your thoroughly understanding the differences between *restrictive* and *nonrestrictive* clauses.

Back in 1975, when I was serving as the Director of Legal Writing at the University of Virginia School of Law, I remember reading a book written by a noted law professor. In that book, the professor sometimes used *that* and other times used *which*. I looked and looked for some slight difference in meaning. Finding none, I consulted my unabridged dictionary, looked up *that*, and discovered:

That: a relative pronoun used to introduce a restrictive clause.

Thanks a bunch. Flipping back to the *w's* I looked up *which* and found:

Which: a relative pronoun used to introduce a nonrestrictive clause.

Terrific. Trying another approach I found *restrictive clause* defined:

A restrictive clause is a defining clause necessary to the meaning of the sentence.

Wonderful. Undaunted but teeth clenched, I skipped over to the *n's* and checked out *nonrestrictive clause.* You guessed it:

A nonrestrictive clause is a nondefining clause unnecessary to the meaning of the sentence.

Whoopie. Why couldn't one of these Ph.D.-types *explain* anything?

I searched the halls of academe for some soul who knew the difference between *that* and *which.* I found one such professor, and his discussion of the differences between these two words and the differences between restrictive and nonrestrictive clauses has stuck with me to this day. I'll share it with you in the hope that these differences stay with you as well.

Let's set up a sample clause and show you this professor's approach to *that-which identification.* Here's my clause:

I always buy his books *that receive rave reviews.*

Here's the professor's approach. Focus your attention on the noun you're modifying. Here we're modifying the noun *books.* How many books has *he* written? Presumably a whole slew. Do I buy all his books? No, I just buy the ones that receive rave reviews. I do not buy all the other ones that receive bad reviews. I would not buy those that receive mediocre reviews. I only buy the ones that receive rave reviews.

So I ask myself this question: *Which* group of books? *That* group of books. A restrictive *that* clause is *defining* which books I mean. Out of all the books that he has written, which ones do I buy? Those *that* receive rave reviews.

A restrictive *that* clause is ? finger-pointer. A singler-outer. The clause is singling out one or a group among many. Which one? Which group? Which noun? Which books? That one. That group. That noun. That group of books. Not all the others. *That* one. Ironically, a *that* clause answers the question: *which one?*

Now let's use the same clause but make it nonrestrictive:

I always buy his books, *which receive rave reviews.*

Here's the professor's approach. Focus your attention on the noun you're modifying. Here we're modifying the noun *books*. How many books has *he* written? Presumably a whole slew. Do I buy all of his books? Yes. And guess what? All receive rave reviews. I do buy all his books. None receives a bad or mediocre review. There is not one book he has written that I do not buy.

A nonrestrictive *which* clause is not a finger-pointer. Not a singler-outer. The information in the clause merely adds information about the modified noun. It does not single out the modified noun. The reader already knows *which one* or *which group*. The reader does not need the information in the clause for the sentence to make sense. Of most importance, the nonrestrictive clause *must* be set off by commas from the rest of the sentence. The nonrestrictive clause *must* be introduced by the word *which* and never by the word *that*.

Unfortunately, these days it is also proper to use *which* as the restrictive relative pronoun. It is proper to say: *I always buy his books which receive rave reviews.* That sentence, without the commas, means that I buy only those books that receive rave reviews and not those that receive bad or mediocre reviews. Thus, there are some of his books that I do not buy.

I say *unfortunately* for a very good reason. We had such a good system going. *That* meant restrictive, and *which* meant nonrestrictive. If everyone knew the difference, then no one's meaning ever could be confused.

I have it on good authority that *that's* don't sound too intelligent. Law professors, therefore, and other real smart people decided to declare war on *that's* and to use *which's* instead. (Have you ever noticed that professors rarely say *that*? Instead they like to use lots of *which's*. Perhaps that explains all the mistakes they make with restrictive and nonrestrictive clauses.) Because of this conspiracy, the rest of us mortals must now cope with dual relative pronouns *that/which* can introduce restrictive clauses.

The importance of punctuation, therefore, becomes paramount. The nonrestrictive clause must be set off by commas. The restrictive clause must never be set off by commas.

Ordinarily, I advise writers to use *that* to introduce restrictive clauses and *which* to introduce nonrestrictive clauses. In one situation, however, use of *which* is mandatory for a restrictive clause, for *which* will permit a preceding preposition while *that* will not. If you refuse to end a clause with a preposition, then you must use *which* as the restrictive relative. Consider this example:

The books that I told you about have arrived at the store.

Now that's a grammatically correct sentence. And, no, there's nothing wrong with ending a sentence or a clause with a preposition. You've heard the old Winston Churchill story? Arguing with a stuck-up grammarian about whether one could end a sentence or clause with a preposition, Churchill snarled:

"My friend, that's an arcane rule of grammar up with which I shall not put."

That ended that.

But in formal writing, you might not want to end a sentence or clause with a preposition. To avoid ending the above clause with a preposition, you must use *which* as the restrictive relative pronoun as follows:

The books about which I told you have arrived at the store.

Before moving on to the adverb clause, I should make two additional comments about the pronouns introducing adjective clauses. First, if the noun modified is a person, then ordinarily you must use either *who* or *whom* or *whose* to introduce the clause. You can decide on the proper *case* of the pronoun by using the following trick. The case must be subjective (who) if the main verb in the clause does not have some other subject. Thus: The candidate *who runs the best race* usually wins. Here the main verb of the clause *runs* does not have its own subject. It needs a subject. The relative pronoun will serve as its subject. It must be in the subjective case. The correct word is *who*.

If, on the other hand, the main verb in the clause already has some other subject, it cannot have yet another one. Indeed, the clause is really yearning for an object. The relative pronoun fills this need for an object. It must be in the objective case (whom). Thus: Mr. Keyes, *whom we all admire,* will address the convention. The main verb of the clause *admire* has its own subject *we.* It cannot have another subject. It needs an object. The correct word, in the objective case, is *whom.*

If the noun you modify is a generic type of person, however, you may use *that* as the relative. Thus: The candidate *that runs the best race* usually wins.

Second, to avoid awkward *of which* constructions, you may use the personal pronoun *whose* even though the noun modified is not a person. Thus: The case, *whose decision started a revolution in products liability law,* prompted radical changes in the doctrine of privity of contract. That sentence is preferable to: The case, *the decision of which started a revolution in products liability law,* prompted radical changes in the doctrine of privity of contract.

Now, before learning to cut down some of these clauses, let's look quickly at the final type of clause—the adverb clause.

The Adverb Clause

The adverb clause modifies the main verb of the independent clause to which it is attached. Or it might modify the entire sentence, as adverbs often do. Keep in mind that adverbs answer the following questions about the verbs they modify: *when, where, how*, and *why*. To gain precision in language, you should try to choose the *clause starter* that most precisely answers the adverbial question you intend. Here, again, is a partial list of adverb *clause starters*, also called *subordinating conjunctions*:

Subordinating Conjunctions

after	insofar as
although	like
as	since
as long as	though
as soon as	when
as well as	where
because	whereas
before	whether
even though	while
if	

Adverb clauses actually cause little trouble in legal writing style. If anything, legal writers probably don't use enough adverb clauses. The reason is simple. As we've seen in previous chapters, legal writers have forgotten the action verb. If they don't use many action verbs, then they don't use many adverb clauses. They just don't have many verbs to modify.

One point legal writers should consider. When preparing Questions Presented in appellate briefs, they tend to overuse their favorite subordinating conjunction *where*. By consulting the list above, they might find some other subordinating conjunctions that would nail down their meaning more precisely.

> *Where* the beneficiary of a decedent's estate procures the appointment of a nonresident administrator, *where* the sole purpose of such appointment is the bringing of a wrongful death claim against an instate defendant, and *where* other, more suitable candidates for appointment reside in state, is there a violation of title 28, section 1359 of the United States Code, which prohibits collusive joinder of parties?

The writer here really means *if* and *when*. Try this:

> *If* the beneficiary of a decedent's estate procures the appointment of a nonresident administrator to bring a wrongful death claim against an instate defendant *when* more suitable candidates for appointment reside in state, does the beneficiary violate title 28, section 1359 of the United States Code prohibiting the collusive joinder of parties?

The Art of Clause-Cutting

The biggest deal in the English language is the main verb—the conjugated verb. It, and it alone, distinguishes a clause as a clause. The main verb forms the independent clause. Along with its subject, the main verb forms the milestone of every sentence. On this milestone hang all other sentence parts: adjectives, adverbs, prepositional phrases, verbal phrases, appositives, adverb clauses, adjective clauses, noun clauses, and a host of others.

The big-deal main verb also forms the dependent clause. The main verb forms the noun clause, serving any one of the eight noun functions. The main verb forms the adjective clause, modifying nouns in a restrictive or nonrestrictive way. The main verb forms the adverb clause, modifying the verb of the independent clause.

Because the main verb is such a big deal, you should be careful in building clauses. You need at least one independent clause for each sentence. On it you can hang a multitude of big-deal dependent clauses.

If you hang too many clauses on a single sentence, however, all sorts of horribles come about. The sentence becomes long-winded. The sentence has too many subordinate thoughts. The sentence has so many big deals that it detracts from those messages that truly are big deals.

The legal writer, especially, must learn to cut clauses. The art of cutting the clause and the product left over after the cutting is done vary with the type of clause. That's why I spent most of this chapter reintroducing you to noun clauses, adjective clauses, and adverb clauses. To learn to cut them, we'll deal with noun clauses separately and adverb and adjective clauses together.

Cutting Noun Clauses

What's a clause? A bunch of words with a main verb in it. When the clause is a noun clause, it satisfies the meaning of a noun in the sentence. In short, a noun clause uses a verb to satisfy the meaning of a noun.

Does all this sound familiar? In Chapter 3, we explored the irony of using derivative nouns and derivative adjectives to satisfy the meaning of a verb. When a sentence begged for a verb, we learned to give it a verb. If the sentence wants to say *the court concluded*, why should we say *the court reached a conclusion*? That sentence wanted a verb. Give it one.

Now the shoe is on the other foot. Now we must look at situations where sentences are pleading for nouns. They are on bended knee. They pine for a noun form. When does a sentence beg for a noun? Whenever you begin a grammatical structure that needs one of the eight noun functions to complete it, your sentence will beg for a noun. For example, if you use a preposition, then your sentence needs a noun to complete the prepositional phrase. If you use a transitive verb, then your sentence is begging for a noun to act as the object. What does the awkward and verbose writer do to the poor, pleading sentence? You got it. Deny it the noun. Give it a verb. Give it an awkward noun clause.

If you have lots of *that's* and *the fact that's* in your writing, you are a prime candidate for some serious exercise in the art of noun clause-cutting. Pay attention. Cutting noun clauses requires a rather sophisticated grammatical analysis. Fortunately, no more 10-minute grammar lessons are needed at this point. Everything you need to know has already been covered.

To have some examples to work with, let's go back to our *the fact that* clauses that we ran through all eight noun functions. Here are the first seven again (I've omitted the object complement, which was kind of bogus anyway):

<u>Seven Noun Functions</u>	<u>Italicized Example</u>
1. Subject	*The fact that you came to this course* shows your interest in clear writing.
2. Direct Object	Your boss applauded *the fact that you came to this course.*
3. Indirect Object	Your boss gave *the fact that you came to this course* her undivided attention.
4. Object of a Preposition	The reason for your success is found in *the fact that you came to this course.*
5. Object of a Verbal Phrase	Emphasizing *the fact that you came to this course,* your boss gave you a raise.
6. Appositive	In authorizing your Christmas bonus, your boss stressed one thing, *the fact that you came to this course.*
7. Subject Complement	The reason you succeeded was *the fact that you came to this course.*

All these sentences are pleading for revision. All they want is a noun—a subject, a direct object, an indirect object, an object of a preposition, and so on. Instead, the wordy writer satisfies this need for a noun with a main verb. The careful writer recognizes this anomaly and cuts the noun clause. Here are the two tricks of cutting noun clauses. First of all, identify the main verb in the noun clause as either (1) not the verb *to be* or (2) the verb *to be*. Then use the *not "to be" trick* or the *"to be" trick*.

Noun Clause-Cutting Trick #1

Not "To Be"—The Similar Noun Approach.
If the verb is not the verb *to be*, then look for a similar noun meaning the same thing as the verb form.

Not "To Be"—The Gerund Approach.
If the verb is not the verb *to be* and if you cannot find a suitable noun substitute, try adding *-ing* to the main verb. Its present participial form can act as a gerund and satisfy the *noun urge* that your sentence is begging for.

Because the verb in our sample noun clause above is not the verb *to be*, let's try converting the main verb by using the *similar noun approach* and the *gerund approach*. Though either one works, I tend to favor the *similar noun* solution for our sample noun clause.

In our example, the similar noun form *your attendance at this course* means the same as the main verb form *the fact that you came to this course*. Try the noun substitute. Not having any verb, the clause will go away. If the noun substitute sounds better and less awkward, then use it.

Seven Noun Functions	Italicized Example
1. Subject	*Your attendance at this course* shows your interest in clear writing.
2. Direct Object	Your boss applauded *your attendance at this course.*
3. Indirect Object	Your boss gave *your attendance at this course* her undivided attention.
4. Object of a Preposition	The reason for your success is found in *your attendance at this course.*
5. Object of a Verbal Phrase	Emphasizing *your attendance at this course*, your boss gave you a raise.

6. Appositive

In authorizing your Christmas bonus, your boss stressed one thing, *your attendance at this course.*

7. Subject Complement

The reason you succeeded was *your attendance at this course.*

Now for the *gerund approach*. In our examples, the gerund form *your coming to this course* means the same as the main verb form *the fact that you came to this course.* If the gerund fits, sounds better, and feels less awkward, then use it. Here are the same examples above:

Seven Noun Functions

Italicized Example

1. Subject

Your coming to this course shows your interest in clear writing.

2. Direct Object

Your boss applauded *your coming to this course.*

3. Indirect Object

Your boss gave *your coming to this course* her undivided attention.

4. Object of a Preposition

You succeeded b/c you came to this course.

The reason for your success is found in *your coming to this course.*

5. Object of a Verbal Phrase

Emphasizing *your coming to this course,* your boss gave you a raise.

6. Appositive

In authorizing your Christmas bonus, your boss stressed one thing, *your coming to this course.*

7. Subject Complement

The reason you succeeded was *your coming to this course.*

A Special Note on the Gerund Approach

If you use gerunds to avoid noun clauses—and many top writers do—you must be careful when you modify the gerund with a personal pronoun. If you need to modify the gerund, be sure to use the possessive case of that personal pronoun. If you use the subjective or objective case, your meaning will change completely. Consider these examples.

You spend Saturday night with Mom. On Sunday morning she gets up and begins frying chicken. The aroma awakens you. You come into the kitchen and correctly say:

"I smelled your frying chicken."

That's right. You smelled the *frying*. *Frying* served the noun function as direct object of the transitive verb *smelled*. The case of the personal pronoun, in order to modify the gerund-noun, had to be possessive.

Many people, however, would make a dramatic mistake and say:

"I smelled you frying chicken."

That's incorrect. The *you* in the objective case changes the meaning. *You*, in the objective case, becomes the direct object of *smelled*. Now you are smelling *you*. *Frying chicken* becomes a present participial phrase modifying *you*. Mom, of course, is miffed and will likely clean your clock with a skillet upside the head.

The same kind of mistake can occur with other nouns used to modify the gerund. Consider how the meaning shifts in these two examples below. In the first, the court is aware of the *Senate*. In the second, the court is aware of the *passing*.

The court was aware of the Senate passing the Clean Harbor Act.

The court was aware of the Senate's passing the Clean Harbor Act.

Now let's use the noun clause-cutting technique when the main verb in the clause *is* the verb *to be*. Here's the second trick

Noun Clause-Cutting Trick #2

"To Be" + Predicate Adjective—Similar Noun Approach.
If the verb in the clause is the verb *to be*, it will probably be followed by a predicate adjective or a predicate nominative. If a predicate adjective is present, you can often find a similar noun, which, when used, will obliterate the clause.

"To Be" + Predicate Nominative—the "Status" Approach.
If the verb *to be* is followed by a noun, there's not a whole lot you can do to get rid of the clause. One solution I've been able to devise is to use the noun *status*, which provides an approximate noun form for the verb *to be*. Sometimes, of course, you can make *to be* a gerund (*being*) to obliterate a noun clause.

Here are some examples of these two approaches to noun clause-cutting.

To Be Noun Clauses	Proposed Revisions
The court emphasized the fact that the plaintiff was negligent.	The court emphasized the plaintiff's negligence.
Congress was aware of the fact that he was President.	Congress was aware of his status as President.

Writing as Good Writers Write

Do good writers use the noun clause-cutting device? Without doubt. Consider the Justice Black example in Chapter 1. Here's one of his sentences:

> The Framers knew, better perhaps than we do today, the risks they were taking.

Mr. Justice Black's sentence was begging for a noun. His transitive verb *knew* yearned for a direct object. He could have satisfied that noun need with a noun clause like this:

> The Framers knew, better perhaps than we do today, that they were taking risks.

But knowing that noun clauses often are tongue-twisters, he went ahead and gave the sentence a noun—*risks*—and modified it with an adjective clause—*they were taking.*

Each day when I pick up a national newspaper or magazine, I find examples of the rule: *When a sentence wants a noun, give it a noun.* A few years back, when the movie *The Right Stuff* premiered in Washington, I read the following sentence in *The Washington Post*:

> I dredge up, with some glee, Washington's losing its mind over the premiere of *The Right Stuff.*

I was struck by what the writer did not say:

> I dredge up, with some glee, the fact that Washington is losing its mind over the premiere of the *The Right Stuff.*

> I dredge up, with some glee, Washington's loss of its mind over the premiere of *The Right Stuff.*

The first has an awkward noun clause. The *similar noun approach* to cutting the noun clause in the second fails to convey the expression *losing one's mind.* The *gerund approach* to cutting the noun clause seems to work best.

The bottom line? Learn the eight noun functions. Watch for them as they inevitably play out in your sentences. Learn to satisfy these noun urges with noun forms. When you truly need the main-verb meaning, then use the noun clause. But if a true noun form states your meaning best, use it. Your writing, as a result, will achieve a natural grace.

Cutting Adjective and Adverb Clauses

Writing with too many clauses clutters up your prose. Above we saw how to cut noun clauses by substituting true nouns or noun forms to satisfy the noun function of the clause. Now let's turn our attention to the other two kinds of dependent clauses, the adjective and adverb clauses. Because these clauses serve the same function of *modifying,* we can deal with them together.

As you know, adjectives modify nouns. Adjective clauses also modify nouns. Adverbs primarily modify verbs, although they can modify other adverbs, adjectives, or entire sentences. The adverb clause, however, typically modifies either the main verb in the independent clause or the entire sentence.

The trick in cutting unnecessary clauses is to find some other structure that will serve the adjective or adverb function of the clause you're cutting. The question thus becomes: *What else in the English language can serve as adjectives and adverbs?* The answer readily comes to mind. We can cut clauses down to adjectives, adverbs, prepositional phrases, verbal phrases, adjective appositives, noun appositives, absolutes, and truncated adverb clauses. Examples will show the trick in action:

Cut Clause Down to Adjective

The court considered the *issues which were vital.*	The court considered the *vital* issues.

Cut Clause Down to Adverb

There are instances in which consumers are abused by false advertising.	Consumers are *sometimes* abused by false advertising.

Cut Clause Down to Prepositional Phrase

While the meeting was in progress, the lawyers excluded the summer associates.	*During the meeting,* the lawyers excluded the summer associates

Cut Clause Down to Verbal Phrase

Remember Mr. Justice Cardozo's paragraph in the *Palsgraf* case. Guess which one he used? Clause or verbal phrase?

The other man, *who was carrying a package, jumped aboard the car . . . .*	The other man, *carrying a package,* jumped aboard the car . . . .

Here's another example:

The statute, *which was enacted in the 1960s,* dramatically expanded our civil rights.	The statute, *enacted in the 1960s,* dramatically expanded our civil rights.

Here's another example:

If citizens are to obtain information, they must file the proper request with the Agency's Freedom of Information Office.	*To obtain information,* citizens must file the proper request with the Agency's Freedom of Information Office.

Each of these requires comment. The first (Cardozo) example: you can cut virtually every progressive tense clause to a present participial phrase. The second example: you can cut virtually every passive voice clause to a past participial phrase. Be very careful when using present or past participial phrases. If the phrase is nonrestrictive, it *must* be set off by commas. If the phrase is restrictive, it *must not* be set off by commas. In the first two examples, both phrases are nonrestrictive. They do not point out *which man* or *which statute*. From context the reader would already know *which man* or *which statute*. The third example: the clause is reduced to an infinitive phrase, an often effective way to convey hard-hitting verb meaning without the big deal of a clause.

Cut Clause Down to Adjective Appositive

Adjective clauses having the verb *to be* followed by a predicate adjective can often be cut to a structure called the *adjective appositive*. You've already seen the noun appositive in our discussion of the eight noun functions. The adjective appositive is similar. Like the noun appositive, it follows the noun it modifies. Also like the noun appositive, it is set off by commas if nonrestrictive and is not set off by commas if restrictive. However, unlike the noun appositive, which can consist of just one word, the adjective appositive usually must have more than one word. Study this example, which shows a *to be* adjective clause cut down to an adjective appositive:

The issues *that are pertinent to our case* include the admissibility of evidence and the application of the hearsay rule.	The issues *pertinent to our case* include the admissibility of evidence and the application of the heresay rule.

Do good writers use adjective appositives? In the following sentence, taken from Mr. Justice Black's passage, can you find the adjective appositive? Check out the last 14 words of the sentence:

> With this knowledge they still believed that the ultimate happiness and security of a nation lies in its ability to explore, to change, to grow and ceaselessly to adapt itself to a new knowledge born of inquiry free from any kind of governmental control over the mind and spirit of man.

Cut Clause Down to Noun Appositive

The same clause-cutting device often produces noun appositives. You should check your writing to see if you use appositives at all. If you do not, the chances are good your writing is too *clausy*. Consider this example:

The evidence impeached the the plaintiff's witness, *who had been convicted of having committed a felony.*	The evidence impeached the plaintiff's witness, *a convicted felon.*

Cut Clause Down to Absolutes

You might use *absolutes* without knowing you use them. If, after learning about them here, you find you don't use them at all, then try them out. They enable you to pack a lot of information in a small amount of space. An absolute is an incomplete sentence attached to a complete sentence; it has in it either a present participle, a past participle, or some other adjective modifying a noun; it must be set off by commas. The distinguishing feature of the absolute is the presence of the subject of the discarded clause. Note the retained subjects and adjectives in these examples:

His research was complete, and he began to build his arguments.	*His research complete,* he began to build his arguments.
Because the court had decided the case, the attorneys searched for ways to appeal.	*The court having decided the case,* the attorneys searched for ways to appeal.

Cut Clause Down to Truncated Adverb Clause

The final product of clause-cutting is the *truncated adverb clause*. Like the absolute, it might not be familiar by name. You should search your writing for the structure, and not finding it, begin to use it. It, too, can pack information down into a tight, hard-hitting package.

The truncated adverb clause uses a subordinating conjunction with an unconjugated verb, typically a present participle or a past participle. Here are examples:

When it decides a case, the court usually relies on precedent.	*When deciding a case,* the court usually relies on precedent.
When it is delivered, process is served.	*When delivered,* process is served.
If it is deserved, the victory is sweet.	*If deserved,* the victory is sweet.

That-Dropping

Finally, when any adjective clause has an independent subject of the main verb, you may, at your discretion, drop the *that* or *which* introducing the clause. If the adjective clause is short, dropping the *that* often produces a tighter, more effective style. If the adjective clause is long, however, it is usually best to retain the *that* to anchor the clause. Obviously, if the clause does not have an independent subject, the *that* or *which* (or *who*) is needed to serve as that subject. Here are some examples:

The result *that we want* is total victory.	The result *we want* is total victory.
He likes the words *that start the clauses.*	He likes the words *that start the clauses*

Remember that the word *that* also starts noun clauses. When such clauses follow *cognitive* verbs, you should retain the *that*. Cognitive verbs include *know, assume, learn, remember,* and many others. Hence: I assume *that* you know *that* you are late.

Do good writers use *thats* after cognitive verbs? Here's Mr. Justice Black, again:

> They *knew that* free speech might be the friend of change and revolution. But they also *knew that* it is always the deadliest enemy of tyranny. With this knowledge they still *believed that* the ultimate happiness and security of a nation lies in its ability to explore, to change, to grow and ceaselessly to adapt itself to a new knowledge born of inquiry free from any kind of governmental control over the mind and spirit of man.

Summary

It's been a long chapter. I hope you've learned the role played by the three dependent clauses—noun clauses, adjective clauses, and adverb clauses. By now, you are familiar with those special words, the *clause starters*, which set up dependent clauses. You know the subordinating conjunctions, which start adverb clauses; the relative pronouns, which start adjective clauses; and those unnamed words that start noun clauses.

Though the role of clauses is vital, too many clauses do clutter up our language. Learning to cut clauses is one of the most important skills the careful writer can acquire. Learning to cut requires an appreciation of the byproduct of clause-cutting. You must know that noun clauses convert to true or substitute nouns and that adjective and adverb clauses convert to one of a variety of other adjective or adverb structures: adjectives, adverbs, prepositional phrases, verbal phrases (present participial, past participial, and infinitive), adjective appositives, noun appositives, absolutes, and truncated adverb clauses.

That's clause-cutting. But before leaving clauses altogether, I'll close by dispelling some popular clause myths.

Three Strange Clause Myths

For some reason, over time, three strange myths have developed about dependent clauses. Discussing these issues with some people can be difficult. They tenaciously cling to lifelong beliefs, no matter how persuasive the arguments against them. The myths are widespread. No doubt you've heard about them yourself.

Myth: Do Not Begin a Sentence with "Because"

I've talked with some highly qualified experts. They can't figure out where this myth came from. But many people believe that you *can't* begin a sentence with a *because clause*. Because they believe this myth so firmly, these people rob themselves of perfectly good, introductory adverb clauses. Because they forbid beginning a sentence with the *cause*, they fail to stress the *effect* by placing it at the end of the sentence. Because they single out the subordinating conjunction *because* for special treatment, they might even neglect ever to use an introductory adverb clause.

Can I not say what I just said in the preceding three sentences? If you say "no," then can I say the following?

> If I were you, I'd join the club.

> While he watched TV, he ate and ate and ate.

> When the court admitted the evidence, it committed reversible error.

Of course I can begin those sentences with adverb clauses. Of course I can use the subordinating conjunctions *if*, *while*, and *when* to begin a sentence. Why is the subordinating conjunction—*because*—any different? The answer? It's not.

Myth: "Since" Never Means "Because"

The subordinating conjunction *since* does have a highly temporal meaning. As a rule, it's best to confine your use of *since* to show relationships in time. Thus:

> Since he became of age, he has enjoyed the privileges of adulthood.

But some people believe that *since* never, ever can mean *because*. Of course it can. Here's the definition found in *Webster's Third New International Dictionary* at 2122 (Merriam-Webster, Inc. 1981):

> For the reason that: because of the fact that (since it was raining, he wore a hat).

The best rule to follow is this: If your sentence using *since* to mean *because* could convey the temporal meaning of *since*, then use *because* to avoid the possible ambiguity. Suppose in the following example I really mean *because*. You can see the ambiguity resulting from the temporal meaning of *since* and the consequent need to use the word *because*.

> Since Reagan was elected and missiles were deployed in Europe, the Soviets more readily bargained in the INF negotiations.

Myth: "While" Never Means "Although"

The same analysis applies to our last clause myth. *While* also has a highly temporal meaning. But it can also mean *although*, *though*, or *even though*. Here's the dictionary definition:

> in spite of the fact that: although (while the evidence he has obtained may be said to fit the theory, the importance of some of it is questionable).

Id. at 2604.

In deciding which word to use, follow the same rule that applies to *because*: If your sentence using *while* to mean *although* could convey the temporal meaning of *while*, then use *although* to avoid the possible ambiguity. In the following example, I mean *though*. Note the possible ambiguity.

> While the price of a barrel of oil declines, the price of a gallon of gas goes up.

Those are the three strange clause myths. And that's clause-cutting.

The Rules of Good Writing

Your list of the rules of good writing now looks like this:

1. Use an average of 25 words per sentence.

2. Avoid putting too many messages in a single sentence.

3. Put most of your messages at the subject-predicate position.

4. For variety or emphasis, invert your sentences.

5. Use the art of subordination to smooth out choppiness.

6. Avoid disrupting your sentences with thought-stopping gaps.

7. Watch out for the rule of parallel construction.

8. Tabulate particularly complex information.

9. Hammer home your point with the powerful, versatile verb.

10. Use the verb *to be* only when you mean it.

11. Get rid of compound prepositions.

12. Cut adjective, adverb, and noun clauses to other structures satisfying the same functions.

On to the Great Debate, the Active vs. the Passive Voice.

Chapter 7

The Great Debate
Active vs. Passive Voice

It was decided that a meeting would be held.

—Letter from a federal official.

Chapter 7

The Great Debate

Active vs. Passive Voice

Introduction

One day in 1975, shortly after I took charge of the writing program at U.Va., I was enjoying a cup of coffee in the faculty lounge. As I was reading my *Washington Post*, I heard a well-known law professor say the following: "I never use the passive voice. I always use the active voice."

My heart pounded. As the new "resident expert," I was about to be asked to join the conversation. I slid down in my seat and raised my *Post* for protection. That was one conversation I had to avoid. For the life of me, I couldn't recall the precise differences between the active voice and the passive voice. Certainly I didn't remember enough nuances to join the level of conversation expected in the faculty lounge.

When the moment was right, I sprinted for the door, made a beeline for my office, and grabbed the closest grammar guide I could find. I began to bone up. I began to study the difference. I learned all about the bad reputation of the passive voice and the many reactions against it. I got to the point where I could detect the passive voice in patterns of speech.

In the faculty lounge, it's too bad the subject never came up again.

Through the years, I've encountered several strange events concerning the passive voice. First, I saw a memorandum from the head of a federal government agency:

To: All Employees
From: Name Deleted
Re: The Passive Voice

The passive voice is used exclusively in the federal government. [The memo continued to criticize the passive voice and strongly suggest that employees avoid it entirely.]

Second, the head of one of the federal departments outlawed the passive voice from all correspondence going out over his signature. Third, an article in a paralegal magazine urged that "the passive voice should be avoided."

There's a much better way to deal with this great debate. Joining the hysteria to rant and rave against the passive voice will educate no one. Instead, a sense of balance is definitely in order. Thus, in this chapter, I'll back up to square one and assume that you aren't exactly sure of the precise differences between the active voice and the passive voice. We'll learn that *voice* pertains only to transitive verbs. We'll study the differences between the active voice and the passive voice. Then, and only then, we'll learn not only to prefer the active voice but to avoid a knee-jerk reaction against the passive voice and instead to use it to our advantage.

Verbs: Transitive or Intransitive

Before learning the differences between the active and the passive voice, you must first recall the differences between transitive and intransitive verbs. Transitive verbs are *action verbs* that carry action from the subject of the sentence to the direct object—the recipient of the action. Put another way, a transitive verb is an action verb capable of being followed by a noun. Put yet another way, a transitive verb is an action verb that is begging for a noun to follow it and receive the action of the transitive verb. Here are some examples:

Subject	Transitive Verb	Direct Object
John	hit	the ball.
The court	decided	the case.
Congress	enacted	the statute.

To test whether a verb is transitive or intransitive, just plug in the verb and ask this question: *Can I [verb] something or somebody?* If the answer is "yes," the verb is transitive. Thus, I can hit something (or somebody), decide something, or enact something.

Before using the test on some verbs, let's examine the other kind of verb, the intransitive verb. The intransitive verb is also an *action verb*. It does not, however, *carry action* from a subject to a direct object. Indeed, the intransitive verb cannot be followed by a noun. It cannot have a direct object. Applying the *can I verb something* test, you will always answer "no." An intransitive verb, therefore, does not have a direct object. The intransitive verb does not beg for a noun. Rather, it typically begs for an adverb.

Thus, consider the verb *walk*. Apply the test: *Can I walk something?* Typically the answer is "no." I do not walk some*thing*. Rather, I walk somehow, somewhere, sometime, or for some reason. The verb begs not for a noun, but for an adverb or adverbial phrase:

> I walk quickly (somehow).

> I walk to the store (somewhere).

> I walk on Sundays (sometime).

> I walk for exercise (for some reason).

Another *question test* is helpful in classifying a verb as transitive or intransitive. You can follow a transitive verb with a *what* or a *whom* question. Try this: *[verb] what?* or *[verb] whom?* If this question makes sense, the verb is transitive. Thus: *hit what?* or *enact what?* or *decide what?* All those questions make sense. Notice that the questions are *noun* questions. These action verbs want nouns. They want direct objects.

On the other hand, you can follow an intransitive verb with four different questions: *how, where, when,* or *why.* Note that these questions are adverbial.

> walk how (quickly)

> walk where (to the store)

> walk when (on Sundays)

> walk why (for exercise)

All those questions make sense as well.

Parenthetically, I do not mean to imply that you cannot adverbially modify a transitive verb. Of course you can hit the ball *out of the park*, decide the case *quickly*, or enact a statute *without much thought of the consequences*. The point I make is this: a transitive verb wants a noun whereas an intransitive verb is searching for an adverb.

Let's use the above tests to classify some verbs as transitive, intransitive, or both. First, the verb *walk*. As noted above, typically you do not walk *something*. Instead, you walk *how, where, when,* or *why*. But if you take the dog along, you can *walk the dog*. In this sense, *walk* is transitive. Similarly, you could *walk a refrigerator up the stairs*. Let's try some others:

1. *Comply*. Can you *comply* something? No. You comply *with* something. The verb, therefore, is intransitive.

2. *Provide*. Can you *provide something?* Yes. As a transitive verb, *provide* means to furnish, to afford, or to stipulate. But you can also provide *for* something. The verb is also intransitive. As an intransitive verb, *provide* means to take measures in advance (as in *to provide for the common defense*) or to furnish subsistence (as in *to provide for his family's needs*).

3. *Delve*. Can you *delve something*? No. You delve *into* something. The verb is intransitive.

4. *Impact*. I just couldn't resist including the favorite word of the 1980s. Not only do people misuse it, but they have magically transformed the verb from the transitive verb that it is to an intransitive verb that it isn't. *Impact*, according to the dictionary, is a transitive verb. Guess what it means? *To strike with great force*. A good synonym would be *to nuke*. The example given in the dictionary: *The antitank missiles impacted the target area*. Yet people these days use this verb to mean *to affect*. Listen carefully and you'll hear somebody say, "We must decide whether our policies will impact the economy." Folks, if there's the slightest chance of your policies *blowing away* the economy, I sincerely hope you'll do away with the policies.

The verb *impact* is transitive. It is therefore incorrect to say: "We must decide whether our policies will impact *on* the economy."

Before you can possibly understand the differences between the active and the passive voice, you must first learn to spot transitive verbs. The reason is simple: you can use transitive verbs either in the active voice or the passive voice. *Voice* has nothing to do with intransitive verbs. There's only one way to say *I walked to the store*. Thus, from this day forward, every time you use any transitive verb, you've got a decision to make—to put the verb in the active voice or the passive voice. Undoubtedly, most writers don't really choose a voice. Instead, they write habitually. The careful writer, the winning writer, strategically chooses voice to achieve a particular objective.

Voice of Transitive Verbs

Whatever one says in the active voice, I can translate into the passive voice. Watch. *Whatever is said in the passive voice can be translated into the active voice.* I just did it. *It was just done.*

You can conjugate every transitive verb in two ways: in the active voice or in the passive voice. Let's look carefully at each.

The Active Voice

In the active voice, the actor precipitates the action. The active-voice verb then carries that action to the recipient of the action, the direct object. Thus, in popular legal parlance:

Actor	Action	Actee
John	hits	the ball.

Notice in the active voice that the action flows left to right. Indeed, in the active voice, we encounter the words in the same order as the represented action would unfold: *John*, the batter, steps up, takes a swing, and *hits* a round sphere we call *the ball*.

The Passive Voice

In the passive voice, the sentence flip-flops. The recipient of the action becomes the grammatical subject of the sentence. The actor, the precipitator of the action, is revealed at the end of the sentence, usually as the object of a prepositional *by* phrase. Take a look:

Actee	Action	Actor
The ball	is hit	by John.

Notice in the passive voice everything is backwards. We see the result or consequences or recipient of the action first. We then see the action. And finally we're introduced to the culprit—the whodunit—at the tail end of the sentence.

We can now understand the definitions of *active voice* and *passive voice*. The definitions derive from the grammatical subjects of the respective sentences. In the active voice, the subject of the sentence is active. In the passive voice, the subject of the sentence is passive. In the active voice, John—the subject—actively does the hitting. In the passive voice, the ball—the subject—passively sits there and gets hit.

Forming the active voice, of course, is a piece of cake. Just conjugate the verb in the twelve major tenses. Here's a third-person conjugation of the transitive verb *show* in the twelve major tenses:

Present	John shows the movie.
Past	John showed the movie.
Future	John will show the movie.
Present Perfect	John has shown the movie.
Past Perfect	John had shown the movie.
Future Perfect	John will have shown the movie.
Present Progressive	John is showing the movie.
Past Progressive	John was showing the movie.
Future Progressive	John will be showing the movie.
Present Perfect Progressive	John has been showing the movie.
Past Perfect Progressive	John had been showing the movie.
Future Perfect Progressive	John will have been showing the movie.

Adding various auxiliary verbs produces an almost endless array of possible verb meanings—all in the active voice: John *might have been showing* the movie. John *must show* the movie. John *could have shown* the movie.

Forming the Passive Voice: *To Be* + Past Participle

Look at the progressive tenses shown above. They are formed by conjugating the auxiliary verb *to be* and adding the present participle. The passive voice is quite similar in structure. You form the passive voice by conjugating the verb *to be* and adding the *past* participle of the transitive verb.

The first hurdle is identifying the past participle of every transitive verb in the English language. You might protest that you don't remember all past participles of all transitive verbs in the English language. And I respond that you probably do know most past participles of most verbs in the English language. You know them because you routinely use them in the *perfect tenses*. To identify any past participle, just complete this sentence: *I have [plug in the past participle]*. Try it with these verbs:

Transitive Verb	I have	Past Participle
show	I have	shown.
decide	I have	decided.
see	I have	seen.
ride	I have	ridden.
write	I have	written.

To form the passive voice, follow this formula: *to be* + past participle of transitive verb = passive voice of the transitive verb. Here is the same transitive verb *show* conjugated in the passive voice in most of the twelve major tenses:

Present	The movie is shown by John.
Past	The movie was shown by John.
Future	The movie will be shown by John.
Present Perfect	The movie has been shown by John.
Past Perfect	The movie had been shown by John.
Future Perfect	The movie will have been shown by John.
Present Progressive	The movie is being shown by John.
Past Progressive	The movie was being shown by John.
Future Progressive	None.
Present Perfect Progressive	None.
Past Perfect Progressive	None.
Future Perfect Progressive	None.

Notice that the progressive tenses have only two passive voice constructions. The other four make no sense: *The movie "will be being shown" by John?*

Notice also that all passive constructions are formed by tacking on the past participle to some form of the verb *to be*. Just as we can form almost endless verb meanings in the active voice by using auxiliary verbs, so too can we form similar meanings in the passive voice: The movie *can be shown*. The movie *must be shown*. The movie *ought to have been shown*.

Remember infinitive phrases? Here's one in the active voice: *To show the movie* was John's goal in life. Here's one in the passive voice: *To be shown the movie* was the children's goal in life. Remember present participial phrases? Here's one in the active voice: *Showing the movie,* John charged an admission fee. Here's one in the passive voice: *Being shown the movie,* the children paid an admission fee. Virtually every active voice construction has a corresponding passive voice construction. And vice versa. Which will it be? Active or passive?

Three Strikes Against the Passive Voice

As noted above, the passive voice has a very bad reputation. Style books love to say terrible things about the passive voice or to extol the virtues of the active voice. When praising the active voice, some experts even rely on the passive. Strunk and White observed:

> Many a tame sentence of description or exposition *can be made* lively and emphatic by substituting a transitive in the active voice for some such perfunctory expression as "there is" or "could be heard" [emphasis added].

They also said:

> The need of making a particular word the subject of the sentence will often, as in these examples, determine which voice is *to be used* [emphasis added].

W. Strunk & E. White, *The Elements of Style* 18 (3d ed. 1979).

Is this preference for the active voice valid? Is the bad reputation of the passive voice deserved? Yes, to both questions. The passive voice has three strikes against it. First, in the passive voice it takes more words to say the same thing:

> John hit the ball (active, 4 words).

> The ball was hit by John (passive, 6 words).

Second, the passive voice is, by definition, passive. It's weak. It's wimpy. Use the passive voice exclusively and you'll produce a string of sentences where no subject acts. Every grammatical subject just sits there and gets acted upon. Every subject sits there and takes it. Nothing ever seems to *happen* in the passive voice. Third, the passive voice is potentially irresponsible. Only in the passive voice can the writer cover up "whodunit" without obviously covering up. Watch this. Here's the passive voice: *The ball was hit.* Now here's the same sentence in the active voice: *Somebody hit the ball.* In the active voice, concealing the actor is obvious. In the passive, the coverup is more subtle.

Nowhere is the passive voice more tyrannical than in the press and in the government. Consider the Dan Quayle affair. Here's the press (quoted from a report by CBS's Dan Rather):

> Tonight, questions are being asked about J. Danforth Quayle's military experience in the National Guard.

Here's the active voice translation:

> Tonight, my colleagues in the press and I are asking questions about J. Danforth Quayle's military experience in the National Guard.

The government official, of course, uses the same trick. Here's Mr. Quayle's response to accusations about his service in the National Guard:

> Calls to the National Guard office were made.

Here's the active voice translation:

> My family and my contacts made calls to the National Guard office.

If you want to detect when someone else is fudging, covering-up, or hemming and hawing, watch for their use of the passive voice. It'll give them away every time.

Most of all, this biggest strike against the passive voice—its ir- responsible nature—accounts for its popularity in organizations. Maybe policies and decisions do indeed unaccountably bubble out of an or- ganization. Maybe decisions *are made.* Maybe *it was decided* that your petition for review *would be denied.* Perhaps *it was thought* that the policy *should be developed* at the upper levels of the organization. Maybe *it was decided* that a meeting *would be held.* Maybe so. But for God's and society's sakes, wouldn't it be nice if someone, somewhere would take the rap for deciding, denying, thinking, and developing?

Is anybody out there *doing* anything?

Or is it just *being done.*

A bad reputation, indeed. But we need not reflexively jerk our knees and abolish the passive voice. Certainly it *was developed* to satisfy some perceived need of human beings who wanted to communicate with each other. Assuredly, it didn't just arrive on the scene, the result of some dark conspiracy of briefcase-toting bureaucrats. It must have some redeeming social value.

It does. Eight, to be exact. At least I've been able to detect eight situations when the passive voice *is preferred*. Perhaps there are more. If you discover any, send me a letter and I'll give you credit in the next printing of this book. Promise.

When the Passive Voice *Is Preferred*

1. When you are generalizing and you want to avoid using *one* as the subject of too many sentences.

   Active: Here are eight situations where one prefers the passive voice.

   Passive: Here are eight situations where the passive voice is preferred.

   Commentary: Let's face it, folks. One who uses lots of *ones* as the subjects of too many of one's sentences might indeed offend one's listeners or one's readers. One might even sound a bit snooty. Mightn't one? Translation: If too many *ones* are used, many readers and many listeners might be offended. Get it? Professors should get it. They are the worst offenders. In the faculty lounge (my, what goes on in there!), I once heard a professor ask: "Where might one find the coffee cream?" For heaven's sake, guys, try the passive: "Where is the coffee cream found?" Or better yet, forget the transitive verb *find* and inquire about the coffee cream's location. Go ahead. You can do it. Just use the verb *to be*: "Where in hell is the damn coffee cream?"

2. When the identity of the actor is the *punch* of the sentence and you want to place it at the end.

   Active: The President of the United States hid the tapes.

   Passive: The tapes were hidden by the President of the United States.

Commentary: This rule can work the other way as well. Sometimes the *beginning* of the sentence is the more emphatic place, as it is in a parallel *series* of sentences all opening with the same subject. If the punch is the recipient of the action, then passive voice constructions provide the only way to put recipients as grammatical subjects. See situation #8.

3. When the identity of the actor is irrelevant and you simply want to omit it.

Active: Congress enacted the statute in 1968.

Passive: The statute was enacted in 1968.

Commentary: This situation often comes up in legal writing. When discussing a case, you frequently will not care which court decided the case. Thus: *The case was decided to remedy police abuses in interrogations.*

4. When the identity of the actor is unknown.

Active: Somebody mysteriously destroyed the files.

Passive: The files were mysteriously destroyed.

5. When you want to hide the identity of the actor.

Active: I regret to inform you that I misplaced your file.

Passive: I regret to inform you that your file has been misplaced.

Commentary: Seriously, you sometimes have to cover your, uh, self. However, let a healthy dollop of ethics restrict your use of situation #5.

6. When you want to avoid sexist writing but also want to avoid those horrible *s(he)'s, he/she's, him/her's,* and *his/her's.*

Active: An applicant for employment must file his/her application with the personnel office. He/she should include his/her complete educational background.

Passive: An application for employment must be filed with the personnel office. A complete educational background should be included.

Commentary: Gross overreaction to the very real problem of sexist writing threatens the very foundations of our language. The

problem is so vast that I've devoted Chapter 9 to a plague en-
dangering every corner of the globe — his/hermaphrodism.

7. When the passive voice sounds better.

Active: A disreputable seller sometimes abuses and exploits consumers. (Too many sssssssssss's!)

Passive: Consumers are sometimes abused and exploited by a
disreputable seller.

Commentary: Watch out for this one. If you are a passive-voice
addict in desperate need of your passive-voice fix every other
sentence, then naturally the passive voice will always sound better
to you. Test your writing. Search for and find the passive voice.
Try the active. Get used to the active. Then, and only then, settle
for the passive as the *better-sounding* construction.

8. When the recipient of the action is the subject matter of the rest of the paragraph.

Active: Smith, because he knows the workings of the Department,
has lasted for more than a year. The President, nevertheless,
probably will ask him to resign.

Passive: Smith, because he knows the workings of the Depart
ment, has lasted for more than a year. Nevertheless, he will
probably be asked to resign.

Commentary: Here the focus is on Smith. He should be kept as
the subject of the sentence.

Reread the previous sentence. Funny. This stuff really works.

The Rules of Good Writing

Your list of the rules of good writing now looks like this:

1. Use an average of 25 words per sentence.

2. Avoid putting too many messages in a single sentence.

3. Put most of your messages at the subject-predicate position.

4. For variety or emphasis, invert your sentences.

5. Use the art of subordination to smooth out choppiness.

6. Avoid disrupting your sentences with thought-stopping gaps.

7. Watch out for the rule of parallel construction.

8. Tabulate particularly complex information.

9. Hammer home your point with the powerful, versatile verb.

10. Use the verb *to be* only when you mean it.

11. Get rid of compound prepositions.

12. Cut adjective, adverb, and noun clauses to other structures satisfying the same functions.

13. Prefer the active voice, but use the passive to satisfy certain objectives concerning the identity or placement of the actor or recipient.

Chapter 8

Losing Weight
Miscellaneous Matters

Proicit ampullas et sesquipedalia verba.

Throws aside his paint-pots and his words a foot-and-a-half long.

—Horace

Chapter 8

Losing Weight

Miscellaneous Matters

Introduction

Every book has one of these chapters—a place for authors to put stuff that fits no where else. Kind of a boutique for the browser or shopper. Or a trash bin for the collector. Depends on your point of view.

In this chapter, in any event, I include a collection of dietary devices to help you trim down your writing. Lean writing wins arguments. Fat, ponderous writing typically loses. Legal writing, though it seeks to win, is usually ponderous and heavy, not lean and aggressive. By using the tricks we've discussed so far, enhanced by the miscellaneous matters in this chapter, you can achieve leanness in your writing. Then you'll be ready to write your way to the top of the legal profession.

Long Words

Remember the passage of Justice Black's writing quoted in Chapter 1? Remember the passage from Justice Cardozo? In each of those passages, the writers used approximately 180 words. Also in each, two-thirds of the words were monosyllabic words. Simple, one-syllable words. Yet how many times have we made a beeline for our *Roget's* to find a longer word, a fancier word to express our meaning. Indeed, in college, trips to *Roget's* to find words no one knows—much less uses— were often awarded *A's* on term papers and book reports.

It's time to break those habits. It's time to learn to use short words. It's time to learn the power of short, Anglo-Saxon words. In legal writing? Yes, especially in legal writing. Black did it. Cardozo did it. So should you.

Fowler had a good time putting down those in love with long words. In a most entertaining passage entitled *Love of the Long Word*, he urged us not to confuse "bulk with force":

> It need hardly be said that shortness is a merit in words. There are often reasons why shortness is not possible; much less often there are occasions when length, not shortness, is desirable. But it is a general truth that the short words are not only handier to use, but more *powerful* in effect; extra syllables reduce, not increase, vigour. This is particularly so in English, where the native words are short, and the long words are foreign. [Emphasis added.]
>
> . . . .
>
> Good English does consist in the main of short words. There are many good reasons, however, against any attempt to avoid a polysyllable if it is the word that will give our meaning best; moreover the occasional polysyllable will have added effect from being set among short words. What is here deprecated is the tendency among the ignorant to choose, because it is a polysyllable, the word that gives their meaning no better or even worse.

H. Fowler, *Modern English Usage* 344-45 (2d ed. 1965).

Though I always get a feeling of country English tweed and a whiff of pipe smoke when I read Fowler, the man does have good opinions about our language. In a similar vein, Mr. E. B. White advised:

> Avoid the elaborate, the pretentious, the coy, and the cute. Do not be tempted by a twenty-dollar word when there is a ten-center handy, ready and able. Anglo-Saxon is a livelier tongue than Latin, so use Anglo-Saxon words.

W. Strunk & E. White, *The Elements of Style* 76-77 (1979).

Thus, consider the following translations of long words into short words. Notice the other devices used as well (denounification, passive voice obliteration, and clause-cutting):

Long Word Style	Short Word Style
The record which has been compiled in the instant proceeding indicates that there is no evidence of any character or kind in support of the causes of action that have been claimed by the plaintiff.	The record in the current case shows no evidence whatsoever supporting the plaintiff's causes of action.

| Invocation of the above-mentioned principles of accounting will result in a reduction of losses that have been shown on the books of the company. | Using the above rules of accounting will dramatically reduce the paper losses of the company. |

Changing long words to short words increases the vigor of your writing. Thus, don't say *indicates*, try *shows* instead. Don't say *invocation of*, try *using*. Changing long words to short words might even have a salutary effect on the clarity of your thinking.

Long words often are highly abstract. Because the meaning of abstractions might reside only in the reader or listener, long and abstract words often fail to pin down precise meaning. Another trick in making your writing leaner and meaner is preferring concrete words over abstract words.

Favoring Concrete Words over Abstract Words

Concrete words create more vivid images. Consequently, concrete words carry more clout. In law especially, which is already filled with so many abstract ideas, the careful writer will seek to use as many concrete words as possible, rather than heaping abstraction on abstraction. Why? Because concrete words will (are you ready?) staple your thoughts to your reader's mind. Good speech writers won't decry *hunger* in America. They'll speak instead of those eating dog food from a can. Good speech writers won't extol *opportunity* in America. They'll speak instead of the successful chocolate-chip cookie tycoon starting an empire from scratch. So too must good writers seek to grab the reader's attention with concrete images. Here, once again, is what Fowler had to say on the issue:

> Turgid flabby English is full of abstract nouns; the commonest ending of abstract nouns is *-ion*, and to count the *-ion* words in what one has written, or, better, to cultivate an ear that without special orders challenges them as they come, is one of the simplest and most effective means of making oneself less un-readable. It is as an unfailing sign of a nouny abstract style that a cluster of *-ion* words is chiefly to be dreaded. But some nouny writers are so far from being awake to that aspect of it that they fall into a still more obvious danger, and so stud their sentences with *-ions* that the mere sound becomes an offence . . . .

H. Fowler, *Modern English Usage* 640 (2d ed. 1965).

Modification

While working for the Federal Judicial Center in Washington, D.C. during the late '70s, I watched an editor ply her trade with a report I was writing. She savagely ripped it to shreds, leaving behind a blood-like trail of red ink. Shrinking in horror, I asked, "What on earth are you doing?"

"Modification," was her terse reply.

"Who?"

She proceeded to show me how to pare down my language with a device called *modification*. Basically, the trick of modification derives from the effective use of adjectives and adverbs. Using modification is really quite simple. Search your writing for piles of words struggling to act as adjectives or adverbs. Find other, simpler, and often one-word adjectives and adverbs and use them instead. The device sometimes just repeats the trick of cutting clauses or destroying compound prepositions. Here's some simple modification:

Before Modification	After Modification
the issues which were vital	the vital issues
trial by jury	jury trial
There are instances in which consumers are abused	Consumers are sometimes abused

In the above examples, the writer recognized that the clause *which were vital* was trying to be a one-word adjective, that the prepositional phrase *by jury* could just as easily form a compound noun, and that the *there are instances in which* wanted to say *sometimes*. That's modification.

A few words of caution are in order. English is a remarkably versatile language. We can indeed change *legs of the chair* to *chair legs*. But watch out. When using modification, be careful you don't overdo it and use nouns as adjectives when perfectly good adjectives will do the job.

No one, for example, would arrange things in *alphabet order*. No. *Alphabetical order*. Know anybody who goes to *medicine school*? No. *Medical school*. Thus, on your resume don't tout your *communication skills*, or you'll show your lack of them. Use the correct adjective *communicative skills.* If you misuse modification or overuse modification, you might then fall into the trap of . . .

The Noun Modifier Proliferation Problem

If you overdo it, you might end up sounding like a page from the Pentagon Name Identification Procedure Manual Appendix. See the problem? These days, nouns used as modifiers have gotten completely out of control. Ironically, the device does derive from a genuine desire to be terse and pithy. (More likely it springs from the urge to produce a memorable acronym.) But if you use a whole slew of nouns to modify other nouns, you can create streams of words offending an ordinary sense of grace.

How far you cut down prepositional phrases is a judgment call. Thus, *judgment call* is a fairly well-recognized *compound noun* and doesn't overdo it. Is *defendant's summary judgment motion* too modified? If so, the way to smooth it out is to reinsert an absent prepositional phrase: *defendant's motion for summary judgment.*

Do Not Tie Yourself Up In *Not's*

I just broke the rule. Let me follow it: *Try to avoid expressing negative conditions in negative terms.* It is awkward to use lots of *no's* and *not's.* Plenty of words in English can express the absence (there's one) of something without relying on awkward *no's* and *not's.* Thus, the *employee who is not present* is the *absent employee.* The *building that does not have adequate fire escapes* is the same one *that lacks adequate fire escapes.* If you *do not want to use too many negative expressions*, you might try *avoiding them.* If you *do not agree*, then you *disagree* or *dispute.* Finally, in legal writing, especially, writers should avoid the multiple negative. You'll twist your sentences (and your reader's brain) all out of shape:

> It is not unusual to be unable to find no cases totally inapplicable to the case at hand.

I'm not quite sure what that means.

The Rules of Good Writing

Your list of the rules of good writing now looks like this:

1. Use an average of 25 words per sentence.
2. Avoid putting too many messages in a single sentence.
3. Put most of your messages at the subject-predicate position.
4. For variety or emphasis, invert your sentences.
5. Use the art of subordination to smooth out choppiness.
6. Avoid disrupting your sentences with thought-stopping gaps.
7. Watch out for the rule of parallel construction.
8. Tabulate particularly complex information.
9. Hammer home your point with the powerful, versatile verb.
10. Use the verb *to be* only when you mean it.
11. Get rid of compound prepositions.
12. Cut adjective, adverb, and noun clauses to other structures satisfying the same functions.
13. Prefer the active voice, but use the passive to satisfy certain objectives concerning the identity or placement of the actor or the recipient.
14. Favor short words over long, fancy words.
15. Use concrete words to staple your thoughts to your reader's mind.
16. Use modification to trim down the fat in your language.
17. Use phrases to smooth out the choppy noun-noun modifier.
18. Do not use too many negative expressions.

Chapter 9

His/hermaphrodism

Multa renascentur quae iam cecidere, cadentque
Quae nunc sunt in honore vocabula, si volet usus,
Quem penes arbitrium est et ius et norma loquendi.

Many terms that have now dropped out of favor will be revived,
and those that are at present respectable will drop out, if usage
so choose, with whom resides the decision and the judgment and
the code of speech.

—Horace

Chapter 9

His/hermaphrodism

Introduction

Anyone who has ever written anything—especially recently—has faced the problem of his/hermaphrodism. You know the problem well. To be fair, you don't want to favor one sex over the other. To solve this problem of fairness, we seem to have developed a new gender, one that shares maleness and femaleness simultaneously, equally, and therefore fairly. We have, in short, created—out of nowhere—a his/hermaphrodite.

A writer will try to make a point about something. He or she needs an actor, yet because he or she is generalizing, he or she must pick a pronoun to convey his/her meaning. Sometimes (s)he will concoct all sorts of new words. Although these his/hermaphroditic expressions might sound fine to her/him, the reader can become somewhat confused about who is who. He or she isn't quite sure what he/she is trying to say to her or him. I mean the reader isn't sure what the writer is trying to say because the writer can't seem to decide whether he or she is a him or a her or a what.

There has to be a better way. In fact, there are three better ways. But before I get to the cures, let me make a lonely plea to preserve some of the grammar of the language.

Agreement in Number—Agreement in Gender

Recall the use of personal pronouns. Also recall the *case* of personal pronouns (subjective, objective, and possessive) and the *number* of personal pronouns (singular and plural). Singular, third-person, personal pronouns include *he* and *she* in the subjective case, *him* and *her* in the objective case, and *his* and *her* in the possessive case. Obviously, each of these *singular* personal pronouns reveals gender. Plural, third-person, personal pronouns include *they* in the subjective case, *them* in the objective case, and *their* in the possessive case. Notice that *plural* pronouns do *not* reveal gender.

When you use a pronoun as a substitute for a noun, you typically reveal the noun first and then refer to that noun with a personal pronoun. Thus: *The girl (noun) announced her (pronoun) plans.* Or: *Tom Jackson (noun) announced his (pronoun) plans.* Or: *The plaintiff (noun) announced his (pronoun) plans.* In the above sentences, *girl*, *Tom Jackson*, and *plaintiff* are the *antecedents* of the later pronouns. Because in each case the writer knows the sex of *girl*, *Tom Jackson*, and *plaintiff*, the writer can use the correct pronouns in the correct *gender*. Also, because each antecedent is singular, the writer can use the correct pronouns in the correct *number* to restate those singular nouns—those singular antecedents.

One of the cardinal rules of grammar—and, with a little effort, it can remain so—requires that a singular pronoun refer to a singular antecedent and a plural pronoun refer to a plural antecedent. Thus, you would not say: *The plaintiff announced their plans.* If you did, your meaning would totally change. The plaintiff doesn't solely possess a set of plans. Rather, he jointly owns some plans with at least one other person, whose identity remains a mystery.

The problem of his/hermaphrodism arises when the writer is generalizing (as I am now generalizing about a *writer*). If I later refer to this writer as *he*, I unfairly exclude girls and women from the generalized class of writers. And if I later refer to this writer as *she*, I unfairly exclude boys and men from the class as well. Reacting to an overwhelming urge to be fair, the writer succumbs to his/hermaphrodism and proceeds to botch up his or her writing with lots of extra words that might obscure his or her meaning.

One thing a writer might do to wreak havoc on the language is break the rule of *number agreement*. A writer might use a singular antecedent and then use plural pronouns when they later want to refer to that singular antecedent. The writer forgets that their reader will lose faith in them if they insist on referring to a previously identified, singular antecedent with a later plural pronoun. All in the name of fairness— thus do we tear our language apart.

Before getting to some solutions to this very real dilemma, I should point out one recognized exception to the *number agreement* rule. Many times in writing, someone will use an *indefinite* pronoun. They may then follow that singular, indefinite pronoun with a later plural pronoun. Reread the last two sentences, and you'll see the rule in action. *Someone* is an indefinite pronoun. It is also singular. Rules of grammar permit a plural pronoun to restate a singular antecedent when that antecedent itself is an *indefinite pronoun*. Hence, the word *they* is correctly used to refer to the singular *someone*. Indefinite pronouns include: *someone, anyone, each, one, everyone*, and some others. Thus, it is correct to say: *Anyone may bring their lunch.* It is also correct to say: *Everyone is entitled to their own opinion.*

The Problem

Here's the problem:

> An applicant for employment must file his or her application with the personnel office. He/she should include his/her educational background, a listing of three of his/her references, and a summary of his/her employment experience.

The Plural Antecedent Solution

One very easy solution to the problem is to make your antecedents plural. Typically, you'll be generalizing about *an applicant, a writer*, or *a taxpayer*. It's quite easy to say the same things about *applicants, writers*, or *taxpayers*. When you do, you have the plural pronouns readily available. And, of most importance, *they, their*, and *them* do not discriminate on the basis of sex. Watch it work:

> Applicants for employment must file their applications with the personnel office. They should include their educational backgrounds, listings of three of their references, and summaries of their employment experience.

A word of caution. Writers should use their heads when using this approach. After all, writers have *heads*—plural—just as *applicants* have *applications, backgrounds, listings*, and *summaries*. When the antecedent is plural, take care to make all succeeding elements plural.

The Passive Voice Solution

You learned in Chapter 8 to manipulate the voice of transitive verbs to achieve certain objectives. One of those objectives was to avoid sexist writing. By using the passive voice, you obviate the need to reveal actors. Hiding the identity of the actors also hides their sex. Discriminatory writing disappears as well:

> An application for employment must be filed with the personnel office. An educational background, a listing of three references, and a summary of employment experience should be included.

The Second-Person Pronoun Solution

We can thank the Department of the Navy's Office of the Judge Advocate General for this solution. While teaching my writing course to attorneys in Washington, I received this suggestion from a Navy attorney: use the second-person pronoun when your writing is instructional. The second-person pronoun, he correctly pointed out, is not gender-based.

> To apply for employment, file an application with the personnel office. You should include an educational background, a listing of three of your references, and a summary of your employment experience.

Bingo. His/hermaphrodism loses. The language wins.

The Pick-a-Pronoun Solution

Sometimes these three solutions just won't work. The passive voice is just too wimpy, plural antecedents don't sound right, or second-person pronouns are out of place. In that case, use *he or she* if the occurrence is infrequent and doesn't get out of control. Otherwise, pick *he* or *she* and use it consistently.

Combating his/hermaphrodism is certainly worth the effort. Being fair is worth the effort, too. By fighting to preserve the language while simultaneously promoting fairness, you can justifiably look upon yourself as one of the English language's most steadfast spokesindividuals. By all means, be fair. But don't be stupid.

The Rules of Good Writing

At last, your list of the rules of good writing looks like this:

1. Use an average of 25 words per sentence.

2. Avoid putting too many messages in a single sentence.

3. Put most of your messages at the subject-predicate position.

4. For variety or emphasis, invert your sentences.

5. Use the art of subordination to smooth out choppiness.

6. Avoid disrupting your sentences with thought-stopping gaps.

7. Watch out for the rule of parallel construction.

8. Tabulate particularly complex information.

9. Hammer home your point with the powerful, versatile verb.

10. Use the verb *to be* only when you mean it.

11. Get rid of compound prepositions.

12. Cut adjective, adverb, and noun clauses to other structures satisfying the same functions.

13. Prefer the active voice, but use the passive to satisfy certain objectives concerning the identity or placement of the actor or the recipient.

14. Favor short words over long, fancy words.

15. Use concrete words to staple your thoughts to your reader's mind.

16. Use modification to trim down the fat in your language.

17. Use phrases to smooth out the choppy noun-noun modifier.

18. Do not use too many negative expressions.

19. Be fair and nonsexist, but don't be stupid.

That's all there is to it. I'll try to tie it all together in some final, parting shots on matters of style. Then we'll turn our attention to the content of persuasive legal writing.

Chapter 10

Some Parting Shots
on Matters of Style

Et semel emissum volat irrevocabile verbum.

And once sent out, a word takes wing irrevocably.

—Horace

Chapter 10

Some Parting Shots

on Matters of Style

What makes good writing good and bad writing bad? Here's the "final" list of the rules of good writing:

The Rules of Good Writing

1. Use an average of 25 words per sentence.
2. Avoid putting too many messages in a single sentence.
3. Put most of your messages at the subject-predicate position.
4. For variety or emphasis, invert your sentences.
5. Use the art of subordination to smooth out choppiness.
6. Avoid disrupting your sentences with thought-stopping gaps.
7. Watch out for the rule of parallel construction.
8. Tabulate particularly complex information.
9. Hammer home your point with the powerful, versatile verb.
10. Use the verb *to be* only when you mean it.
11. Get rid of compound prepositions.
12. Cut adjective, adverb, and noun clauses to other structures satisfying the same functions.
13. Prefer the active voice, but use the passive to satisfy certain objectives concerning the identity or placement of the actor or the recipient.
14. Favor short words over long, fancy words.
15. Use concrete words to staple your thoughts to your reader's mind.
16. Use modification to trim down the fat in your language.
17. Use phrases to smooth out the choppy noun-noun modifier.
18. Do not use too many negative expressions.
19. Be fair and nonsexist, but don't be stupid.

To write powerfully—to wield your mighty sword—you must pay attention to sentence structure. You've got to know that sentences typically appear in one of four forms. They will consist of a subject plus transitive verb plus object, subject plus intransitive verb plus adverb, subject plus *to be* plus adjective, subject plus *to be* plus noun, or subject plus linking verb plus adjective. From these basic structures comes the first rule of style: Keep your sentences short. Your reader is not too excited about sticking with one of your sentences for more than 25 words. To grab your reader's attention and not let go, keep your sentences short and to the point. Second, dish out your messages a bite at a time. Avoid putting too many messages in one grammatical sentence. Third, your reader fully expects to find your main message placed at the strategic part of your sentences. Let your subject and your main verb carry most of your messages. Vary that approach only for emphasis or variety. Fourth, when you tire of straightforward writing, flip your sentences with the art of inversion. Fifth, if you carry these rules to the extreme, your writing will be too short and choppy. Develop, therefore, an ear for those sentences crying out for subordination. Learn to weave the information in one sentence into another nearby. Recognize situations calling for subordinate clauses, prepositional phrases, verbal phrases, or appositive phrases. Sixth, remember to keep strategic parts of your sentences close together. Keep subject next to verb, verb next to object, and complex-verb words next to one another. In short, avoid gaps. Seventh, remember those extraordinarily important conjunctions—the coordinating and correlative conjunctions. Your readers expect them to join equal grammatical units, so keep your writing parallel. Also remember to use the notion of parallel construction as a way not only to identify those constructions you use but to uncover those constructions missing from your written language. When was the last time you used a correlative conjunction to join two infinitive phrases? I just did. Three sentences ago. It works. After all, parallelism helped me write this book. The eighth and final trick to fine-tune your sentences is the device of tabulation. Go ahead and make lists in your writing, but be sure to follow rules of grammar and style in making those lists. Do all these things to your sentences and your writing will improve.

Then turn your attention to your words. The ninth item on our list of the rules of good writing is perhaps the most important of all. Denounification. The mere sound of the word alone should prove the worth of the goal it seeks. Unstuff your language. Cut out those piles of pillowy nouns. Bare your fists with hard-hitting, action-packed verbs. That's the way to win the battle of words in the legal profession. Or anywhere else. Tenth, learn to use the verb *to be* only when you really mean it. If you're a part of the *new generation*, pay special attention to your language. *Like, go, waslike*, and other parts of nonspeech threaten thought itself. Really and truly, you'll go nowhere talking and thinking that way. Eleventh, declare war on compound prepositions. They really are quite tyrannical, never fessing up with respect to their precise meaning. Twelfth, watch out for clauses. Too many of them inevitably get in the way of clear writing. Learn to substitute true nouns or gerunds for noun clauses. Learn to replace adjective or adverb clauses with verbal phrases, prepositional phrases, one-word adjectives or adverbs, adjective appositives, truncated adverb clauses, and absolutes. Thirteenth, as a rule, you should prefer the active voice over the passive voice. If the majority of your sentences appear in the passive voice, no subject ever does anything. All subjects just sit there and take it. Your writing, in the passive voice, will lack a sense of activity, a sense of urgency. Your writing, in the passive voice, will just be weak and wimpy. Not exactly a prescription for victory. Fourteenth, use short words. They always do a better job than long ones, even in the law, perhaps especially in the law. Fifteenth, concrete words usually paint more vivid images in the reader's mind. Though attorneys must necessarily deal with abstractions, using concrete words to express or exemplify those abstract doctrines will do much to staple your thoughts to your reader. Sixteenth, you can put your writing on a diet by using the device of modification to trim out excess verbiage. Useless clauses and prepositional phrases can often be replaced by one-word adjectives and adverbs. Seventeenth, keep modification within reasonable bounds. Don't overdo it and produce long-winded chains of nouns used as adjectives. Eighteenth, avoid negative expressions. That says it just fine. And lastly, nineteenthly, please keep our language. It has done a good job for so long. The language, the ear, and good sense recoil at *he/she's* and *s(he)'s*.

That's the way to write. Learn these rules of grammar and a good, powerful style will necessarily follow. The rules of grammar, after all, didn't just pop up overnight. They didn't just materialize out of your eighth-grade grammar book. Your teachers didn't just make them up to trip you up. They rule the language—these rules of grammar. They rule the language that conveys our thoughts. Without them, we can't talk, we can't write. Indeed, without them, we can't even think. So use these rules of grammar. They aren't really leering over your shoulder waiting to pounce on your slightest error.

They are, instead, your weapons in whatever battles you must fight with words.

Chapter 11

Content of Legal Writing

Semper ad eventum festinat et in medias res
Non secus ac notas auditorem rapit.

He always hurries to the main event and whisks his audience
into the middle of things as though they knew already.

—Horace

Chapter 11

Content of Legal Writing

Introduction

Right up front I should set the stage for this chapter. My primary audience is the first-year law student and the first-year paralegal student. They must learn, after all, to write that first, dreaded Memorandum of Law. They must know what a Statement of Facts is. They must learn about Questions Presented. They must master the art of discussing a case. To the novice, strange and frightening stuff. To the attorney, pretty basic stuff.

This chapter must begin with these basics. But it will go further. I urge the more seasoned practitioner to stay with this discussion, for it will also treat some sophisticated matters of content and contain some observations that can go a long way toward increasing the power and effectiveness of legal writing. The chapter will delve into problems of structure, strategies of paragraphing, and ways of sticking your writing together. It will discuss effective ways to present legal authority, analyze legal authority, and demonstrate conclusions made or arguments set forth. It will, I believe, articulate some matters of legal content in a way that's new and, I hope, helpful to the legal profession.

My focal point is the Memorandum of Law. I will not separately discuss appellate advocacy or even trial advocacy. The content discussed here can be easily transferred to other settings or documents and adapted as necessary to situations requiring argumentation, exposition, academic communication, or even judicial decision-making. For after all, a case discussion is a case discussion. It matters not that it appears in a Memorandum of Law written by a first-year law student, in a trial brief written by an ace litigator, or even in an opinion of law written by a state or federal judge. The setting and thrust will change, but the basics of legal content remain pretty much the same.

To focus on a Memorandum of Law, I needed a frame of reference. I needed a statute to talk about. I needed a fact situation. I needed some case law to refer to. Case law. That's the ticket. I needed a casebook.

I remember back in law school, envying all those law professors who wrote those big, heavy casebooks. Not a bad deal, I thought. All they had to do to have a best-seller on their hands was to dispatch their eager—and inexpensive (they're all on Federal Work Study)—student assistants to the law library to find noncopyright-protected case law waiting to be reproduced word for word in a big, heavy casebook. Follow each case with some unanswerable, but highly intelligent questions. Include a few research notes to law review articles asking equally unanswerable questions. Throw in a few citations to the *Restatements of the Law*. Voila! Book! Instant tenure!

Not to be outdone, I've prepared my own casebook in the next chapter. There you will find the almost full text of the following opinions:

McSparran v. Weist, 402 F.2d 867 (3d Cir. 1968), *cert. denied*, 395 U.S. 903 (1969).

Bishop v. Hendricks, 495 F.2d 289 (4th Cir.), *cert. denied*, 419 U.S. 1056 (1974).

Hackney v. Newman Memorial Hospital, Inc., 621 F.2d 1069 (10th Cir.), *cert. denied*, 449 U.S. 982 (1980).

Bianca v. Parke-Davis Pharmaceutical Division of Warner-Lambert Co., 723 F.2d 392 (5th Cir. 1984).

Joyce v. Siegel, 429 F.2d 128 (3d Cir. 1970).

These cases concern our Statement of Facts, which follows below. They involve a relatively simple question concerning the diversity of citizenship jurisdiction of federal courts. They comprise only a small part of the case law governing the issue found in our Statement of Facts. They do not contain all the law that would be needed to analyze our hypothetical facts thoroughly. They just provide some law we can use to focus this discussion of legal content.

I urge you to stop reading this chapter right now and turn to the next chapter. Read each case. Take some research notes. Try to figure out how you would organize these cases in a Memorandum of Law. Think about what information you would include or leave out. Begin to picture various ways you could arrange a series of presentations of each case.

When you've completed reading my casebook, return to this chapter for a discussion of legal content. Then, in the final chapter, I've included a sample Memorandum of Law to give you some idea of what legal writing looks like and sounds like.

The Purpose of a Memorandum of Law

Contrary to my style above, *Memorandum of Law* should not be capitalized. To a first-year law student, it just feels like it ought to be capitalized. Sheer terror alone should justify the upper case. Add the endless hours spent during the first semester of law school and a first-year student is likely to type *MEMORANDUM OF LAW* (to be spoken in a suitably imposing voice with a slight trace of an English accent like the ones you hear on National Public Radio).

Let's cut it down to size and call it a *memo*. Or *legal memo*. At least it sounds a little friendlier. Let's explore its function and its content, for the elements and structure of a legal memo also appear in most other forms of legal writing.

A legal memo typically addresses a given *Statement of Facts*. In the practice of law, a senior partner might want a Memorandum of Law (senior partners insist on the upper case) in order to analyze a new case, to plan trial strategy, to decide on the suitability of various defenses, to advise a client, or to prepare pleadings. Lurking in the Statement of Facts are various *Questions Presented*. These questions articulate legal questions, not factual questions. They point the way for legal research and provide broad outlines for organization. We'll return to them in detail below. Then, the *Discussion of Authority* occupies the main portion of the memo (and the main portion of the writer's time and energy).

The legal discussion found in a legal memo seeks to fulfill three main functions. First, the discussion *collects* and *preserves* the fruits of legal research. The writer has spent hours researching the issue. The writer has read or at least skimmed scores of cases. The writer has studied a host of law review articles. The writer has decided to discard some authority and to include only those cases, statutes, regulations, rules, other primary authority, and secondary authority needed to *reach* and *demonstrate* a legal conclusion.

Second, the discussion *teaches* the reader what the reader needs to know to understand the law applying to each question presented. The discussion should not assume full knowledge on the part of the reader. Instead, the discussion should assume relative ignorance and seek to bring the reader's knowledge up to the same level as the writer's. The writer has spent the time in the law library and should seek to share with the reader the knowledge gained.

Third, the discussion should *reveal the rationale* of the writer. The writer should not assume that the reader automatically *gets it*. Instead, through careful organization and careful development of each legal issue, the writer should methodically show each step of the analysis or argument so that the reader winds up at the same conclusion. The reader should finish the last page of the memo, put it down, nod, and say, "I see."

Other functions do exist. Some firms might instruct their associates to write legal memos in such a way that they can be slightly changed and transformed into a piece of advocacy suitable to serve as a trial or appellate brief. A judge might instruct his law clerk to prepare a *bench memo* that can serve as the basis of an opinion of law. Some law offices want legal memos to appear in an argumentative style, while others insist on strict objectivity. Regardless of function or style, however, the *content* of legal writing remains pretty much the same.

Various Formats

In your first-year legal writing course, in your law firm, in your government agency, or in your court, you'll encounter a variety of *formats* used for legal memos and other forms of legal writing. Though none is necessarily superior to another, the formats exist for a reason. The first-year law student should learn early to follow the prescribed format. Deviating with clever changes inevitably meets with the disdain of those having power over your professional life.

A typical format for a legal memo is likely to include a caption (To, From, Re, Date), a Statement of Facts, Questions Presented, Discussion of Authority, and Conclusion. The format I used at the University of Virginia appears on the following page.

MEMORANDUM OF LAW

To: Recipient's Name

From: Writer's Name

Re: Case Name or File Name or Brief Description of Contents

Date: Date of Final Preparation

Statement of Facts:

A complete statement of relevant facts appears here. Though length will vary with complexity, an average Statement of Facts should consume two or three typewritten, double-spaced pages.

Questions Presented:

1) State the first question presented.

2) State the second question presented.

3) And so on.

Conclusion:

In a series of well-constructed paragraphs, state broadly the conclusions to each question presented.

Discussion of Authority:

1) Repeat the first question presented here.

Discuss the law governing the first question presented. Length will range from two to three pages right on up to 10 or 20 pages.

2) Repeat the second question presented here.

Discuss the law governing the second question presented. Again, length will vary.

The Statement of Facts

In your first-year legal writing course, you will be given a fact situation. In the real world, lawyers must derive the facts from client interviews, witness interviews, truck loads of documents, pretrial discovery, and untold other sources. The fact situation given to first-year students—like the real world—typically contains extraneous matter. In fact, legal writing professors have a great deal of fun concocting statements of facts, and the more extraneous detail they can include, the better.

The Statement of Facts should begin with the procedural posture of the case. Who is suing whom for what and where are we in the legal proceedings? Provide this information first so that the reader has some idea of a context before tackling the facts.

To present the facts cogently, the writer must distill them (from the real world or from the professor's wild imagination) down to a Statement of Facts appearing in a legal memorandum. The Statement of Facts should give the reader those facts that are relevant to the legal discussion and exclude any information the reader does not need to follow the legal discussion in the memo. For example, if a case involves a statute of limitations issue, then exact dates of the transaction become crucial. On the other hand, if exact dates have no legal relevance, the writer should not include a host of dates that tend to baffle the reader. As another example, don't say the plaintiff was injured in a collision between his 1985 two-tone blue and white Buick Regal and a 1987 bright red Mazda RX-7 Turbo. Just say the plaintiff was injured in a collision between his sedan and defendant's sports car.

The Statement of Facts should also seek to simplify complex fact patterns. Thus, the reader can follow the facts more easily when parties are referred to by their legal status or by some shortened name, not by their given names. Instead of constantly referring to *Consolidated Import-Export Unlimited*, shorten the name to *Consolidated* or to a legal status such as *parent corporation*. Instead of referring to *Lieberman, Stanley, Fix*, and *LeFleur*, use their legal or other status such as *plaintiff, defendant, appellant, appellee, petitioner, respondent, decedent, administrator, landlord, tenant, wife #1, wife #2, wife #3*, and the possibilities are truly limitless.

In the Statement of Facts, resist the urge to sound like a police report, which adores the word *subject*, or, worse, a lawyer who uses *said* as an adjective. Don't say: *While traveling in said automobile plaintiff Linda Fix suffered extensive injuries in the subject accident.* Resist the urge to drop articles. Don't say: *Plaintiff sued defendant for injuries sustained in automobile accident.* Instead say: *Plaintiff sued defendant for injuries sustained in an automobile accident.* It's all right to drop articles when referring to parties to lawsuits (plaintiff, defendant, appellant, appellee, petitioner, respondent) or when referring to a generalized noun, e.g., injuries. It is not all right to drop articles for all nouns, e.g., automobile accident.

Finally, the Statement of Facts should include all facts that come up in the Discussion of Authority. Do not introduce new facts in the Discussion of Authority. Every factual element appearing in the Discussion of Authority should also appear in the Statement of Facts.

Following is the fact pattern we'll use for our sample memorandum of law. The facts given below are similar to the type of fact presentation you're likely to receive in your first-year legal writing course. It is stuffed with irrelevancies and detail. Your task is to strip the facts down to those essentials the reader needs to follow your legal analysis. A proper Statement of Facts appears in the sample memorandum in Chapter 13.

Sample Fact Pattern

It was a clear and sunny day, January 17, 1985. At approximately 3:30 PM, Barbara Jean Goss, age 12, alighted from her school bus and began to cross in front of the bus to get to the other side of the street. The school bus driver, Mr. Frank Simpson, had been driving buses for the Guilford County School System since 1965. His driving record was spotless, and he had received a Driving Safety Award during the 1983-84 academic year. Before Barbara Jean alighted from the bus, Mr. Simpson followed the standard procedure of activating the "School Bus Stop System," which entailed the automatic display of a "STOP" sign on the side of the bus facing oncoming traffic. State law requires all oncoming traffic to come to a complete stop when confronted with such a sign. Similarly, traffic behind a school bus must come to a complete stop and must not pass the bus. Satisfied that the way was clear and safe, Mr. Simpson opened the door to let Barbara Jean off at her usual stop. Also alighting were 10-year-old Fred Salazar and 12-year-old Vince Pierce. They lived on the right side of the road and, consequently, did not cross in front of the bus to the other side.

As was her usual practice, Barbara Jean began to run in front of the bus to the other side of the road. She paused briefly to look right to see if oncoming cars had stopped. Seeing no cars at all to the right, she proceeded to the other side.

Meanwhile, Mr. Frederick Joseph Mulligan was approaching the stopped bus from the rear. Later evidence would show that Mr. Mulligan had just spent three hours at the Friendly Horse Pub, a popular drinking spot on the outskirts of Greensboro, North Carolina. According to witnesses at the pub, Mr. Mulligan consumed at least three "Super Pitchers" of "light beer." His blood alcohol level, tested during his autopsy, showed him to be legally intoxicated. Mr. Mulligan was a successful businessman, owning a chain of printing companies throughout the South. His net worth totalled more than $3.2 million at the time of his death. He was a permanent resident of Greensboro, North Carolina, having lived there most of his life.

Mr. Mulligan failed to see or ignored the red lights flashing on the back of the bus. He failed to see or ignored the "STOP" sign appearing on the left side of the bus. As he approached the bus in his 1984 black Cadillac Coupe de Ville, he accelerated, right before Barbara Jean began crossing to her side of the street.

Barbara Jean had not looked left when crossing to the other side of the street. When she was halfway across, she sensed motion to her left, turned, and saw the black Cadillac bearing down upon her. She screamed and made a desperate leap to the other side. Mulligan, seeing the little girl, slammed on his brakes, veered sharply to his left, and smashed head-on into a steel telephone pole. Mr. Mulligan was killed instantly. He barely missed Barbara Jean.

Barbara Jean died instantly of a heart attack. Her medical records show a congenital heart defect. Medical witnesses will testify that the sudden fright caused a massive myocardial infarction resulting in death. They will also testify that Barbara Jean died instantly and probably felt little, if any, pain.

Barbara Jean's mother, Susan Goss, witnessed her only child's death. Having her usual afternoon cocktail, she peered from behind the curtains in her bedroom just as the car crashed into the telephone pole and Barbara Jean collapsed. She rushed in terror to the scene. A neighbor had the presence of mind to call the police and an ambulance.

Barbara Jean's father died when Barbara Jean was two years old. Her uncle, Fred Jackson—Susan's sister's husband—resides in High Point, North Carolina and earns a six-figure income as a traveling sales representative. Susan's other sister, Sally McAllister, lives in Richmond, Virginia, and runs a fashion boutique in a popular shopping mall.

Barbara Jean had an estate valued at $10,322.48. Because Barbara Jean had no will, her mother inherited the estate under the law of intestacy in North Carolina.

Following the tragic death, Susan turned to alcohol for solace. She entered a substance abuse program in early 1986 but suffered a relapse in the fall of 1986.

On November 10, 1986, Susan retained a personal injury law firm with slick television ads to pursue a claim for wrongful death against the estate of Frederick Joseph Mulligan. By that time, Susan had already served as administratrix of Barbara Jean's estate and had disbursed the funds of the estate to herself as the sole statutory beneficiary. Susan resigned as administratrix on November 25, 1986. On the same day, Sally McAllister was appointed as the successor administratrix. On November 30, 1986, Sally McAllister, as plaintiff, filed a wrongful death and survival action against the estate of Frederick Mulligan in the United States District Court in Greensboro. The complaint alleged diversity of citizenship as the basis for the federal court's jurisdiction.

Mulligan's insurance company, one of your firm's most valued clients, does not want to litigate the case in federal court and wants to know whether it can get the case dismissed because the appointment of Sally McAllister violates the provisions of section 1359 of title 28 of the United States Code.

Questions Presented

The Question Presented is quite difficult to write. The Question Presented should pose the *legal* question or questions arising from the Statement of Facts. Each question, if more than one, serves to break down the Discussion of Authority into major, separate discussions. Thus, each Question Presented should be fairly broad.

Mistakes that first-time legal writers make in phrasing a Question Presented are predictable and, therefore, avoidable. First, do not confuse a Question Presented with a legal issue. If you've already read the casebook in the next chapter, then you know that the broad question in the current facts is whether the federal district court will dismiss the action as a violation of title 28, section 1359. Residing within that broad question are a host of *legal issues* and *factual questions*. They might include whether the parties appointed the nonresident administratrix in order to get into federal court or in order to achieve legitimate considerations, whether other candidates could or should have been appointed, and whether the nonresident administratrix has any stake in the outcome of the lawsuit. These are narrower legal issues or factual questions. They are not *Questions Presented*. Resolving each question figures in the overall resolution of the Question Presented, but each one does not rise to the level of full-fledged Question Presented.

Second, make the question generic. Do not use the parties' names in formulating the Question Presented. Rather, use their legal status. Thus, don't refer to *Barbara Jean* in the Question Presented. Instead, refer to her as a *minor decedent* or just the *deceased*.

Third, put the Question Presented in an interrogatory form: Does a federal district court lack jurisdiction . . . ? Does the appointment of a nonresident administratrix . . . ?

Fourth, try to incorporate into the Question Presented the major legal issues that must be resolved to answer the Question Presented. Thus, if *motive* and *stake in the outcome* appear to be the major issues involved, these elements should appear in the Question Presented.

Here are several versions of a Question Presented that might appear in a legal memo on the sample Statement of Facts:

Question Presented:

Will the federal court dismiss this case as "improperly or collusively made or joined" where a nonresident administratrix with no stake in the outcome of the case is appointed to prosecute an otherwise wholly local controversy against a resident defendant and invokes the diversity of citizenship jurisdiction of the federal court?

Where a nonresident administratrix is appointed to bring a wrongful death case in federal court against a resident defendant, is related to the deceased, but has no stake in the outcome of the case, does the federal court lack subject matter jurisdiction under title 28, section 1359 of the United States Code?

If a nonresident administratrix is appointed to bring a wrongful death case in federal court against a resident defendant, may the defendant successfully move for dismissal on the grounds that the court lacks jurisdiction under title 28, section 1359 of the United States Code?

The Conclusion

Most legal memo formats have a *Conclusion* positioned either at the beginning of the memo or at the end. If positioned at the beginning, it might also be called a *Brief Answer*. The Conclusion should answer the Question Presented and hit the major legal issues that must be resolved to reach the particular conclusion. The Conclusion also should paint a broad picture of the status of the law relating to the Question Presented. If some courts go one way and other courts go another, the Conclusion should briefly highlight the conflict.

First-time legal writers typically make two mistakes in writing the Conclusion. First, they go on forever in the Conclusion. It becomes so detailed it might as well be the Discussion of Authority. Instead of revealing the specifics, keep it general. You'll have plenty of opportunity to get into the nuts and bolts in the Discussion of Authority.

Second, many first-time legal writers will cite authority in a Conclusion. It's best only to mention the broad points and the overall result. The reader understands what the Conclusion is and knows you will support the Conclusion with specific authority in the Discussion of Authority.

Here's a stab at a Conclusion for our sample case:

Conclusion:

Since the decision of a landmark case in the 1960s, the courts have liberally interpreted title 28, section 1359 and held that an appointment of a nonresident fiduciary to invoke the diversity jurisdiction of the federal court violates the statute and deprives the court of subject matter jurisdiction. Under that view, the *motive* to get into federal court, without some other legitimate reason supporting the fiduciary's appointment, is fatal and the case will be dismissed. Other cases have emphasized the *stake* the fiduciary has in the proceedings. If the fiduciary has any financial or other legal stake in the case, then the desire to get into federal court is irrelevant, and the provisions of the statute are satisfied.

Here, getting the case dismissed depends to a great degree on which view the court uses. The Fourth Circuit relies primarily on the *stake in the outcome* test and tends to downplay the role of motive. Thus, even though the administratrix is related to the deceased and to the beneficiary of the wrongful death claim, she stands to gain no interest in any potential damage award. On this ground alone, the case might well be dismissed.

The record is silent on the issue of motive and on the availability of other persons who could have served as administrator. If we can show the availability of other candidates—the mother or the resident uncle or perhaps a resident aunt—then the arguments for dismissal grow ever stronger.

The Discussion of Authority

Now comes the tough one—the Discussion of Authority. What follows are some observations on the content of legal writing. These observations apply not only to a legal memo but to almost any form of legal discussion. The first-time writer, however, encounters this content first in a legal memo. But more seasoned practitioners, law professors, judges, and government officials can increase the effectiveness of their legal writing by studying the structures and strategies we are about to discuss, comparing their own approaches, spotting their weaknesses (if any), and going about making the necessary changes.

This discussion of legal content stretches on for quite a few pages and covers a host of different topics. To give you some idea of our destination, here are the mileposts we will visit: *Organizational Devices, Introduction, Paragraphing and Topic Sentences, Transitions, Legislative Presentations, Case Discussions, Other Legal Presentations, Proper Quotations, Legal Comparisons, Application of Law to Facts*, and *Reaching and Stating the Final Result*.

As noted above, the Discussion of Authority seeks to collect and preserve the fruits of legal research, to teach the reader about the law applicable to the Statement of Facts, and to reach a conclusion that answers the Question Presented. To accomplish these tasks, the Discussion of Authority will adapt a discernible organizational scheme, cite and discuss applicable law and secondary authority, apply law to facts, compare various cases to isolate *dispositive factors* in the courts' analyses, make arguments where needed, and attempt to predict the outcome of the case under discussion.

Throughout the Discussion of Authority, you should never forget that a given case prompted you to toil endlessly in the law library. A given set of facts is under discussion, and you should frequently relate legal discussions to those facts. Too often, first-time (and even experienced) legal writers will produce a legal memo that looks, sounds, feels, and smells like an *A.L.R.* Annotation or a passage from *C.J.S.* The writers go merrily along, oblivious to the *instant case*. Finally, perhaps at the tail end of the memo, they will mention—oh so briefly—the facts prompting all that toil. As an afterthought—a footnote, almost—they reach a conclusion by saying, "Therefore, the federal court will dismiss the current case as a violation of title 28, section 1359 of the United States Code."

"Why?" the reader begs.

"What do you mean 'Therefore'?" the reader pleads.

If you will keep your case at the forefront of your mind and as the focus of your writing, you'll have a much better chance of landing an *A* on that first legal writing assignment or of winning a case by impressing a judge or intimidating an opponent.

Let's begin our discussion of the Discussion of Authority by look-ing at various organizational devices you might use in structuring legal content.

Organizational Devices

At the conclusion of research, a big, blank, leering piece of paper (or computer screen) stares back at you. Your job, of course, is to fill it up with erudition. As a first step, you might consider the various ways to organize legal material, for your discussion not only should *have* an organization but should *reveal* it to the reader. Too many legal writers seem to write a whole bunch of case discussions on note cards, shuffle them and cut, throw them wildly into the air, type them up as they land, and declare the memo at an end. The content has no apparent structure. The points discussed don't seem to flow. They don't connect. The forest has no shape. The trees get in the way.

You have plenty of trees, no doubt about that. You've got the relevant statute or statutes, the implementing regulations, if any, scores of cases, several law review articles, and perhaps other material such as legislative history. "But how do I put it together?" you ask. "How do I arrange all this stuff?" "What comes first?" "What next?"

I don't pretend to have isolated and described the shape of all possible forests in legal writing. Indeed, as I teach persuasive writing to attorneys, they invariably suggest additional ways to organize legal content. Naturally, I've borrowed freely from their ideas. I'll set them out here, along with some brief commentary, and then point out those structures we might best use to organize the sample case concerning Barbara Jean Goss. Here are some structures you might use to organize any legal discussion.

The Type-of-Law Approach

Most legal questions logically break down into a type-of-law or-ganizational device. If a question is governed by a statute, then naturally you'll present the statute first. If regulations implement that statute and are pertinent to the question presented, they come next. If bills, hear-ings, committee reports, or floor debate help to flesh out the meaning of a statute, then this legislative history might come next. Inevitably, in our system of law, we turn to case law to find out the meaning of statutes, so they will probably come next. Finally, because courts do pay attention to scholarly writing, you might add secondary authority along with or immediately after your discussion of case law. Along the way, of course, you must decide when to apply the law to the facts of your case. (We'll discuss Application of Law to Facts below.) The type-of-law outline, thus, might look like this:

Introduction

Statute

Regulations

Legislative History

Case Law

Secondary Authority (law reviews, treatises, Restatements of the Law)

Conclusion

The legal writer usually encounters the greatest difficulty in organizing case law. Which case comes first? Which one comes next? Where does this one fit? All these are typical cries for help. Though the following organizational devices can and do apply to questions controlled by statutes, regulations, case law, and other forms of authority, I will limit my discussions to the organization of case law. This approach will simplify the discussion and enable you to apply these devices to other forms of law.

The Historical Approach

Often, history is relevant to a particular legal question. If a doctrine has developed in a dramatic way, then understanding the current view might depend on an understanding of the old view. Thus, chronology might dictate the ordering of your cases. Chronology, however, should only dictate the positioning of those milestone cases that significantly extended or changed a legal doctrine. Once those major organizational milestones are fixed in your paper, you're likely to use one or more of the other organizational devices to order cases within these broader historical segments.

Let's consider the sample topic. In the field of manufactured diversity of citizenship, we find a significant change in 1968 when *McSparran* overruled *Corabi*. Thus, right away, we can see a potential organizational device. We could begin with a brief discussion of *Corabi* (the old view) and then include a broader discussion of *McSparran* (the new view). The organizational problem then becomes the ordering of cases in the post-*McSparran* period. Chronology, you can readily see, loses its relevance. Thus, after discussing *McSparran*, you'd abandon the historical approach and shift to one of the other devices shown below.

The Yes-No Approach

One convenient way to group cases broadly is by their outcomes. Your memo can first deal with those cases going one way (yes) and then deal with those cases going the other way (no). The *yes-no* dichotomy can relate to any broad outcome: *yes*-liability-imposed, *no*-liability-not-imposed; *yes*-evidence-admissible, *no*-evidence-inadmissible; *yes*-case-dismissed, *no*-case-not-dismissed; and so on. The trick, from a legal analytical point of view, is to glean from each group those elements prompting the courts to reach a *yes* and to distinguish those elements from the ones found in the *no* cases. Then, of course, the trick is to show the close similarity of your facts with the *yes* cases and the vast differences of your facts with the *no* cases (if that is the desired result). On the other hand, the trick is to show the vast differences of your facts with the *yes* cases and the close similarity of your facts with the *no* cases (if that is the desired result).

The Yes-No Approach readily lends itself to our sample topic as one way to group the cases in the post-*McSparran* period. We could group all opinions dismissing the cases under section 1359 and figure out the *dispositive elements* prompting the courts to reach that result and then deal, in a similar way, with all opinions refusing to dismiss the cases. Because we want a dismissal, we would try to show the close similarity of our case with the *yes*-dismissal cases and the vast differences of our case with the *no*-nondismissal cases.

The Case-by-Case Approach

Many legal writers just take it one case at a time. They deal with *Jones*, then *Smith*, then *Jackson*, and so on to the end of the list of cases. Each case, confronting the same legal question, necessarily deals with the same legal issues. Thus, if a legal question is resolved by applying three factors (X, Y, and Z) in a particular way, each case discussion necessarily entails discussing these three factors—over and over again. The outline might look like this:

The *Jones* Case

Issue X

Issue Y

Issue Z

The *Smith* Case

Issue X

Issue Y

Issue Z

The *Jackson* Case

Issue X

Issue Y

Issue Z

The Case-by-Case Approach might be appropriate when you use the Yes-No approach and the focus is on the *result* of the case. If, however, resolving the question depends upon an understanding of the factors present in the case and an application of those factors to your set of facts, then the Case-by-Case Approach tends to bog down. The Issue-by-Issue Approach definitely does the better job.

The Issue-by-Issue Approach

I tend to favor the Issue-by-Issue Approach over the Case-by-Case Approach. When you organize *issues* rather than *cases*, you are more in control of the subject matter. You govern the exact place where a particular issue is introduced to your reader. The approach forces you to grapple with the entire subject matter, identify and articulate the controlling issues (called *issue spotting* on your exams), and slant (in an ethical but adversarial way) those points favoring your client. These issues, of course, do come from cases, and you do use cases to reveal those issues. But in an Issue-by-Issue organizational scheme, you include in your case discussion just those issues you wish the case to reveal. Contrast this approach with the Case-by-Case Approach in which you would discuss all issues that each case concerns. Also, in the Issue-by-Issue Approach, you can *chop up* your discussion of a single case. If the *Jones* case deals effectively with two of your issues—X and Y—you can cite and discuss *Jones* twice, once under the discussion of X and once under the discussion of Y. Your outline, thus, might look like this:

Issue X

 the *Jones* case

Issue Y

 the *Smith* case

 the *Jones* case

Issue Z

 the *Jackson* case

 the *Smith* case

Think about the sample topic. What are the issues in resolving a question under section 1359? The two biggies are *motive* and *stake in the outcome*. Other issues include: *policy of diversity jurisdiction, other available candidates, estate to administer, other duties of the fiduciary,* and perhaps *family turmoil*.

A potential organizational scheme for our sample topic thus unfolds. It begins with the Historical Approach (*old view/new view*) and switches to an Issue-by-Issue Approach:

Old View

 the *Corabi* case

New View

 the *McSparran* case

Motive

 the *McSparran* case

 the *Bianca* case

Stake in the Outcome

 the *Bishop* case

 the *Hackney* case

Other Factors

 policy of diversity (the *McSparran* case)

 estate to administer (the *Joyce* case)

 other available candidates (the *Joyce* case)

 duties of the fiduciary (the *Bishop* case)

Another organizational scheme could combine the Historical Approach with the Yes-No Approach. Your outline might look like this:

Old View

the *Corabi* case

New View

the *McSparran* case (motive, policy of diversity, stake in the outcome)

Dismissal

the *McSparran* case (motive, policy, and stake)

the *Bishop* case (stake)

No Dismissal

the *Bianca* case (motive)

the *Hackney* case (stake, family member)

the *Joyce* case (family turmoil, other candidates, estate to administer)

You can readily see plenty of room for creativity in legal writing. No single organizational device is necessarily the best one. Many memos, however, fail to adopt any organizational scheme at all. Let's look at some other possibilities.

The Theory-by-Theory Approach

Many times, courts facing the same set of facts will use entirely different legal theories to dispose of the cases. If you detect the existence of different theories in your subject matter, you can discuss the cases using one theory and then move on to other cases using a different theory.

The Definitional Approach

The resolution of many legal questions depends on the meaning of a word or phrase. The definition might entail a three-part conjunctive test. The organization of the memo thus follows the line of reasoning a court would use to decide whether the facts of a given case fit within the definition of a legislative, regulatory, or judicial term of art.

Throughout the entire memo, of course, the writer should constantly relate discussions of law to the facts prompting the research in the first place. Because my outlines above do not include *Application of*

Law to Facts does not mean you should write a classic *A.L.R.* Annotation without any references whatsoever to a given set of facts. I'll deal with the importance of *Application* later in this chapter.

The above devices don't necessarily comprise the universe of possible organizational schemes. Others, no doubt, do exist. But these, I believe, can help the first-time writer begin to fill up that blank piece of paper or that blank computer screen laughing at you at the end of research. Jot down an outline using one or more of these approaches, and you're well on your way to writing your first Memorandum of Law.

Having decided on your organizational scheme, the time has come. Put pen to paper or fingers to keyboard. What do you produce? Simple. An Introduction, Paragraphs, Transitions, Legislative Presentations, Case Discussions, Other Legal Presentations, Proper Quotations, Legal Comparisons, Applications of Law to Fact, and the Final Result. Let's look at each in turn.

Introduction

Too much legal writing lacks any introduction whatsoever, thereby resembling the writing described by Horace 2,000 years ago (see the Latin quote beginning this chapter). The writer grabs the reader by the scruff of the neck, "whisks [him] into the middle of things," yanks him up to the first tree, presses his face firmly against the bark, and says:

> See that? That's a tree. Look at it. See what it's like? Now [writer grabs reader and smooshes him up against another tree] here's another tree.

> Get it? Here's another. And another. See the picture? We're in a forest, dear reader. And I'm not going to let you see it for the trees.

Readers don't like having their faces smooshed against trees. Neither do they like being "whisked into the middle of things."

There's a much better way. The first paragraph in the Discussion of Authority should introduce the entire discussion relating to that Question Presented. You should generally alert your readers to the issues they'll encounter in the discussion. Paint the big picture. Let your reader know what the forest looks like—broadly, in general. Then, when you introduce your readers to each tree, they'll have a sense of context, a sense of direction.

The introduction not only reveals the general content of the discussion. It also should reveal your organizational scheme. You don't necessarily do this by expressly stating what your organization is. Law review *Notes* do precisely that. In a section entitled *Introduction*, the Note will say something like this: "This Note will first explore the historical origins of the doctrine of privity, examining the origins of the doctrine in early English legal development. It will then show the early applications of the doctrine in Colonial America. To trace the doctrine to its current stage of development, the Note will . . . ."

In a Memorandum of Law, generally much shorter than a law review Note, it's probably best to show the organizational scheme by *implication*. In other words, the order in which you mention the key elements of the discussion is the same order as your organizational scheme. By having some idea of the big picture and of the order in which the information will appear, your readers will more readily ingest each major point as it comes.

Although we'll deal with *Legislative Presentations* later in this chapter, I should point out here that it is usually best to cite and quote any governing statute right up front, especially if the statute is short and relatively uncomplicated. If the statute is long and complex, it's probably better to introduce the statute and the applicable case law before proceeding to quote the statute and to discuss the cases.

To give you some idea of an introduction, the following might introduce the memo on the sample topic:

Discussion of Authority:

1. Where a nonresident administratrix is appointed to bring a wrongful death case in federal court against a resident defendant, is related to the deceased, but has no stake in the outcome of the case, does the federal court lack subject matter jurisdiction under title 28, section 1359 of the United States Code?

Several legal situations allow the beneficial parties of a lawsuit to pick the plaintiff to prosecute the action. Guardians must be appointed to represent the interests of minors in court. When an accident causes the death of a person, an administrator must be appointed to prosecute any wrongful death claim. Often, the parties standing to gain from such actions will appoint a nonresident plaintiff to pursue an otherwise local action against a resident defendant. The nonresident plaintiff then uses his diverse citizenship to pursue the action in federal court, invoking the court's diversity of citizenship jurisdiction.

Such appointments have traditionally been attacked as *collusive*, made only to confer jurisdiction on a federal district court. The defendant can seek to have the case dismissed as a violation of title 28, section 1359 of the United States Code:

> A district court shall not have jurisdiction of a civil action in which any party, by assignment or otherwise, has been improperly or collusively made or joined to invoke the jurisdiction of such court.

Before 1968, the federal courts routinely held that the motive to get into federal court was irrelevant in finding a violation of the statute. *Collusion*, under the old view, had to rise to the level of fraud. However, in 1968, the courts overruled the old view and held that motive was a relevant factor in determining the validity of the appointment of a nonresident fiduciary. Since that time, the courts have adjudicated a host of cases involving appointments of nonresident administrators. Though appointing a nonresident by itself does not violate the statute, the courts look disfavorably on such appointments and insist on *legitimate considerations* supporting the appointment. Chief among these considerations are the stake the administrator has in the outcome of the case, other duties the administrator must undertake, the availability of other candidates who could have been appointed, and particularly stressful family situations. Most circuits seem to emphasize *motive* as the key factor in a section 1359 analysis, whereas at least one circuit—the Fourth—has moved away from motive and has emphasized *stake in the outcome* as the decisive factor.

Now the reader knows what the problem is, what the statute is, and generally how the courts have responded. The reader knows what the forest looks like. It's time to smoosh his face up against a tree. It's time to discuss the law. It's time to remember some pretty basic rules on expository writing. It's time to rediscover the paragraph.

Paragraphing and Topic Sentences

I used to worry about teaching paragraphing to professionals. Too basic, I thought. Too elementary. I was wrong. If you'll read some particularly tortuous legal writing, the chances are overwhelming you'll find egregious errors in basic paragraphing.

So let's back up and recall the definition of a paragraph: *a bunch of sentences all dealing with one central idea.* Here's another crucial definition, that of a topic sentence: *a topic sentence generally states the central idea of a paragraph.* A paragraph deals with one idea, not six. That idea should be generally revealed in a topic sentence—*generally* revealed, not specifically discussed.

Typical paragraphing mistakes break these two definitions. A paragraph might wander on forever, dealing with a host of ideas. A topic sentence—especially in legal writing—often goes ahead and gets hopelessly specific, losing any claim it might have had to the status of topic sentence.

Perhaps some examples of good paragraphs will show the rules best. Consider the following paragraph from the Supreme Court decision of *In re Gault*, 387 U.S. 1, 14 (1967):

> From the beginning of the juvenile court system, wide differences have been tolerated — indeed insisted upon — between the procedural rights accorded to adults and those of juveniles. In practically all states, there are rights granted to adults which are withheld from juveniles. In addition to the specific problems involved in the present case, for example, it has been held that the juvenile is not entitled to bail, to indictment by grand jury, to a public trial or to trial by jury. It is frequent practice that rules governing the arrest and interrogation of adults by the police are not observed in the case of juveniles.

Notice that the broad topic of the paragraph resides in the two words *wide differences*. But do those two words tell the whole story about the procedural rights of adults and juveniles? Who ends up on the short end of the stick? Without the second sentence, the reader doesn't know. Thus, the second sentence narrows the topic with the word *withheld*. Notice what the writer didn't do until the third sentence. Before the third sentence, the reader doesn't know precisely what rights an adult has that a juvenile doesn't. The writer kept the topic sentences general to state the point and then provided the specifics in the balance of the paragraph.

Must the topic sentence always be the first or the first two? Check out a paragraph by Mr. Justice Blackmun in *Nevada v. Hall*, 440 U.S. 410, 429-30 (1979):

> The Court's expansive logic and broad holding—that so far as the Constitution is concerned, State A can be sued in State B on the same terms as any other litigant can be sued—will place severe strains on our system of cooperative federalism. States in all likelihood will retaliate against one another for respectively abolishing the "sovereign immunity" doctrine. States' legal officers will be required to defend suits in all other States. States probably will decide to modify their tax collection and revenue systems in order to avoid the collection of judgments. In this very case, for example, Nevada evidently maintains cash balances in California banks to facilitate the collection of sales taxes from California corporations doing business in Nevada. Under the Court's decision, Nevada will have strong incentive to withdraw those balances and place them in Nevada banks so as to insulate itself from California judgments. If respondents were forced to seek satisfaction of their judgment in Nevada, that State, of course, might endeavor to refuse to enforce that judgment, or enforce it only on Nevada's terms. The court's decision, thus, may force radical changes in the way States do business with one another, and it imposes, as well, financial and administrative burdens on the States themselves.

The topic sentence idea is found in the first sentence, in the two words *severe strains*. Then, after developing the idea with specifics, the writer returns to the same idea, but with much harsher language: "The court's decision, thus, may force radical changes in the way States do business with one another, and it imposes, as well, financial and administrative burdens on the States themselves." The writer brought us all the way from a *severe strain* (a stretching) to a *radical change* (a break).

The paragraph above shows a terrific technique of paragraphing strategy. When you have a point to make, state it as a topic sentence, but don't ask your reader to agree with very much. Use relatively mild language. Then, after developing the idea, state it again—as a knockout blow—in more strident language. The good legal writers do it. To become one, so should you.

If you encounter some writing that seems difficult to read, subject it to the paragraphing test. Look at each paragraph to see if it deals with only one idea. Look for topic sentences. Do they even exist? Are they broad and general, or do they tend to get highly specific? By keeping it simple, by stating your points one by one in well-structured paragraphs, you can grab your reader's attention and not let go.

Legislative or Regulatory Presentations

There are two ways to present statutes or regulations. First, you can quote the provision verbatim or *in pertinent part*. Second, you can paraphrase the provision. Both require special care.

When you quote a statute or regulation, you should introduce that quotation with its main point. Though it might seem redundant to do so, the redundancy is necessary to the reader. The reader needs a context and needs to know where the statute fits into the overall analysis. If you just haul off and throw your statutory quote at your paper like a dart and put the quote in abruptly wherever it lands, your reader will be disoriented. So introduce your statutory quote with the main point of the statute. It might be as simple as this:

> The defendant can seek to have the case dismissed as a violation of title 28, section 1359 of the United States Code:
>
> > A district court shall not have jurisdiction of a civil action in which any party, by assignment or otherwise, has been improperly or collusively made or joined to invoke the jurisdiction of such court.

Paraphrasing a statute can be particularly difficult, primarily because legislative writing is so downright awful. Any editor will tell you that transforming terrible writing into a work of art is next to impossible. Legislative writing is often so complex and incomprehensible that legal writers throw up their hands and *paraphrase* the statute in a loose quote.

When legal writers paraphrase legislative or regulatory material, they often will use a popular, but rather ineffective, method of expression. They will say that *section 101 provides that* . . . . Then the major legislative message will appear in the dependent clause. Here are some samples:

> Section 2056(a) of the Internal Revenue Code provides that a marital deduction is allowed for the value of any interest in proper-

ty that is included in the decedent's gross estate and that passes from the decedent to the surviving spouse.

Section 20.2056(b)-1(b) of the Estate Tax Regulations provides that a "terminable interest" in property is an interest that will terminate or fail on the lapse of time or on the occurrence or the failure to occur of some contingency. Section 20.2056(b)-1(c) of the regulations provides that a property interest that is a terminable interest, as defined above, is nondeductible if another interest in the same property passed from the decedent to some other person for less than an adequate and full consideration in money or money's worth, and because it passed, the other person may possess or enjoy any part of the property after the termination or failure of the spouse's interest.

Section 2032(a) provides that the executor may elect to determine the value of the property included in the gross estate as of six months after the decedent's death. However, property distributed, sold, exchanged, or otherwise disposed of within six months after death must be valued as of the date of distribution, sale, exchange, or other disposition.

This tradition of discussing legislative or regulatory provisions has two negative effects. First, as a matter of content, the device encourages writers to include legislative or regulatory material that does not really relate to the subject matter of the paper. The readers are forced to wade their way through extraneous legislative or regulatory materials while trying to find and comprehend the *pertinent parts*. Second, as a matter of style, the device muddies up legal writing. Under the rules of good style, the main message of a sentence should appear at the subject-verb position of the sentence. The *section 101 provides that* approach to writing shoves each message to a subordinate clause, which, by definition, is usually reserved for subordinate information. When discussing legislative or regulatory material, the writer is trying to show the law as found in the Code or Regulations. The provision is the main message, not the statutory cite. Thus, the writer should subordinate the statutory cite and put the summary of the provision in the sentence's independent clause.

Two devices will cure the problem. First, the writer can put the legislative or regulatory cite in a prepositional phrase like *Under section 101* or *According to section 101*. Second, the writer might keep *section*

101 as the subject of the sentence but search for a more precise verb such as *allows, prohibits, restricts, decreases, increases, eliminates* and so on.

Finally, as a general rule, it's best to quote or paraphrase the statute and then precisely state the issue that arises under the statute. Don't for a minute think that it's obvious to the reader what the issue is. It isn't obvious. You're the one who has read and ingested the statute and thought at length about its applicability to your set of facts. Your reader, on the other hand, has only a few minutes in the field and is relying on you to show the way.

Case Discussions

Most legal memos will consist primarily of discussions of case law. The reason is simple: *stare decisis*. All legal questions ultimately bump up against the stark reality of going to court. A court will decide your case just as courts have decided the hundreds of cases you've sought, overlooked, found, read, digested, groaned over, weeded out, and pared down to a number manageable for inclusion in your memo. Not surprisingly, because of its prevalence, case law presents the biggest problem for first-time legal writers.

If you'll think about a case discussion in terms of good paragraphing, writing an effective discussion will become easier. First and foremost, you should begin each case discussion with a general topic sentence that states the point you—the writer—are trying to make. You've included the case at a particular point in your overall discussion for a particular reason. What is that reason? What point are you trying to make? Don't think the reader automatically knows how a case fits into your discussion. Make it evident by stating an effective, to-the-point topic sentence.

One trick you might use is this: avoid starting any paragraph with the classic prepositional *In* phrase with the case citation serving as the object of the preposition. In many legal memos, a series of paragraphs might start like this:

In *McSparran v. Weist*, 402 F.2d 867 (3d Cir. 1968), *cert. denied*, 395 U.S. 903 (1969), the mother of a minor procured the appointment of a nonresident guardian. Shortly after the appointment, the guardian brought a diversity of citizenship action against a resident defendant to recover damages sustained by the minor in an instate automobile accident. At trial, the lower court . . . .

In *Bishop v. Hendricks*, 495 F.2d 290 (4th Cir), *cert. denied*, 419 U.S. 1056 (1974), decedent was killed in an automobile accident. The beneficiaries of the estate procured the appointment of an out-of-state administrator to bring a wrongful death case in federal court. The record at trial showed that the administrator was related to the beneficiaries by marriage and that the decedent had no estate to administer, other than the potential recovery in the wrongful death action. The defendant moved to dismiss the case as a violation of section 1359. The trial court . . . .

Undoubtedly, we learned this device of case discussion in our early days in the study of law when our professors taught us to *brief* cases by revealing facts-issues-holding-reasoning. The case brief is fine as a note-taking device, but not so fine as a method of presenting law in formal legal writing.

This technique of case discussion has several serious drawbacks. First, the device encourages writers to stick cases in *any ole place*. Such writing resembles a series of disjointed presentations that bear little if any relationship to each other or to any discernible whole. Second, the device forces the readers to engage in two simultaneous mental functions. The readers not only must take in the facts-issues-holding-reasoning but make the necessary analytical connections to figure out the case's relationship to the entire legal discussion. Third, the device allows mental flabbiness on the part of the writer and forces the reader to exert considerable mental effort. The roles should reverse. The writer is charged with informing the reader, not vice versa.

If you're trying to show that one case did something a bit differently than another case, then say so in an introductory topic sentence:

The Fifth Circuit rejected *Bishop's* *stake in the outcome* approach and returned to the *motive* approach of *McSparran*. The court in *Bianca v. Parke-Davis Pharmaceutical Division of Warner-Lambert Co.*, 723 F.2d 392 (5th Cir. 1984), relied on the "improperly or collusively" language of the statute in holding that the district court must inquire into the issue of motive before dismissing a case under section 1359. *Bianca* involved the death of an 11-year-old girl from complications from a medication . . . .

Or if you're showing that a particular case is unique, say so in an introductory paragraph. Then, if you must, use the *In [case name]* approach:

> The new rule of *McSparran* does not preclude the appointment of any nonresident administrator or guardian to bring otherwise local cases in federal court. *McSparran* itself left the door open for such appointments by declaring that section 1359 "does not ban the appointment of nonresident fiduciaries . . . ." McSparren v. Weist, 402 F.2d at 874-75. The Third Circuit, just two years after the *McSparran* decision, confronted a case where the appointment of a nonresident did not offend the collusive joinder provisions of section 1359. In *Joyce v. Siegel*, 429 F.2d 128 (3d Cir. 1970), decedent, a resident of Pennsylvania, was killed in an automobile accident . .

Several questions inevitably arise concerning the proper discussion of case law. Let me anticipate some questions you might have.

Question: Do I cite all the cases I found in research?

Answer: The research of many legal questions often uncovers hundreds of cases. Though you might indeed cite them all in a law review note or other scholarly paper, you should not cite them all in a legal memo, trial brief, or appellate brief. Indeed, your role as researcher is to sift through the mass of information and just present those controlling cases necessary for a thorough legal analysis.

Question: Which cases do I include?

Answer: Certain cases obviously stand out and must be included. It's the others that'll bug you to death. To determine whether a particular case merits your time, attention, and space, you might consider these factors: (1) recentness, (2) on-pointness, (3) quotability, (4) reputation of judge or court, (5) quality of opinion, and (6) frequency of citation by other cases.

Question: How extensively do I discuss the facts-issues-holding-reasoning of a case?

Answer: The extent of case discussion varies with your use of the case in your overall analysis. At one end of the spectrum, you'll just state a proposition of law and follow it with a case citation and no discussion at all. At the other end, you'll discuss a case completely.

For example, in the sample memo you would discuss *McSparran* completely. Once the setting of a typical manufactured diversity of citizenship case is established, however, you can shorten later discussions substantially.

When presenting the facts of a case, be sure to strip the facts down to essentials, to omit irrelevant dates, and to identify parties primarily by their legal status rather than by their given names. Also, watch out for and avoid the temptation to write in legalese, using lots of *saids* as adjectives and dropping articles right and left.

Question: What tense do I use when discussing a case?

Answer: Legal writing should not resemble literary criticism, where you learned to say that "Fitzgerald then uses color when he develops the mood of life on East Egg." When discussing a case, use the past tense. Thus: "The court held . . . ." If, however, you are referring to the present impact of an opinion, the present tense would be correct. Thus: "*McSparran* requires the lower court to inquire into motive." Finally, when revealing an ongoing rule of law, you should use the present tense. Thus: "*McSparran* held that a district court lacks jurisdiction if section 1359 is violated."

Other Legal Presentations

Good legal writing definitely should include the views of scholars. A legal memo devoid of citations to and quotations of law reviews and treatises isn't much of a memo. Why not? Because judges are definitely influenced by the views of expert commentators. And if that's not reason enough for litigators, students should recognize the importance of citing and analyzing secondary authority to impress their professors.

You can use secondary authority in a variety of ways. First, it can help bolster an argument otherwise lacking direct judicial support. Second, you can and should quote the views of commentators in your analysis of the law. Third, often a law review article will provide an ideal organizational structure for your own discussion. Fourth, you can cite a law review article to support a factual statement about the law, e.g., "twenty-six states have adopted the no-privity rule."

In your writing, you should present other legal authority in the same way you discuss cases and statutes. Make your point first. Introduce the material. When you quote, precede each quote with the point it seeks to make. And finally, be sure to relate the material from the secondary authority to your particular set of facts.

Proper Quotations

I've already dealt somewhat with techniques of quoting legal authority. Above I pointed out that you—the writer—should state the point of the quotation first, even though you'll feel you're being redundant to do so. Remember, the material you're presenting is old to you. You've lived with it night and day for weeks. Your reader, on the other hand, is a fledgling. Your reader does not automatically *get it*. Thus, state the point of the quotation and then the quotation itself. Here are some examples of *quotation introduction* taken from discussions of our sample cases.

A Quotation from *McSparran*:

Though *Corabi* had held that motive was irrelevant in applying section 1359, the *McSparran* court considered such an approach too limiting in scope. According to the court:

> [I]t is difficult to see how motive can be entirely ignored in ascertaining the purpose for which the representative is selected in view of the language of section 1359. The statute outlaws the creation of jurisdiction where a party has been improperly or collusively made or joined to invoke the jurisdiction of the court. While the statute does not ban the appointment of nonresident fiduciaries, the artificial selection of a straw representative who has no duty or function except to offer the use of his citizenship is a violation of its provisions.

Id. at 874-75.

A Quotation from *Hackney*:

The court pointed out the inevitable delay occasioned by defendants challenging the appointments and the motivations of nonresident family members. In the words of the court, "We think the better view is to make immune from challenge, for diversity purposes, an appointment of a fiduciary who has a substantial beneficial interest in the litigation being conducted." *Id.* at 1071.

A Quotation from *Bianca*:

Motive is not just *a* factor in a section 1359 analysis. It is *the* factor, according to the Fifth Circuit.

> If an out-of-state administrator has not been selected with the purpose of manufacturing diversity, the administrator's lack of a stake in the outcome of the litigation cannot alone trigger section 1359's jurisdictional bar.

Id. at 398.

If you're a first-time legal writer, you'll be tempted to make some drastic mistakes in quoting legal material in your memorandum. Here is a list of proscriptions:

1. Do not quote headnotes.

2. Do not quote the prefatory statement of a case (the long-winded and terribly written paragraph preceding the court's opinion).

3. Do not quote a court's presentation of the facts.

4. And do not quote *too much.*

How much is *too much*? That's a judgment call. Two or three typewritten inches is about right. The problem of too-lengthy quotation has been around the legal profession for a long time. Heed the words of this turn-of-the-century opinion:

> Extended quotations from authorities have no place in the [brief], which, after stating the facts fairly, should set forth the positions insisted upon by counsel, the heads of the argument and the authorities relied upon to support it. *When every lawyer wrote his points with a pen* there was no occasion for complaint in this regard, but since the use of stenographers has become general the evil has grown until it is so serious that repression is necessary.

Stevens v. O'Neill, 169 N.Y. 375, 377, 62 N.E. 424, 425 (1902) (emphasis added). One can only wonder what the *Stevens* court would do with today's high-speed laser printers, optical character readers, and Xerox machines.

I think it appropriate at this point to pause and consider a few rules of style governing quotation in legal writing. I use as my source *A Uniform System of Citation* (14th ed. 1986), the notorious *Harvard Bluebook*. The *Bluebook* is the single best, but most difficult to understand, system of legal citation in the country. Few legal writers ever master its demanding rules of citation and style. They especially ignore rules of proper quotation. I'll hit the highlights and encourage the reader to spend some valuable time with the *Harvard Bluebook*. The reader is also encouraged to study C. Good, *Citing & Typing the Law, A Guide to Legal Citation and Style* (Blue Jeans Press, 1986), which contains a complete explanation of the system of citation and style found in the *Harvard Bluebook*.

The *Bluebook* requires you to indent and single space any quotation of 50 words or more. If you're writing your first Memorandum of Law and you've been instructed to "follow the *Bluebook*," then you'd better count words. If you're in the real world, you might consider some matters other than *word count* when deciding to indent or not to indent. For example, the Solicitor General of the United States points out in his style manual that the indented quote is a two-edged sword. On the one hand, an indented quote stands out on the page and is thereby emphasized. On the other hand, the reader can easily see where an indented quote begins and ends and might be tempted to rush through the quote. Thus, urges the Solicitor General, if you want to make sure the reader actually reads your quote, don't indent.

If you do indent, then here is the correct format. Indent 10 spaces from the left-hand margin. Indent a further five spaces to show paragraphing in indented quotes. Thus, if your first-quoted word begins a paragraph in the original, you should show paragraph structure. But if your first-quoted word does not begin a paragraph in the original, do not further indent the first-quoted word. Here's the indented quote from *McSparran* shown above.

Though *Corabi* had held that motive was irrelevant in applying section 1359, the *McSparran* court considered such an approach too limiting in scope. According to the court:

> [I]t is difficult to see how motive can be entirely ignored in ascertaining the purpose for which the representative is selected in view of the language of section 1359. The statute outlaws the creation of jurisdiction where a party has been improperly or collusively made or joined to invoke the jurisdiction of the court. While the statute does not ban the appointment of nonresident fiduciaries, the artificial selection of a straw representative who has no duty or function except to offer the use of his citizenship is a violation of its provisions.

Id. at 874-75.

Notice that the citation supporting the quote does not come within the indentation. Rather, it is the first nonindented material two lines down from the indented quote. If the writer then continues within the same paragraph, the writing would continue on the same line as the citation. If the writer begins a new paragraph, then the next passage appears two lines down from the citation.

One final, but important point on proper quotation merits your close attention. Often you must vary the quote to make it fit your grammar or your style. For example, you might want to emphasize words, add words, or omit words. When you emphasize words, be sure to fess up and include *(emphasis added)* after the citation. When you add words, be sure to enclose them in brackets. Finally, when you omit words, you should use the ellipsis signal, which is formed by "three periods separated by spaces and set off by a space before the first and after the last period." *A Uniform System of Citation* 27 (14th ed. 1986). The first two of these quote-alteration devices cause little trouble. The third, however—the ellipsis signal—causes serious confusion in formal legal writing.

To understand the rules governing the ellipsis signal, you must first recall some basic rules of grammar and style. Whenever you quote and that quotation is a complete sentence and is not an integral part of the grammar of your own sentence, the quotation must begin with a capital letter. On the other hand, when you quote and the quotation *is* an integral part of the grammar of your own sentence, the quotation should *not* begin with a capital letter. Thus, this quotation should begin with a capital letter: The court said, "The law is wonderful." This quotation, however, should begin with a lowercase letter: The court pointed out that in Virginia jurisprudence "the law is wonderful." In the first quotation, the quoted matter is a complete sentence. In the second, the quoted words are needed to complete the writer's sentence.

With these rules in mind, the rules governing the ellipsis signal become easier to understand. According to the *Harvard Bluebook*, the ellipsis signal should *never* begin a quotation. *Id.* The reason? Most quotations will not need the ellipsis signal to show an omission of words leading up to the first-quoted word. Why? Because of the above *uppercase/lowercase* rule. Watch it work.

Suppose the original court's opinion reads as follows: "According to our research, the law is wonderful." Suppose the writer wishes to quote the court as follows: The court said, "the law is wonderful." If the writer does it that way, he has broken the *uppercase/lowercase* rule. To follow the rule, the writer must begin the word *The* with an uppercase letter, yet the word was in the lower case in the original. To follow the rule and also to show the omission of words leading up to the first-quoted word, the writer puts it this way: The court said, "[T]he law is wonderful." The bracketed uppercase *T* shows that the *T* was a lower-case *t* in the original, which, in turn, shows that words in the original leading up to the first-quoted word were omitted. The writer has followed correct rules of grammar and has shown the omission. Notice that the ellipsis signal is simply not needed. Also, if the writer picks up the quotation in the middle of a sentence and the first-quoted word should begin with a lowercase letter anyway, then the omission is shown as well. Again the ellipsis signal is not necessary.

There is only one situation where the ellipsis signal would be needed to begin a quotation. If the first-quoted word is a proper noun but words leading up to it have been omitted, then an ellipsis is needed to show the omission. Suppose, in our example above, the original had read this way: "According to our research, Virginia law is wonderful." If the writer says it this way, omission is not shown: The court said, "Virginia law is wonderful." In that situation, the *Bluebook* still says *"never"* begin a quotation with the ellipsis signal. I think the *Bluebook* is incorrect. In law, any omission *must* be shown. Not to do so opens the door for potential abuse that we should not tolerate in legal writing.

Thus, the better rule is to begin a quotation with an ellipsis signal only in that rare situation where the first-quoted word is a proper noun but words leading up to that first-quoted word have been omitted from the original.

If you only rarely begin a quotation with the ellipsis signal, when *do* you use the device? When words are omitted within a quotation, use the ellipsis signal. Or if words ending the last-quoted sentence are omitted, then end your quotation with the ellipsis signal. When ending a sentence with the ellipsis signal, be sure to include a fourth dot to serve as the period ending the sentence.

For a more elaborate discussion of this problem and the rules of omitting paragraphs, please see *Citing & Typing the Law, A Guide to Legal Citation and Style*.

Transitions

You can write the world's best paragraphs and still not produce a work of art. Paragraphs and sentences within paragraphs must *stick together*. They must *flow together*. If they don't flow, the reader gets the sensation that you wrote a bunch of paragraphs on note cards, shuffled, cut the deck, played 52-pickup, and produced your paper. To avoid this *shuffle approach*, you must learn the art of transition.

Transition involves what I am now doing in the sentence you are now reading. I ended the preceding paragraph with the word *transition* and began this paragraph with the same word. That's one technique of transition. There are others and we should deal with all forms of sticking paragraphs and sentences together in an integrated whole. But before getting to the precise methods, let's pause and consider the need for transition.

Earlier in this chapter, I wrote about the importance of the introduction. I pointed out that you've done the research and presumably know what the law is. Your readers haven't done the research. Indeed, that's why they told you to do it. The senior partners, law professors, judges, or other powerful people in your life didn't have the time or inclination to do the drudge work. So you did the work. You now know the law. They don't. It's your job to tell them what that law is. To do it, you must engage in the function of teaching.

To teach something to someone, you should tell them where you're going, go there, and tell them where you've been. Constantly. Always look ahead. And always look back. Doing so will keep your readers glued to your work.

That's why the introduction is so important to good writing. That's why topic sentences are so important to good paragraphing. And that's why transition is so important to hang it all together. The art of transition consists, in the main, of looking ahead and of looking back. The good writers pull it off primarily by using five transitional devices: (1) connective expressions, (2) the demonstrative pronoun device, (3) the word pickup device, (4) look-back summaries, and (5) look-ahead discussions.

Connective expressions are primarily bits of *sentence glue* to keep your prose rolling along within paragraphs. Such expressions might show order in time: *first, next, the second, finally.* They might show order in arrangement: *next, second, a further reason.* They might add specifics: *especially, in particular, at least, for example.* They might show additions: *moreover, in addition, furthermore, besides, also, indeed.* They might indicate exceptions or the contrary: *but, however, nevertheless, yet, on the contrary.* Finally, they might show cause or effect: *therefore, thus, accordingly, as a result, consequently.*

A terrific type of *paragraph glue* to keep your thoughts flowing from one major idea to the next is the *demonstrative pronoun* trick. If the preceding paragraph was dealing with legislative history, your next paragraph might begin: "Against *this background* of legislative history . . . ." If your preceding paragraphs were discussing a particular line of cases, your next paragraph might begin: "*These cases* should prompt the court to grant the defendant's motion in the present case." If your preceding paragraphs summarized certain provisions of the Internal Revenue Code, your next paragraph might begin: "Applying *these provisions* to the taxpayer's case . . . ." The trick is simple. Use the demonstrative pronouns in the English language—*this, these, those, that*—to point back to the subject matter you were just talking about. (As a general rule of style, try to avoid using a demonstrative pronoun as a noun substitute. Don't say: "Applying this to our case . . . ." Instead, repeat the *this what* you were talking about.)

The demonstrative pronoun trick is not the only form of paragraph glue. I just used another. The word pickup device. If your preceding paragraph mentioned *the demonstrative pronoun trick,* then your next paragraph can *pick up* those precise words to begin the next paragraph.

Courts use this approach (how about that one?) all the time. Here are two paragraphs from a court's opinion. Notice how the court *picks up* the words *presumption of validity* in the second paragraph as a form of *paragraph glue.* Notice also that the court is not afraid to repeat the word *presumption* yet again to keep the flow going in the second paragraph.

> State laws are generally entitled to a presumption of validity against attack under the Constitution. Legislatures have wide discretion in passing laws that have the inevitable effect of treating some people differently from others, and legislative classifications are valid unless they bear no rational relationship to a permissible state objective.

> Not all legislation, however, is entitled to the same presumption of validity. The presumption is not present when a state has enacted legislation whose purpose or effect is to create classes based upon racial criteria, since racial classifications, in a constitutional sense, are inherently suspect . . . .

When material is complex or lengthy, instead of charging ahead with additional material, pause and summarize what you have just discussed. Look back and review what you've just discussed so the reader does not become lost and confused. Lookback writing might look like this:

> From these cases it appears . . . .
>
> So interpreted, section 501(c)(3) permits . . . .
>
> When read together, the three provisions discussed above show a congressional intent to . . . .

Finally, keep in mind that transition is bi-directional. Transitional writing not only looks back but looks ahead as well. Thus, after discussing several cases, you might include a paragraph that wraps up those cases *and* anticipates the cases you're about to discuss. For example, in the sample memorandum, look-ahead writing might appear like this:

> As another factor, many cases have considered the impact of appointing a relative of the beneficiaries. Though family relationship can play some role in determining the validity of the appointment under section 1359, the factor alone is not dispositive. [Then proceed with a discussion of those cases considering the importance of family relationship.]

Application of Law to Facts

Too many legal writers produce what I call the law-law-law-therefore approach to legal analysis and legal writing. They string together a series of legal discussions, fully expecting the readers instantaneously to get it. They want the readers to make all the necessary analytical steps to distill the key elements from the legal discussions, apply them to the facts of the current case, and reach some sort of ineluctable conclusion.

But the readers don't *get it*. The readers have to go back, reread, scratch their heads, ponder the points, examine the current facts, line up the law, look at the law in light of the current facts, and then . . . *get it.* Readers don't like that. The writer should do the job for them.

At some point or points in your legal discussions, you should produce what I call *Application of Law to Facts.* You should compare the facts of the decided cases with the facts of your case, comment on the similarities, and point out the distinctions. You should try to come up with some result and share with your reader the mental reasoning required to reach that result.

Application of Law to Facts can occur in a variety of spots in your Discussion of Authority. If a case you've discussed is particularly complex or particularly important, you might go ahead and apply that case to your facts immediately after discussing the case. When you get really good at it, you can apply a case while simultaneously discussing it, pointing out similarities or distinctions between the cited case and the case under discussion. On the other hand, you might discuss a series of cases, compare them one with another, distill out the key elements, and apply those elements to your set of facts.

Here's a sample Application of Law to Facts, which might follow a discussion of *Bishop v. Hendricks*:

> Thus, the Fourth Circuit, whose law will govern the current case, stresses *stake in the outcome* in determining a violation of section 1359. Though the *Bishop* administrator was related to the beneficiaries of the wrongful death claim, he stood to gain nothing from any recovery. Similarly, the administratrix in the current case is the decedent's aunt, but any recovery in the wrongful death claim will go directly to the mother. *Bishop* also pointed out that the administrator in that case had nothing substantial to do because the decedent left no estate to administer. Although the decedent in the current case did leave a modest estate, those funds have already been distributed to the statutory beneficiary—the mother. The nonresident administratrix, like the administrator in *Bishop*, has nothing whatsoever to do.

Legal Comparisons

After all cases have been discussed, or while they are being discussed, it's usually profitable to compare cases with each other. By doing so, you can often identify those factors that sway the courts one way or the other, check your facts for the presence or absence of those factors, and argue whatever you need in order to win.

For example, in the model topic, many of the courts mentioned *family relationship* as a factor to be considered in applying section 1359. To highlight this factor, we can *compare* the various cases like this:

> Many cases have considered the impact of appointing a relative of the beneficiaries. Though family relationship can play some role in determining the validity of the appointment under section 1359, the factor alone is not dispositive. In *Bishop*, for example, the administrator was related to the decedent by marriage. According to the court, however, "mere kinship" was not enough. *Bishop v. Hendricks*, 495 F.2d at 293. "[T]he fact that the beneficiaries . . . are related to the out-of-state administrator . . . will not justify diversity based on the administrator's citizenship." *Id.* at 295. In wrongful death actions, of course, those who stand to gain from any tort recovery typically are family members. At least one court has stated that such a family member appointed to serve as administrator will be "immune from challenge" under section 1359. *Hackney v. Newman Memorial Hospital, Inc.*, 621 F.2d at 1071. *Hackney*, however, can be explained as merely supporting the *stake in the outcome* standard of *Bishop*, rather than establishing family membership as the significant factor in a section 1359 analysis. If family membership alone would justify an out-of-state appointment, then section 1359 could be easily thwarted, for it is the rare American family that lacks some out-of-state relative.

Reaching and Stating the Final Result

As I mentioned earlier in this chapter, many legal writers will string together a series of case discussions and continue for page after page without even mentioning the current case—the facts prompting the research in the first place. Then, maybe, at the end of the memo, the writer will say, "Therefore, the federal court should dismiss the case at bar as a violation of title 28, section 1359." The reader, of course, wants to scream. The writer thinks it's self-evident how the entire discussion applies to the current case. But it isn't self-evident. The reader is still a novice. The reader only has the amount of time it took to read your memo. You, the writer, have amassed untold hours of research and thought. It's your job not only to reach a result but to demonstrate that result to your reader.

If you've discussed cases properly, applied cases to your facts, and compared cases with one another, then you've set a good foundation for reaching and stating the final result. It can often be as short as a paragraph or two. Your task is to tie everything together, to draw out of the law the key elements, and to reach some conclusion on the applicability of those elements to your facts. In the model topic, the *final result* might appear like this:

When the district court considers all these factors and analyzes the situation in the current case, it should be persuaded to dismiss this action as a violation of section 1359. Certainly if the *stake* test of *Bishop* continues in the Fourth Circuit, the case should be dismissed. The assets of the decedent have already been distributed to the sole statutory beneficiary—the mother. Nothing remains for the administratrix to do. She has no stake in this proceeding. She has nothing to gain from its successful completion. She can only lend her name to the proceedings and her citizenship to the complaint to support an allegation of diversity. Even if the *motive* test of *Bianca* should prevail or make inroads on the *stake* test, the court still should dismiss the suit. Though additional investigation might fail to uncover evidence of the *impure motive* of manufacturing diversity jurisdiction, the factors mentioned in *Bianca*, which can show improper motive, seem to weigh heavily in the defendant's favor. Next, though the current administratrix is the sister of the statutory beneficiary, *Bishop* made it abundantly clear that a familial relationship is not enough. And unlike *Hackney*, the family member here is not a statutory beneficiary who stands to collect part of the proceeds of any wrongful death recovery. Finally, the turmoil of the mother's drinking problem and understandable grief does not come close to approaching the level of turmoil experienced by the family in *Joyce*. Even if it did, the administrator in *Joyce* had substantial duties to perform in administering a $50,000 estate. Here, the estate has been administered. All that remains is picking a plaintiff to bring a wrongful death case. That duty alone is clearly not the kind contemplated by the courts. Indeed, that duty alone should show the *impropriety* of the current appointment. For these reasons, the case should be dismissed.

Conclusion

I hope this chapter will help that first-time legal writer, befuddled with the mysteries of legal research and overwhelmed at the prospect of putting it all down on paper. I also hope it will help practicing attorneys, judges, and other members of the profession. As a law student, I can remember reading and rereading case law, law review articles, statutes, and reams of other stuff. I can remember scratching my head and wrinkling my brow. I can remember sneaking a peek at other students, wondering if they were similarly confused. I can remember that feeling of dread when it dawned on me that I had accidentally been admitted to law school. "All these other students must be getting it," I thought. "How did I get in?"

If only I knew then what I know now. I would have felt much better had I known that what I was reading was, quite simply, some of the worst prose ever put to paper.

As the profession charged with preserving liberty and justice, we've really made a mess of things. We—the lawyers, judges, legislators, regulators, professors, and students of law—are charged with putting down on paper what people are supposed to do and what they are not supposed to do. We—the legal profession—are bound to think and reason and analyze and conclude what is *right*. What is *constitutional*. What is *legal*. What *will work*. Indeed, what is *moral*. We—the legal profession—are supposed to fashion rules of conduct and put them down on judicial, legislative, or regulatory paper.

But just look at the paper we produce. Read some of it. Pick a page or two from the *Federal Register*, the *United States Code*, a West Company reporter, a treatise, or your own filing cabinet. Read some of it. Aloud. With a straight face. Read some of it to the people whose life it governs. Will they continue to cooperate? Will they continue to pay the bill? Do they cheer? Are they stirred?

No, they're not.

We—the legal profession—have a job to do. I hope, in some small way, this book will help.

Chapter 12

A Big, Heavy Casebook

O imitatores, servum pecus.

O imitators, you slavish herd.

Atque inter silvas Academi quaerere verum.

And seek for truth in the groves of Academe.

—Horace

Chapter 12

A Big, Heavy Casebook

Introduction

Following are a federal statute and five cases interpreting that statute. They all relate to the sample Statement of Facts found in Chapter 11. They *do not* comprise a complete set of cases one would ordinarily use to write a Memorandum of Law on the sample Statement of Facts. They merely provide some law you and I can use to discuss the nature, organization, and presentation of legal content.

I strongly urge you to read this chapter in its entirety *before* reading Chapter 11. Then in Chapter 13, you'll find a completed Memorandum of Law on the case of Barbara Jean Goss.

Here are the statute and the cases (in no particular order).

The Statute

28 U.S.C. § 1359 (1982) provides:

> A district court shall not have jurisdiction of a civil action in which any party, by assignment or otherwise, has been improperly or collusively made or joined to invoke the jurisdiction of such court.

The Cases

McSparran v. Weist, 402 F.2d 868 (3d Cir. 1968), *cert. denied*, 395 U.S. 903 (1969).

This appeal was argued before a panel and we ordered it to be reargued before the court en banc with Esposito v. Emery, 3 Cir., 402 F.2d 878 so that we could review the troublesome question of the jurisdiction of a federal court where diversity of citizenship is created or "manufactured" by the appointment of a nonresident guardian of a minor, selected solely for the purpose of creating diversity. Here federal jurisdiction over the parent's consequential claim is asserted as pendent to the "manufactured" diversity claim of the child for damages.

Richard R. Riegner, a minor, was injured in an automobile accident on November 27, 1966, in Berks County, Pennsylvania, where he lived with his mother, Martha M. Fritzinger. In January 1967, being then just under twenty years of age, he petitioned the Orphans' Court of Berks County with his mother's consent and joinder for the appointment of a guardian of his estate, setting out that the only funds which might come into the guardian's hands were "monies which may be obtained by suit or settlement in an action which the proposed guardian will institute in the * * * [United States District Court for the Eastern District of Pennsylvania sitting] at Philadelphia to recover for injuries sustained by said minor" as a result of the accident. On February 6, 1967, the Orphans' Court appointed Stella McSparran as "guardian". In view of the prayer of the petition we shall assume that it intended her to act as guardian of Riegner's estate.

A few weeks later Stella McSparran, as guardian of Riegner's estate, instituted the present action in which she was joined as plaintiff by Mrs. Fritzinger, who designated herself as "Parent and Natural Guardian of Richard R. Riegner, a Minor, in Her Own Right." Mrs. Fritzinger claimed damages in the amount of $17,500 for loss of the minor's services and earning power until he attained majority and for medical expenses which she had been compelled to expend and would be required to expend until he attained majority.

One of the defendants moved to dismiss Mrs. Fritzinger's claim on the ground that she was not of diverse citizenship from the defendants and that her claim could not be sustained on a theory of pendent jurisdiction. The district court granted dismissal, and in doing so expressed the hope that the question, on which the judges of that court had already expressed differing views, would be resolved by an immediate appeal. [The court then describes some procedural problems in the lower court concerning the issuing of a final judgment.] The district court [then] entered a final judgment against Mrs. Fritzinger within the prescribed time and the appeal is now properly before us for decision.

It is conceded in the record as well as in the briefs and arguments of counsel that the guardian here is a straw party, chosen solely to create diversity jurisdiction. Before we reach the contention that the mother may maintain her pendent claim in her own right, we are therefore required to determine first whether such artificially created diversity is an adequate foundation for federal jurisdiction.

[The court proceeds to analyze the effect of the Federal Rules of Civil Procedure on the issue of whether the citizenship of the fiduciary governs the determination of diversity. The court also explored the differences between various fiduciaries.]

We are not here concerned, however, with capacity to sue under Rule 17, nor with the question whether the fiduciary is the real party in interest. Our problem is whether for purposes of diversity jurisdiction we should look to the citizenship of the representative, here the guardian of the estate of a minor, or to the person on whose behalf he acts. In Mexican Central Railway Co. v. Eckman, 187 U.S. 429, 23 S.Ct. 211, 47 L.Ed. 245 (1903), the Court held that the citizenship of the guardian of the person and estate of a minor governed in the determination of diversity of citizenship, because the guardian "had the right to bring suit in his own name" under the law of the state of his appointment. But in referring to the *Eckman* case with approval in Lumberman's Mutual Casualty Co. v. Elbert, 348 U.S. 48, 51, 75 S.Ct. 151, 99 L.Ed. 59 (1954), the Court characterized the guardian as the real party in interest. In Fallat v. Gouran, 220 F.2d 325 (3 Cir. 1955), we followed the *Eckman* case and held that diversity of citizenship existed on the basis of the citizenship of the guardian of the estate of a mental incompetent and that the citizenship of the incompetent himself was not the test. In that case residents of Pennsylvania were involved in an automobile accident in Pennsylvania and the married daughter of the incompetent, who was a New Jersey citizen, brought suit in her own name as his guardian. We sustained federal jurisdiction because of the diversity of the daughter's citizenship from that of the defendants although no diversity existed between the defendants and the incompetent himself. We declined to follow the decision to the contrary in Martineau v. City of St. Paul, 172 F.2d 777 (8 Cir. 1949).

These decisions deal with the party whose citizenship is to be the test in the determination of the existence of diversity. They do not decide the problem now before us—the effect of the artificial creation or "manufacture" of diversity. As recently as 1954 the Orphans' Court of Philadelphia hesitated to appoint a nonresident guardian because its general rule limited appointment to those who were within its jurisdiction and therefore amenable to its process and to its supervisory authority and control. After a factual determination that larger verdicts were generally obtained in the United States District Court for the Eastern District of Pennsylvania than in the Common Plea Courts of the state the Orphans' Court concluded that, since the only asset of the minor's estate was the personal injury claim, it would yield to the request that it appoint an out-of-state guardian because its primary concern was the financial benefit of its ward. The court had some doubt whether diversity jurisdiction would be found to exist by the federal courts but considered this a question for the federal courts themselves. [Citation omitted.] Since the publication of that opinion the rivulet of "manufactured" diversity cases has swollen to a stream of wide dimensions. The American Law Institute's detailed study of a sample of the diversity cases filed in the Eastern District of Pennsylvania during 1958 and 1959 indicated that 20.5 per cent of them were brought by out-of-state personal representatives of Pennsylvania citizens against Pennsylvania defendants. We are advised that one out-of-state citizen is the guardian of sixty-one pending diversity cases in the Eastern District of Pennsylvania.

The desire of suitors to seek justice in the federal courts carries, of course, no stigma. Where actual diversity exists among the appropriate parties, the choice to resort to the federal courts rather than the state courts cannot be denied them. Nor does a barrier grow simply because an increasing number of litigants prefer the federal to the state jurisdiction. But cases in which a straw or nominal fiduciary is appointed to create diversity stand on totally different ground than those in which the courts are simply concerned with the general question whether the citizenship of the personal representative or his ward or beneficiary should be the test of diversity jurisdiction. In cases of "manufactured" diversity jurisdiction there is brought into play the question of the applicability of 28 U.S.C. § 1359 which provides: "A district court shall not have jurisdiction of a civil action in which any party, by assignment or otherwise, has been improperly or collusively made or joined to invoke the jurisdiction of such court."

"Manufactured" diversity jurisdiction is not a new phenomenon in this Circuit. In Jaffe v. Philadelphia & Western R. Co., 180 F.2d 1010 (3 Cir. 1950), our first case on the subject, we sustained a diversity action under the wrongful death and survival statutes of Pennsylvania although the New Jersey plaintiff who was appointed as administratrix ad prosequendum was a stenographer employed in the office of the widow's attorney. We held that the administratrix ad prosequendum was the real party in interest and that her selection did not amount to collusion under what is now 28 U.S.C. § 1359, although the lawsuit apparently was the only asset under her nominal management. We placed heavy reliance on Mecom v. Fitzsimmons Drilling Co., 284 U.S. 183, 52 S.Ct. 84, 76 L.Ed. 233 (1931), where Mr. Justice Roberts said: "To go behind the decree of the probate court would be collaterally to attack it, not for lack of jurisdiction of the subject-matter or absence of jurisdictional facts, but to inquire into purposes and motives of the parties before that court when, confessedly, they practiced no fraud upon it."

In Corabi v. Auto Racing, Inc., 264 F.2d 784, 75 A.L.R.2d 711 (3 Cir. 1959), the mother of a deceased minor resigned as administratrix of his estate to permit the appointment of a non-resident so that suit could be brought in the federal court. In a unanimous decision by the court en banc we held in an opinion by Chief Judge Biggs that the nonresident administrator d.b.n. had capacity to sue and that his citizenship rather than that of the beneficiaries of the decedent's estate was determinative of diversity jurisdiction. We also held that § 1359 did not bar the action, because there was involved no collusion between plaintiff and defendant in fraud of the court, and the action was not "improperly" brought since there was no impropriety or irregularity involved in the perfectly valid proceeding in the state court for the appointment of the out-of-state fiduciary. [Citation omitted.] Corabi has become a leading case and is the authoritative foundation for the maintenance of "manufactured" diversity jurisdiction.

. . . .

Section 1359 is a combination in simplified form of the old anti-assignment statute [citation omitted] derived from 11 of the Judiciary Act of 1789, with the separate provision originating in the Act of March 3, 1875 and later incorporated as § 37 of the Judicial Code of 1911. [Citation omitted.] In combining these two provisions the reviser intended no alteration in the meaning of § 37 which empowered the district court to dismiss a suit "at any time * * * [when] such suit does not really and substantially involve a dispute or a controversy properly within the jurisdiction of said district court, or the parties to said suit have been improperly or collusively made or joined, either as plaintiffs or defendants, for the purpose of creating a case cognizable or removable * * *." The reviser's note to § 1359 states: "Provisions * * * for dismissal of an action not really and substantially involving a dispute or controversy within the jurisdiction of a district court were omitted as unnecessary [because] * * * any court will dismiss a case not within its jurisdiction when its attention is drawn to the fact, or even on its own motion."

While the preliminary words of § 37 no longer appear in § 1359, we believe they give content to its otherwise indefinite and ambiguous words "improperly" or "collusively." They say in effect that a nominal party designated simply for the purpose of creating diversity of citizenship, who has no real or substantial interest in the dispute or controversy, is improperly or collusively named.

The impropriety or collusion is not any conduct between the plaintiff and the defendant, for as Chief Judge Biggs pointed out in *Corabi*, the defendant may even oppose the guardian's prosecution of the action. The collusion exists between the nonresident guardian and the applicant for his appointment in the state proceeding as a result of which one who would not otherwise have been named as guardian has achieved the status from which he claims the right to sue because of his artificial selection solely for the purpose of creating jurisdiction. He is not chosen because of his capacity to manage the property of his ward, and indeed need have no experience in the management of property. He is outside the jurisdiction of the court which is to supervise his nominal activity. In truth none of the considerations which normally lead to the selection of a guardian affects the local appointing court's determination because it knows that in the "manufactured" diversity case the guardian is not expected to manage any property for his supposed ward and usually will not continue in office or exercise any real function after any funds are recovered in the litigation. He is no more than a representative of the minor's counsel whom counsel provides in order to establish a diversity of citizenship which will permit him to bring the action in the federal court. As a straw party he does not stand in the position of a true fiduciary whose involvement in litigation is incidental to his general duty to protect the interests of those for whom he is responsible.

The multiplication of "manufactured" diversity cases is a reflection on the federal judicial system and brings it into disrepute. Efforts therefore have been made to remedy the evil by legislation recommended by the Judicial Conference of the United States, and the American Law Institute in its recent study of the division of jurisdiction between the state and federal courts has recommended a statute which would test diversity in all cases by the citizenship of the beneficiary or the decedent rather than the personal representative. There would be no need for such legislation in "manufactured" diversity cases but for the interpretation of § 1359 in our leading case of *Corabi,* and similar decisions.

We believe on reconsideration that § 1359 is not so limited in scope as was held in *Corabi,* especially when read in the full background of the language of its predecessor provision originating in the Act of 1875. Further light is supplied by the construction long given to the anti-assignment provision which is now also incorporated in § 1359. It is well settled that the anti-assignment provision of § 1359 bars the creation of diversity jurisdiction by the transfer of a right of action to a collection agent whose only interest in prosecuting the suit is the recovery of his fee, even though he is vested with a portion of the legal title and has been expressly authorized to sue on behalf of the beneficiaries. The appointment of a fictitious guardian or representative selected by counsel for no other purpose than to create diversity jurisdiction in the action which will constitute the only asset in the estate is not substantially different from an assignment to an agent for the purpose of instituting litigation.

There are two obvious differences between the position of an assignee for the purpose of litigation and a straw fiduciary. In the former case there is an assignor in existence who might have sued in the state court in his own name, whereas in the case of an estate or a ward there is no one competent to sue prior to the appointment of a fiduciary. But since the appointee is in effect a straw party there is no reason why he should not be construed to come within the prohibition in § 1359 against invoking the diversity jurisdiction of a federal court by having one made a party improperly or collusively whether by assignment or otherwise. The second distinction in the case of a fiduciary is that he owes his position to a decree of a state court. We do not impugn this decree collaterally by refusing to recognize the citizenship of a straw guardian. Guardian he remains, but since he is acting in the capacity of a straw party we refuse to recognize his citizenship for purposes of determining diversity jurisdiction. His appointment may have authorized him to bring suit but his nominal status does not make his citizenship determinative for purposes of diversity. He occupies in effect the role of a guardian ad litem or a next friend or prochein ami whose function merely is to supply a party on the record responsible for costs [citation omitted] and whose citizenship would not be determinative of diversity jurisdiction.

It has often been said that in judging whether diversity of citizenship exists the courts will not inquire into the motive which led to the appointment of the personal representative. While, of course, the desire to obtain diversity jurisdiction is not in itself improper, nevertheless it is not irrelevant in the determination of the question whether the fiduciary is in fact a straw fiduciary whose citizenship is to be disregarded. Moreover, it is difficult to see how motive can be entirely ignored in ascertaining the purpose for which the representative is selected in view of the language of § 1359. The statute outlaws the creation of jurisdiction where a party has been improperly or collusively made or joined to invoke the jurisdiction of the court. While the statute does not ban the appointment of nonresident fiduciaries, the artificial selection of a straw representative who has no duty or function except to offer the use of his citizenship to create diversity in contemplated litigation is a violation of its provisions. This is made clear by the knowledge that the appointing court normally would not have designated him because of his absence from the jurisdiction and the consequent limitation of its control over him, all of which can be put aside because there is at the time of appointment nothing for him to administer and he is not expected to exercise any real function.

In Jaffe v. Philadelphia & Western R. Co., 180 F.2d 1010 (3 Cir. 1950), we relied heavily on Mecom v. Fitzsimmons Drilling Co., 284 U.S. 183, 52 S.Ct. 84, 76 L.Ed. 233 (1931), for our holding that motive is irrelevant in the artificial creation of diversity jurisdiction. *Mecom* is immediately distinguishable from the present case because it involved an administrator, whereas here we deal with a guardian, who does not have title to the ward's right of action. But we believe § 1359 reaches executors and administrators as well as guardians and therefore put this difference aside. The fundamental distinction between *Mecom* and the present case is that there the collusion statute was not involved because the resignation of the administratrix and the appointment of her successor were acts done not to create federal jurisdiction but to prevent it from attaching. Section 1359, as its language clearly shows, expresses a policy against the creation of federal jurisdiction and not against its avoidance. It proscribes improper or collusive conduct "to invoke" diversity jurisdiction and hence was inapplicable in the *Mecom* case.

In *Corabi* we placed great weight on Black & White Taxicab v. Brown & Yellow Taxicab & Transfer Co., 276 U.S. 518, 48 S.Ct. 404, 72 L.Ed. 681 (1928) for the irrelevance of motive. But the operative facts in *Black & White Taxicab* distinguish it from the present case. There a new corporation created to make diversity jurisdiction possible was not a mere straw. It became the sole party in interest after the old corporate assets were transferred to the successor. While the Court held that jurisdiction existed regardless of the motives of the management and shareholders of the corporation, it did so in the context of a real transaction which had significance beyond establishment of diversity jurisdiction. The Court in *Black & White Taxicab* therefore distinguished Lehigh Mining & Mfg. Co. v. Kelly, 160 U.S. 327, 16 S.Ct. 307, 40 L.Ed. 444 (1895) and Miller & Lux v. East Side Canal & Irrigation Co., 211 U.S. 293, 29 S.Ct. 111, 53 L.Ed. 189 (1908), which we recognized in *Corabi* might have been controlling but for the construction put upon § 37 by the *Black & White Taxicab* case. In those two earlier cases, however, the manufacture of diversity jurisdiction by the creation of new corporations and the transfer of assets to them in order to make it possible for them to bring diversity suits in the federal courts was stricken down as collusive, under the then Act of 1875. The collusion, of course, was not with the defendant but among those having charge of the plaintiff's assets and the cause of action. Those cases were not overruled in *Black & White Taxicab*.

Since plaintiff invoked diversity jurisdiction the burden was upon her to prove all the facts by which it could be sustained. Here plaintiff has added nothing to a record which shows on its face a naked arrangement for the selection of an out-of-state guardian in order to prosecute a diversity suit. It was early said in *Lehigh Mining & Mfg. Co.*, quoted in *Miller & Lux*: "But when the inquiry involves the jurisdiction of a federal court—the presumption in every stage of a cause [is] * * * that it is without the jurisdiction of a court of the United States, unless the contrary appears from the record." This is particularly true in diversity jurisdiction which trenches upon the jurisdiction of the state courts. As Mr. Justice Frankfurter said in City of Indianapolis v. Chase National Bank, 314 U.S. 63, 76-77, 62 S.Ct. 15 20, 86 L.Ed. 47 (1941): "The dominant note in the successive enactments of Congress relating to diversity jurisdiction, is one of jealous restriction, of avoiding offense to state sensitiveness, and of relieving the federal courts of the overwhelming burden of 'business that intrinsically belongs to the state courts,' in order to keep them free for their distinctive federal business. [citations omitted] 'The policy of the statute [conferring diversity jurisdiction upon the district courts] calls for its strict construction. The power reserved to the states, under the Constitution, to provide for the determination of controversies in their courts may be restricted only by the action of Congress in conformity to the judiciary sections of the Constitution. * * * Due regard for the rightful independence of state governments, which should actuate federal courts, requires that they scrupulously confine their own jurisdiction to the precise limits which the statute has defined.'"

In the present case not only was the straw guardian appointed solely to create diversity jurisdiction, but the controversy itself is essentially local, and one of the reasons underlying diversity jurisdiction, the prevention of discrimination against out-of-state litigants, is completely absent. The accident occurred in Pennsylvania, where the injured minor and all the defendants reside and have their citizenship.

We hold therefore that the attempt to confer diversity jurisdiction in the present case offends against § 1359. *Jaffe* and *Corabi* are hereby overruled, and Fallat v. Gouran is disapproved to the extent that it indicates approval of "manufactured" diversity. Whether in an individual case diversity jurisdiction is "manufactured" is, of course, a question of fact. Here "manufactured" diversity is conceded, but in other cases where it is not conceded it will be for the district court to make the factual determination.

[The court ended its opinion with a discussion of the prospective application of the new rule.]

[The dissents of Judge McLaughlin and Judge Kalodner are omitted.]

Joyce v. Seigel, 429 F.2d 128 (3d Cir. 1970).

This case falls within the narrow class in which the question is whether our decision in McSparran v. Weist [citation omitted] barring "manufactured" diversity actions, should be applied retrospectively.

The doctrine of *McSparran,* in which we overruled and disapproved our previous decisions, has since been adopted in a number of circuits, and has its real significance for future cases. We made it clear that in the gradually shrinking class of cases where the parties had a right to rely on our prior rule because the cause of action arose before *McSparran* was decided, such pending actions should not be dismissed by retrospective application of *McSparran* if this would impose serious prejudice on any of the parties or upon the administration of justice.

This is an action brought under the Pennsylvania Wrongful Death and Survival Statutes. Defendant filed a motion to dismiss the action on the ground that diversity was "manufactured." After entering a number of orders in which it successively denied, granted and vacated the dismissal of the action the district court ultimately dismissed the action. From this dismissal the plaintiff has appealed.

Plaintiff attacks the order dismissing the complaint on two grounds. One is that the dismissal was entered without holding a hearing, to which he was entitled and which the district court had indicated would ultimately be held.

We need not rest our decision on the failure of the district court to hold a hearing. For the action of the district court was based on the insufficiency of the facts alleged by the plaintiff in his answer to the motion to dismiss and in various affidavits filed on his behalf to establish, as was his burden, that diversity existed. No counter-affidavits were filed by the defendant and no question of credibility has been raised. We therefore review the decision of the district court on the facts appearing in the record.

On April 6, 1968, the decedent, Richard M. Lane, was killed in a collision between his automobile and a tractor-trailer of defendant in Elk County, Pennsylvania. Decedent was a citizen of Pennsylvania and so is defendant. Decedent's wife had died a year before the accident. They had three children, two of them adopted daughters aged 16 and 14 at the time of the accident, and a five-year old son born of the marriage. After decedent's death the two adopted daughters lived with friends of the decedent, Mr. and Mrs. Lee Grosch at Shippenville, Pennsylvania, and the boy lived with his paternal grandmother, Mrs. Bertha Lane, at Marienville, Pennsylvania.

This was a family afflicted by tragedy and troubled by family discord. The wife, whom decedent had named in his will as executrix and who would become the guardian of the children, had predeceased him. His father-in-law, Darwin L. Sayres, whom he had named as alternate executor and guardian, was old and so ill that he died a short time later. He renounced the executorship after other members of the family indicated through Leroy F. Grosch that they did not believe it would be in the best interest of the family for him to serve.

Decedent's mother, Mrs. Bertha Lane, was 58 years of age, and in ill health and distress because of the death of her husband in an accident a short time before. She also renounced, and then selected as administrator John W. Joyce, the decedent's uncle, because he "would be able to handle all the problems connected with the estate without getting involved in any of the personal problems such as custody and guardianship of minor children." Her choice was approved by Mr. Sayres, as well as by Neal Fiscus, the husband of decedent's sister, who was the only other relative mentioned in the record residing in Pennsylvania. Mr. Fiscus also averred in his affidavits that the family did not wish Mr. Sayres to act as administrator and that he himself did not wish to serve because of a family conflict over custody of the two adopted daughters.

The assets of the decedent's estate, aside from the present cause of action, were worth approximately $50,000, and Mr. Joyce attended to them before instituting the present action.

The ultimate determination whether diversity has been "manufactured," as we made clear in *McSparran*, is a question of fact to be determined from the circumstances of the individual case. A number of factors which ordinarily will be encountered were specified in Groh v. Brooks, 421 F.2d 589, 595 (3 Cir. 1970). These, of course, are but illustrations and not definitive, for the ultimate factual decision must be derived from the particular characteristics of the individual case.

In the present case the circumstances make it clear that Mr. Joyce became the administrator c. t. a. for legitimate considerations. His residence and citizenship outside of Pennsylvania was the reason for his selection, but this was because it freed him from close involvement in the family's personal problems, and his selection for this reason and because he was experienced in financial affairs was quite different from an effort to create artificial diversity. In these circumstances the plaintiff was entitled to select the federal courts for the decision of the claim against defendant, and the action should therefore go forward in the district court, where it was brought.

The order of the district court dismissing the action will be reversed and the case remanded for further proceedings.

Hackney v. Newman Memorial Hospital, Inc., 621 F.2d 1069 (10th Cir. 1980).

This is an appeal from an order dismissing a wrongful death action brought by Donna Beth Hackney as administratrix of her deceased mother's estate. The basis for the dismissal was the trial court's ruling that plaintiff was improperly or collusively appointed successor administratrix to create diversity jurisdiction, in violation of 28 U.S.C. § 1359. The propriety of this ruling is the only question in this appeal.

Byrdie Blasdel, a life-long resident of Oklahoma, died November 12, 1975. She was survived by her husband, a severely disabled person, also a resident of Oklahoma, and two daughters, Brenda Sue Rea and plaintiff. Rea was a citizen of Oklahoma; plaintiff was then a citizen of Colorado. The family decided Rea should administer the estate and she was duly appointed. She acted in this capacity until June 6, 1977, when she resigned and plaintiff was appointed successor administratrix. At that time the estate had been fully administered except for the conduct of the wrongful death action. This suit was commenced on August 29, 1977, while plaintiff and her husband were in Oklahoma on a house-hunting trip because of an anticipated transfer of plaintiff's husband by his employer. In September the transfer was finalized, and plaintiff and her husband moved to Woodward, Oklahoma, where they have resided since. All defendants are citizens of Oklahoma.

The trial court held an evidentiary hearing to determine whether plaintiff was a citizen of Oklahoma when the suit was filed and, in the alternative, whether she was improperly or collusively appointed to succeed her sister for the purpose of creating diversity jurisdiction. The trial court found that plaintiff was a citizen of Colorado when the suit was filed, but ordered dismissal on the ground plaintiff was appointed in violation of the anti-collusion statute, 28 U.S.C. § 1359. Plaintiff appeals from this order.

The trial court did not expressly discuss section 1359 in terms of its "improperly or collusively made" language. Instead, it couched the holding in factual terms, referring to the case as "essentially a local controversy" and finding the appointment of plaintiff was for the "primary purpose of invoking federal jurisdiction." Plaintiff argues that the court's reliance upon a "primary" purpose test is erroneous. We do not decide that issue, since we hold the purpose of the appointment is not determinative in this case.

Prior to 1968 the courts construed section 1359 narrowly in determining whether an appointment of a nonresident fiduciary was improper or collusive. The leading case, *Corabi v. Auto Racing, Inc.*, 264 F.2d 784 (3d Cir. 1959), held that such an appointment is not collusive unless there is collusion between plaintiff and defendant in fraud of the court, and is not improper if the state court appointment was valid. But in *McSparran v. Weist*, 402 F.2d 867 (3d Cir. 1968), *cert. denied*, 395 U.S. 903, 89 S.Ct. 1739, 23 L.Ed.2d 217 (1969), *Corabi* was overruled, the court reasoning that the relevant collusion is between the "nonresident [fiduciary] and the applicant for his appointment in the state proceeding as a result of which one who would not otherwise have been named as [fiduciary] has achieved the status from which he claims the right to sue because of his artificial selection solely for the purpose of creating jurisdiction." *Id.* at 873. It also reasoned that a federal court's determination that a fiduciary's appointment violates section 1359 is not a collateral attack on the appointment by the state court. The appointee retains the capacity to act as representative; his or her citizenship is simply disregarded for federal purposes. *Id.* at 874. The court construed the words "improperly or collusively" to "say in effect that a nominal party designated simply for the purpose of creating diversity of citizenship, who has no real or substantial interest in the dispute or controversy, is improperly or collusively named." *Id.* at 873. Shortly thereafter in *Kramer v. Caribbean Mills, Inc.*, 394 U.S. 823, 89 S.Ct. 1487, 23 L.Ed.2d 9 (1969), the Supreme Court held that an assignment of an interest in a contract for purposes of collection only is improperly or collusively made under 28 U.S.C. § 1359 even though the assignment is valid under state law.

Drawing in part upon *Kramer*, other circuits have followed *McSparran*. [Citations omitted.] In several of these cases the parties admitted the sole reason for the out-of-state fiduciary was to achieve diversity jurisdiction, as was permitted under the *Corabi* rule. [Citation omitted.] The courts following *McSparran*, however, have emphasized that the purpose for which the representative was appointed is but one of the factors the court should consider. [Citation omitted.] Although they found appointment of straw parties as fiduciaries solely to obtain diversity jurisdiction was collusive within section 1359, in dictum they declared or inferred that if the appointed representative has a substantial relationship to the litigation the result would be different. [Citation omitted.] The instant case tests the dictum.

the Pennsylvania state courts. The *McSparran* court rejected old decisions holding § 1359 applicable only when the administrator or guardian was not properly appointed under state law, and ruled that "a nominal party designated simply for the purpose of creating diversity of citizenship, who has no real or substantial interest in the dispute or controversy, is improperly or collusively named." *Id.* at 873.

In *McSparran*, the parties candidly admitted that the guardian had been named for the sole purpose of manufacturing diversity; there were no ties to the family, the guardian's sole function was to lend his name to the tort action, and the estate contained no assets save the tort claim. Though the guardian was unquestionably the "real party in interest" under state law, the court held that federal jurisdiction could not rest on so formalistic a base. Rather, the substantive considerations of motive and function would guide the inquiry . . . .

The *McSparran* rule found support the following year in the Supreme Court's decision in *Kramer v. Caribbean Mills, Inc.*, 394 U.S. 823, 89 S.Ct. 1487, 23 L.Ed.2d 9 (1969). *Kramer* involved the collusive— though valid under state law—assignment of a legal claim for purposes of creating jurisdiction in the federal courts, and the Court held that such conduct fell within § 1359's proscription. Though the Court recognized that there are some differences between assignment cases and guardianship or administration cases, and explicitly reserved the question of § 1359's role in the latter types of cases, *id.* at 828 n.9, 89 S.Ct. at 1490 n.9, *Kramer* has been consistently read as marking an end to the period in which citizenship of the formal "real party in interest" under state law was necessarily regarded for purposes of the diversity determination. Such a ruling, the Court noted, does not disparage the states' sovereign power to give effect to certain assignments and appointments made under their laws, but establishes only that "[t]he existence of federal jurisdiction is a matter of federal, not state, law." *Id.* at 829, 89 S.Ct. at 1490.

Bouyed by the *Kramer* decision, the "motive/function" rule of *McSparran* was quickly adopted in many other circuits. [Citations omitted.] This court adopted that rule in *Bass v. Texas Power & Light Co.*, 432 F.2d 763 (5th Cir. 1970), *cert. denied*, 401 U.S. 975, 91 S.Ct. 1194, 28 L.Ed.2d 324 (1971), where the parties admitted that an administrator had been named for the sole purpose of creating diversity, and we accordingly dismissed the action for want of jurisdiction. The admission of improper motive made *Bass* an easy case, but we recognized that ordinarily "[t]he question of whether a device is so lacking in substance as to be improper and collusive under Section 1359 is a question of fact." *Id.* at 766-67.

Such a factual determination had to be made almost immediately thereafter in *Green v. Hale*, 433 F.2d 324, 325 (5th Cir. 1970), where there was no admission that the out-of-state administrator had been named deliberately to create diversity. We held that under such circumstances, "inquiry into the purpose of the appointment is essential," *id.* at 329, thus reaffirming that the motive underlying the naming of an out-of-state administrator is a determinative factor under § 1359. Factors to be considered by the district court in making a § 1359 inquiry include:

> the relationship of the representative to the party represented; the scope of the representative's powers and duties; any special capacity or experience which the representative may possess with respect to the purpose of his appointment; whether there exists a nondiverse individual who might more normally be expected to represent the interests at stake; whether those seeking the appointment of the representative express any particular reasons for selecting an out-of-state person; and whether, apart from the appointment of an out-of-state representative, the suit is one wholly local in nature.

Id. at 329; *accord, Groh v. Brooks*, 421 F.2d 589, 595 (3d Cir. 1970).

Hard on the heels of *Bass* and *Green*, we decided *White v. Lee Marine Corp.*, 434 F.2d 1096 (5th Cir. 1970), wherein the motive underlying the appointment of an out-of-state administrator was hotly contested, but we affirmed as not clearly erroneous the trial court's determination that the administrator had been improperly or collusively named in contravention of § 1359. The inquiry, we stated, was (1) whether there was an intent to manufacture diversity, and (2) whether there is sufficient substance to the appointment to allow it to be recognized in a diversity suit." *Id.* at 1098-99. Our inquiry into the substance of the appointment was spurred by *McSparran's* "heavy emphasis on its finding that the guardian there was only a straw party with no stake in the outcome of the litigation and no fiduciary relationship to the parties represented." *Id.* at 1098. Thus, we perceived a "requirement of substantive as well as formal validity of the representative's appointment." *Id.*

This language, regrettably, has since been misconstrued to imply that we require an administrator to have some substantial stake in the outcome of the wrongful death action he brings for the estate, even in those cases where the administrator's appointment is not infected by any improper motive to manufacture diversity. *Bishop v. Hendricks*, 495 F.2d 289, 294 n. 23 (4th Cir.), *cert. denied*, 419 U.S. 1056, 95 S.Ct. 639, 42 L.Ed.2d 653 (1974). We do not think *White* may be so read. First, *White* relies on *McSparran* as the source of its analysis, and *McSparran* does not suggest that a "substantial stake" test must be passed above and beyond the "proper motive" test. Rather, *McSparran* relies in part on the guardian's lack of a stake in the litigation to establish that there was no proper motive for the appointment of this individual. Second, in reviewing the district court's dismissal of the action in *White*, we analyzed the various indicators of proper and improper motive in the appointment. As there was no indication that the administrator had any stake in the outcome of the litigation, this review would have been pointless if there was a separate "substantial stake" requirement. Moreover, if one examines the district court finding under review—"that the said [administrator] has no real or substantial interest in this litigation; and that said appointment was improperly or collusively made to invoke the jurisdiction of this Court," *id.* at 1100—it is apparent that the only inference which might fairly be drawn from *White* is that, where an administrator does have a substantial stake in the litigation, jurisdiction will be sustained even if there is evidence that this administrator was chosen for the purpose of creating diversity. Third, to the extent *White* may be ambiguous, it must be read in light of *Green v. Hale*, where the emphasis was plainly on motive alone.

The Fourth Circuit in *Bishop* also took note of our observation in *White* . . . that upholding federal jurisdiction where the administrator has no stake in the litigation and no substantial ties to the beneficiaries, "would not advance any of the functions diversity jurisdiction was designed to serve." *White*, 434 F.2d at 1100 . . . . By that statement, however, we meant only that we could not find any affirmative reason to uphold jurisdiction, not that failure to advance the functions of diversity jurisdiction itself inveighs against jurisdiction where statutory requirements are otherwise met. Control over the scope of diversity jurisdiction rests with Congress, and we may not bar a plaintiff—with or without a "substantial stake" in the litigation—from access to the federal courts because we conclude that he is unlikely to encounter any bias in state court against out-of-state plaintiffs.

In sum, we have for many years adhered to the rule that an administrator whose appointment is not motivated by an intent to manufacture diversity does not fall within the proscription of § 1359, and that the existence of diversity will accordingly be determined with reference to his citizenship. Whether the administrator has a substantial stake in the litigation, whether he has duties above and beyond prosecution of the lawsuit, and whether the estate contains assets other than the wrongful death claim may all inform our judgment as to the motive for the appointment, but none of these elements are [sic] independently necessary to sustain jurisdiction if no improper motive underlies the appointment.

In *Bishop v. Hendricks*, the Fourth Circuit abandoned this "motive" test in favor of a "substantial stake" test. The court held that an out-of-state administrator who is named for the purpose of prosecuting a lawsuit but has no substantial stake in the outcome of that suit has been improperly or collusively named under § 1359 even if there is no evidence that the manufacture of diversity was a motive for the appointment. The administrator must have "something more than a nominal interest at stake in the litigation," *id.* at 297:

> [A]ny appointment of an out-of-state administrator, which is nominal and "without substance" and which, if given effect for jurisdictional purposes, has the effect of giving diversity to an action which does not "really and substantially involve a dispute or controversy" between citizens of different states, is violative of the purposes of, and falls under the interdict of, Section 1359.

Id. at 294.

Despite this rather absolute statement of the "substantial stake" test, the *Bishop* court allowed that this test would not apply where it could be shown that the administrator was not appointed predominantly for purposes of prosecuting the lawsuit. "It may be assumed," the court stated, *id.* at 293, "that if there is a valid reason for the appointment of an out-of-state administrator that gives to his representation greater substantiality than a mere administrator *ad litem*, the citizenship of the administrator may be determinative of diversity." However, where the administrator has no material function other than prosecution of the lawsuit, and no stake in the outcome of that suit, § 1359 will be violated even if the administrator was named for perfectly legitimate reasons:

> [T]he fact that the beneficiaries are prostrated by grief, or are related to the out-of-state administrator, or are relying on the administrator for advice or that the out-of-state administrator is "a competent business man," will not justify diversity based on the administrator's citizenship. Confidence in the superior business judgment and ties of friendship, even intimate ones, are equally unavailing.... [O]nly if the Court can conclude that the out-of-state administrator has something more than a nominal relationship to the litigation will the citizenship of an out-of-state administrator sustain diversity, and any reason or motive for the appointment which does not elevate his relationship to the litigation above the level of a nominal party is irrelevant to the issues of diversity.

Id. at 295. The "function" aspect of the Fourth Circuit's rule is evidently designed to ameliorate some of the harshness of a strict "substantial stake" test, and harmonizes with the "function" branch of the traditional "motive" test—though in the latter case the existence of functions other than prosecution of a lawsuit simply evidences the presence of proper motives for the administrator's selection.

The question before us is whether we should join the Fourth Circuit in adopting a "substantial stake" test or retain the old "motive" test. We see much in the Fourth Circuit's approach that is attractive. The "substantial stake" test is simple to apply, and averts the "difficult and perhaps needless litigation of disputed facts [which] might well encourage perjury or manipulation of factual evidence," *White*, 434 F.2d at 1099 n. 8, that attends the "motive" test. The "substantial stake" test may also do more to effectuate the purposes of diversity jurisdiction than the "motive" test. Nevertheless, we recognized in *White*, *id.*, that we are not free to adopt a desirable rule if it is not the rule prescribed by statute.

We conclude that the "substantial stake" test cannot be justified under the language of § 1359. The statutory interdict against jurisdiction where a party "has been improperly or collusively made or joined *to invoke* the jurisdiction" of the federal courts (emphasis added) incontrovertably suggests to us that the motive underlying the naming of the administrator must guide the diversity inquiry. If an out-of-state administrator has not been selected with the purpose of manufacturing diversity, the administrator's lack of a stake in the outcome of the litigation cannot alone trigger § 1359's jurisdictional bar.

Returning to the facts of this case, it is apparent that Bianca has no substantial stake in the outcome of the wrongful death action. Though Bianca asserts that Mississippi's Wrongful Death Statute vests in her substantive powers and duties which belie any claim that she is a "straw fiduciary," she does not lay claim to any portion of any recovery in the wrongful death action, and she does not credibly claim that her function as administratrix was to do more than prosecute this lawsuit. On this basis, the district court found that Bianca was a "straw-party" whose citizenship would be disregarded in the diversity inquiry.

The district court cited our holding in *Green v. Hale* . . . , but we find no support in [this case] for a *per se* rule against parties having no stake in the litigation, absent some improper motive in the administratrix's appointment. Principally, the district court relied on the Fourth Circuit's decision in *Bishop v. Hendricks*, but we decline to follow the principles there enunciated, and accordingly we cannot uphold a § 1359 inquiry which is grounded in the *Bishop* standard. Though the district court did find an attempt to manufacture diversity, the court made plain its view that an attempt to manufacture diversity is presented when the administratrix has no function other than prosecution of the lawsuit and no stake in the outcome of the suit, irrespective of the fact that the administratrix is named in good faith.

We hold, in sum, that § 1359 instructs us to disregard the citizenship of an administratrix only when there is a factual determination that the administratrix was named with a purpose to manufacture diversity. The district court thoughtfully traversed this uncertain terrain but because it chose a path we here make plain was not available in this circuit, we must reverse the dismissal of this suit for want of jurisdiction. On remand the district court's inquiry will be guided by the circumstance that its ultimate inquiry is into motive and purpose with substantiality of stake a relevant but not controlling indicator as we here explain.

Bishop v. Hendricks, 495 F.2d 289 (4th Cir.), *cert. denied*, 419 U.S. 1056 (1974).

This is an action to recover under the wrongful death statute of South Carolina. It arose out of a motor collision occurring in Newberry County, South Carolina. The deceased was a life-long citizen of South

Carolina. The statutory beneficiaries of the action are likewise life-long citizens of South Carolina. The beneficiaries retained counsel to prosecute the wrongful death action on their behalf. After consulting with their counsel, they applied to the local probate court for the appointment of the plaintiff-appellant, a citizen of Georgia and a relative by marriage of the beneficiaries, as administrator in whose name the action might be prosecuted. This action was thereupon commenced as a diversity action in the District Court against the lessee-operator of the other vehicle in the accident. The lessee of the other vehicle, who is the appellee on this appeal, was a citizen of South Carolina. He moved to dismiss the action for lack of diversity claiming in support of his motion that when a deceased leaves, as the deceased did in this case, no estate to be administered and the sole reason for the appointment of an administrator is to provide a nominal party plaintiff to institute the action, the benefits of which, if successful, pass directly to the statutory beneficiaries without any general administration, the citizenship of the administrator should be disregarded and the citizenship of the beneficiaries of the action should control in ascertaining federal diversity jurisdiction. The appellant-administrator countered with the contention that such a rule was applicable only when it could be found that the sole motive for the appointment of an out-of-state fiduciary was to created federal jurisdiction. The District Court, however, concluded, as did the Court in Nickell v. Westervelt (D.C.Va.1973) 354 F.Supp. 111, 112, and Johnson v. Worley (D.C.Va.1972) 353 F.Supp. 1381, 1382, that Miller v. Perry (4th Cir. 1972) 456 F.2d 63, "held that diversity of citizenship" in such a case as that here "is determined by the citizenship of the beneficiaries rather than by the citizenship of the administrator", and it reached that conclusion despite its remark that in its opinion the "motive" for the appointment of the out-of-state administrator in this case was not the creation of federal jurisdiction. It accordingly dismissed the action for want of jurisdiction. The administrator appeals. We affirm.

The appellant would confine the scope of *Miller* to the peculiar facts of that case; and since the facts in this case are different, he argues *Miller* is without application. *Miller*, however, was not phrased in the narrow terms of its own facts. The language of *Miller* was manifestly intended as a declaration of what one commentator has correctly denominated as "a substantial change in diversity jurisdiction". The Court in that case was focusing generally on the broad, fundamental problem of determining the real party in interest, not in a procedural but in a jurisdictional sense, and in making clear what, in the light of the decision in Kramer v. Caribbean Mills (1969) 394 U.S. 823, 89 S.Ct. 1487, 23 L.Ed.2d 9, was an "improper" or "collusive" joinder under Section 1359, 28 U.S.C. The emphasis "was on a fresh appraisal of an old problem." By its decision, the Court was making a choice between the old, purely mechanical or "ritualistic" rule that an administrator, validly appointed, is always the real party in interest whose citizenship fixes diversity jurisdiction and what, on the other hand, has been aptly described as the more recent "substantive real party in interest test" as determined by the facts of the particular case. The Court recognized that "there was nothing sacred in the customary rule that an administrator's citizenship governs, a principle which serves policies of judicial economy rather than federal-state comity" and concluded as a matter of principle that substance should prevail over mere procedure, that federal courts on jurisdictional issues should "assess the substantive relations between the parties to the controversy" and that they should make "a realistic determination with respect to the presence of diversity." It found authority for such an approach in *Kramer*, which directed, as construed in *Miller*, "that the duties and responsibilities of administrators should be taken into account in federal determinations of the relevancy of the citizenship of such a personal representative to the presence of diversity jurisdiction." It held specifically that when the responsibilities of the administrator are solely to institute the wrongful death action—when he is what one Court has described as "an administrator *ad litem*" and no more—the Court would "hinge the diversity determination to the citizenship of the wrongful death action beneficiaries, rather than to that of their representative."

The result reached in *Miller* had long found advocates among legal scholars. It has received wide approval from the legal commentators. It is in conformity with the rule as stated by Professor Moore in his authoritative text:

> "Where a party sues (or is sued) as a receiver, representative of a class, assignee, subrogee, executor or administrator it is normally his citizenship that is material when jurisdiction is dependent upon the character of the parties. This is true also of the general guardian of an infant, or the curator or committee of a lunatic, when under the law of the state where such fiduciary is appointed he has the status of a real fiduciary. But if the law

of the state gives the administrator, guardian, or other representative the status of only a nominal fiduciary then the beneficiary or the ward, not the administrator or guardian, is the real party in interest, and it is the citizenship of the beneficiary or ward, as the case may be, that is determinative." 3A, Moore's Federal Practice, pp. 112-4 (footnotes omitted).

"Such a determination", also, has the virtue that it "insures that federal jurisdiction will be invoked only when necessary to protect the party whose personal interest in the suit might be prejudiced by the presence of local bias", which "has been the historical view for why diversity jurisdiction originated". [Citation omitted.] To permit the appointment of a nominal non-resident fiduciary to create federal diversity jurisdiction would clearly "run counter to the general policy of viewing the federal courts as tribunals of limited jurisdiction whose subject matter jurisdiction principles should be applied with restraint," and, through its artificial creation of diversity, would represent an "improper manufacture of jurisdiction" in obvious violation of the purposes of Section 1359.

Even if it be conceded that the rule in *Miller* is normally of general application, the appellant, however, would restrict it to situations where the reason or "motive" assigned for the appointment of the administrator was to create diversity jurisdiction. It may be assumed that if there is a valid reason for the appointment of an out-of-state administrator that gives to his representation greater substantiality than a mere administrator *ad litem*, the citizenship of the administrator may be determinative of diversity. This exception was implicit in *Miller,* which drew a clear distinction between the situation where the administrator was merely an agent to sue "without stake" in the litigation as it were and where he had some substantial interest or stake in the proceedings. It was, also, recognized by implication in Lester v. McFaddon. But it must be remembered that, in a situation where an out-of-state administrator files a wrongful death action on behalf of resident beneficiaries, involving the death of a resident decedent in an accident occurring within the state, want of diversity will be presumed unless the record provides sufficient support for the conclusion that the representation of the administrator is not nominal but was based on a valid and substantial reason. But for the reason or motive for the appointment to give the necessary substantiality to his representation that his citizenship will be regarded for diversity it must be more than an expression of sentiment or personal preference or mere kinship with either the beneficiaries of the decedent. Nor can it be established by some self-serving profession of good faith in the appointment. The reason or motive that will render the out-of-state administrator's citizenship important for diversity purposes must be one that harmonizes with the thrust and purposes of Section 1359 itself. [The court's review of statutory history is omitted.] That the purpose of the statute remained the same was emphasized by the Circuit Court opinion in *Kramer*, where "improper or collusive" joinder for jurisdiction was declared to result when it rested on "*colorable assignment or other device without substance*" (Italics added.) And this was the construction adopted and applied in *Miller*. Accordingly, any appointment of an out-of-state administrator, which is nominal and "without substance" and which, if given effect for jurisdictional purposes, has the effect of giving diversity to an action which does not "really and substantially involve a dispute or controversy" between citizens of different states, is violative of the purposes of, and falls under the interdict of, Section 1359. The courts should accordingly evaluate the reasons for the appointment and determine whether the reasons given logically or realistically establish that, as a result, the fiduciary sustains more than a nominal relationship to the litigation. The Courts have often done just that and, on the basis of their evaluation, have determined whether the citizenship of the administrator is to be given effect. As we have said, the fact that the beneficiaries are prostrated by grief, or are related to the out-of-state administrator, or are relying on the administrator for advice or that the out-of-state administrator is "a competent business man", will not justify diversity based on the administrator's citizenship. Confidence in the superior business judgment and ties of friendship, even intimate ones, are equally unavailing. On the other hand, O'Brien v. Stover (8th Cir. 1971) 443 F.2d 1013, 1015-1016, instances circumstances in which the appointment will control diversity. In that case, the out-of-state administratrix was the daughter of the deceased and "her sole heir". Under these circumstances, the Court said, "The diversity here is bona fide and plaintiff's appointment as administrator was natural and logical under the circumstances. She was the real party in interest. These facts are sufficient to establish diversity jurisdiction." Again, when a general administrator, having assets other than the wrongful death suit to administer and who, incidental to his duties as general administrator, files a wrongful death suit, it has been held, though not uniformly, that his citizenship may be considered for diversity. In summary, only if the Court can conclude that the out-of-state administrator has something more than a nominal relationship to the litigation will the citizenship of an out-of-state administrator sustain diversity, and any reason or motive for the appointment which does not elevate his relationship to the litigation above the level of a nominal party is irrelevant to the issues of diversity.

In this case, the administrator has failed to establish any substantive facts or to assign any valid reasons for his appointment that would give "substance" to his representation or fix his status in the suit as different from nominal. Without any "real [or] substantial interest in the outcome of the litigation", he possesses "no stake in the litigation". He has nothing to gain by the suit save a fee for the use of his name if successful, and, if the suit is lost, nothing to lose. In fact, it would seem that the beneficiaries of the action, if they chose to, could settle the action, with or without consulting him. Nor is the prosecution of the action incidental to any general fiduciary duties of an administrator. There are no assets in the estate other than this suit. The appellant has no knowledge of the accident out of which the litigation arose and can contribute nothing to its prosecution. He actually had no part in the selection or employment of counsel. The employment of counsel occurred before his appointment and under the circumstances, he, like the representative in Lester v. McFaddon, *supra* (415 F.2d at p. 1103) "can hardly be expected to ride herd upon them (i. e., counsel) or exercise any effective supervision of their conduct of the litigation". It is true, he is the nominal plaintiff but this is simply because the statute so commands . . . .

The only reason assigned for his appointment and sought to justify diversity on the basis of his citizenship was that he was more experienced in business affairs than the father or mother of the deceased, the beneficiaries of the action. This reason is not persuasive. The beneficiaries, either of whom would have been the natural fiduciary, chose the attorney to prepare the suit and to try it. That was substantially the only function the administrator in a case such as this would perform. The suggestion that the father and mother were without business experience was unimportant since there could be no occasion to use business experience in the very limited, nominal role to be played by the administrator.

In summary, the appellant is, so far as this suit is concerned, a "straw party", appointed just as a guardian *ad litem* solely for the purposes of providing a nominal plaintiff for the maintenance of this action. His appointment is manifestly an artificial creation of federal diversity and as such cannot support jurisdiction. It is, for all practical purposes, similar to the situation in First Nat. Bank of Amherst, Mass. v. Fulcher (D.C.Va.1954) 119 F.Supp. 759, p. 763, where the Court, "looking at reality" and determining diversity in the citizenship of the beneficiaries of the Virginia wrongful death statute rather than that of the administrator, said:

> "* * * The personal representative is nominally the plaintiff solely because the statute says that he must be. Should there be a recovery, no creditor could touch it. No administration is necessary. Any recovery would go to the sons as the jury might direct."

We have not overlooked that the District Court stated that, if the issue were properly before him he would find that the "motive" in the appointment of the appellant as administrator was not improper. He gave no reason for such opinion. As we have indicated, however, the propriety of an administrator's appointment in a case such as this is determined under Section 1359 by whether the administrator has something more than a nominal interest at stake in the litigation. The appellant-administrator manifestly did not have such an interest and the District Court properly dismissed the action on jurisdictional grounds.

Chapter 13

Sample Memorandum of Law

Prisco si credis, Maecenas docte, Cratino,
Nulla placere diu nec vivere carmina possunt
Quae scribuntur aquae potoribus.

If you believe Cratinus from days of old, Maecenas, (as you must know) no verse can give pleasure for long, nor last, that is written by drinkers of water.

—Horace

Chapter 13

Sample Memorandum of Law

Introduction

Following is a sample Memorandum of Law on the sample fact pattern you found in Chapter 11. It contains a suggested Statement of Facts, Question Presented, Conclusion, and Discussion of Authority. It uses just the five cases that are reproduced in the Big, Heavy Casebook in Chapter 12. It emphatically does not analyze all cases that should be analyzed to write a complete Memorandum of Law on the model topic. It contains no secondary authority, which a proper memo definitely should contain. It merely gives you an idea of what a Memorandum of Law looks like and sounds like.

Finally, I have no doubt that many readers of this book could improve upon the sample you find below. I offer it only as a suggestion and as a guide.

MEMORANDUM OF LAW

To: Reader's Name
From: Writer's Name
Re: McAllister v. Estate of Mulligan,
        Manufactured Diversity of Citizenship
Date: October 26, 1988

Statement of Facts:

Sally McAllister, administratrix for the estate of Barbara Jean Goss, has filed a wrongful death action in federal court against the estate of Frederick Joseph Mulligan, which is insured by our client. McAllister, a resident of Virginia, bases the jurisdiction of the suit on diversity of citizenship. Our client wishes to avoid litigating the case in federal court and wants to know if the case can be dismissed as an impermissible manufacture of diversity in violation of 28 U.S.C. § 1359 (1982).

On January 17, 1985, Barbara Jean Goss, age 12, was killed in an automobile accident in Greensboro, North Carolina. As Barbara Jean was crossing in front of her stopped school bus, Frederick Joseph Mulligan attempted to pass the bus from the rear, saw Barbara Jean, swerved, narrowly missed her, and slammed into a telephone pole. Mulligan, who had been drinking heavily, was killed instantly. Barbara Jean, who suffered from a congenital heart defect, suffered a fatal heart attack as a result of her intense fright.

Barbara Jean's father died when she was a small child. She has no brothers or sisters. Her mother, who currently suffers from a drinking problem, originally served as administratrix of Barbara Jean's estate, valued at slightly more than $10,000, and paid that amount to herself as the sole legal heir. Recently, however, the mother resigned as administratrix. Her sister, Sally McAllister, a businesswoman from Richmond, Virginia, was appointed to serve and shortly thereafter instituted this action in federal district court, alleging diversity of citizenship as the basis for federal jurisdiction.

Evidence obtained to date does not show whether the plaintiff's attorneys suggested the resignation of the mother or the appointment of the nonresident relative. The mother does have a successful brother-in-law, Mr. Fred Jackson, living in nearby High Point. It is unclear whether Mr. Jackson's wife, Mrs. Goss' sister, also lives in High Point and whether Mr. Jackson or Mrs. Jackson was approached and asked to serve as fiduciary. Under the laws of intestacy of North Carolina, Mrs. Goss, Barbara Jean's mother, is the sole beneficiary of any proceeds that might be recovered in the wrongful death action. McAllister, the aunt serving as administratrix, will not receive any of the recovery.

The client prefers to litigate this case in state court and has asked us to determine if the federal court will dismiss the case as an "improper or collusive" joinder of parties under 28 U.S.C. § 1359 (1982).

Question Presented:

Where a nonresident administratrix is appointed to bring a wrongful death case in federal court against a resident defendant, is related to the deceased, but has no stake in the outcome of the case, does the federal court lack subject matter jurisdiction under title 28, section 1359 of the United States Code?

Conclusion:

Since the decision of a landmark case in the 1960s, the courts have liberally interpreted title 28, section 1359 and held that an appointment of a nonresident fiduciary to invoke the diversity jurisdiction of the federal court violates the statute and deprives the court of subject matter jurisdiction. Under that view, the *motive* to get into federal court, without some other legitimate reason supporting the fiduciary's appointment, is fatal and the case will be dismissed. Other cases have emphasized the *stake* the fiduciary has in the proceedings. If the fiduciary has any financial or other legal stake in the case, then the desire to get into federal court is irrelevant, and the provisions of the statute are satisfied.

Here, getting the case dismissed depends to a great degree on which view the court uses. The Fourth Circuit relies primarily on the *stake in the outcome* test and tends to downplay the role of motive. Thus, even though the administratrix is related to the deceased and to the beneficiary of the wrongful death claim, she stands to gain no interest in any potential damage award. On this ground alone, the case might well be dismissed.

The record is silent on the issue of motive and on the availability of other persons who could have served as administrator. If we can show the availability of other candidates—the mother or the resident uncle or perhaps a resident aunt—then the arguments for dismissal grow ever stronger.

Discussion of Authority:

Several legal situations allow the beneficial parties of a lawsuit to pick the plaintiff to prosecute the action. Guardians must be appointed to represent the interests of minors in court. When an accident causes the death of a person, an administrator must be appointed to prosecute any wrongful death claim. Often, the parties standing to gain from such actions will appoint a nonresident plaintiff to pursue an otherwise local action against a resident defendant. The nonresident plaintiff then uses his diverse citizenship to pursue the action in federal court, invoking the court's diversity of citizenship jurisdiction.

Such appointments have traditionally been attacked as "collusive," made only to confer jurisdiction on a federal district court. The defendant can seek to have the case dismissed as a violation of title 28, section 1359 of the United States Code:

> A district court shall not have jurisdiction of a civil action in which any party, by assignment or otherwise, has been improperly or collusively made or joined to invoke the jurisdiction of such court.

Before 1968, the federal courts routinely held that the motive to get into federal court was irrelevant in finding a violation of the statute. "Collusion," under the old view, had to rise to the level of fraud. However, in 1968, the courts overruled the old view and held that motive was a relevant factor in determining the validity of the appointment of a nonresident fiduciary. Since that time, the courts have adjudicated a host of cases involving appointments of nonresident administrators. Though appointing a nonresident by itself does not violate the statute, the courts look disfavorably on such appointments and insist on *legitimate considerations* supporting the appointment. Chief among these considerations are the stake the administrator has in the outcome of the case, other duties the administrator must undertake, the availability of other candidates who could have been appointed, and particularly stressful family situations. Most circuits seem to emphasize *motive* as the key factor in a section 1359 analysis, whereas at least one circuit—the Fourth—has moved away from motive and has emphasized *stake in the outcome* as the decisive factor.

The leading case espousing the old view was *Corabi v. Auto Racing, Inc.*, 264 F.2d 784 (3d Cir. 1959). In that case, the mother of a deceased child resigned as administratrix so that a nonresident administrator could bring a wrongful death case in federal court. The Third Circuit, sitting en banc, unanimously held that such an appointment did not constitute collusion under section 1359. Such collusion, according to the court, must be between plaintiff and defendant. The mere motive to get into federal court did not rise to the level of the collusion prohibited by the statute.

In 1968, the Third Circuit overruled *Corabi* in the landmark decision of *McSparran v. Weist*, 402 F.2d 868 (3d Cir. 1968), *cert. denied*, 395 U.S. 903 (1969). *McSparran* involved the appointment of a nonresident guardian to sue a resident defendant for damages sustained by a resident minor. The mother of the minor and other interested parties admitted that they appointed the nonresident to create diversity jurisdiction so that they could prosecute the case in federal court. The Third Circuit, again sitting en banc, expressly overruled *Corabi* and stated that the motive of the parties was

> not irrelevant in the determination of the question whether the fiduciary is in fact a straw fiduciary whose citizenship is to be disregarded. Moreover, it is difficult to see how motive can be entirely ignored in ascertaining the purpose for which the representative is selected in view of the language of 1359.

Id. at 874. Thus, *motive,* which was once irrelevant, now became "not irrelevant" in determining whether a nonresident administrator had been improperly or collusively named. *Motive,* therefore, could not be "entirely ignored."

McSparran was not grounded solely on *motive,* however. The court also analyzed the *function* of the appointed fiduciary. In the case before it, the court found that the guardian had no duties to perform other than to lend her name and citizenship to the contemplated litigation. In the words of the court: "[T]he artificial selection of a straw representative who has no duty or function except to offer the use of his citizenship to create diversity in contemplated litigation is a violation of [section 1359]." *Id.* at 875.

Since the decision in *McSparran,* the issue of manufactured diversity of citizenship has been adjudicated by many district and circuit courts. At present, the courts seem to have taken the *McSparran* case and cut it in two. Some courts—particularly the Fourth Circuit—stress the *stake* or *function* of the nonresident fiduciary whereas others emphasize the importance of the *motive* prompting the nonresident's appointment. The *stake* courts look to the duties of the fiduciary and, finding few or none, will dismiss the case. The *motive* courts insist on evidence of intent to manufacture diversity of citizenship. Because the evidence in the current case is incomplete on the issue of motive and because motive can often be difficult to prove, we should urge the continued application of the *stake* test in the Fourth Circuit. Applying that test to the current case should prompt the district court to dismiss for lack of subject matter jurisdiction.

One of the leading decisions supporting the *stake* test is *Bishop v. Hendricks,* 495 F.2d 289 (4th Cir.), *cert. denied,* 419 U.S. 1056 (1974), whose facts are quite similar to those in the current case. There, an out-of-state administrator, related to the statutory beneficiaries by marriage, was appointed to bring a wrongful death action against an instate defendant. The deceased in that case left no estate to administer, so the sole function of the administrator was to pass along any wrongful death recovery to the statutory beneficiaries. The Fourth Circuit upheld the lower court's dismissal of the action as a violation of section 1359 and rejected the administrator's contention that *motive* was the dispositive factor in finding a violation of the statute. On the contrary, according to the Fourth Circuit, *motive* plays only a minor role in a section 1359 analysis. Instead, the focus is on the role and duties of the fiduciary.

Under the *stake in the outcome* test, those duties must be "substantial." Indeed, in cases like the current case, "where an out-of-state administrator files a wrongful death action on behalf of resident beneficiaries, involving the death of a resident decedent in an accident occurring within the state, *want of diversity will be presumed* unless the record provides sufficient support for the conclusion that the representation of the administrator is not nominal but was based on a valid and substantial reason." *Id.* at 293 (emphasis added). In a very telling phrase, the court went on to say that "for the reason or motive for the appointment to give the necessary substantiality to his representation that his citizenship will be regarded for diversity it must be more than an expression of sentiment or personal preference or mere kinship with either the beneficiaries or decedent." *Id.* A sufficient reason or motive "must be one that harmonizes with the thrust and purposes of Section 1359 itself." *Id.*

Put another way, *motives* or *reasons* for an out-of-state appointment under *Bishop*'s *stake in the outcome* test must be *pure motives* and they must "elevate his relationship to the litigation above the level of a nominal party...." *Id.* at 295. Unavailing reasons include "the fact that the beneficiaries are prostrated by grief, or are related to the out-of-state administrator, or are relying on the administrator for advice or that the out-of-state administrator is 'a competent business man'...." *Id.*

It is difficult to imagine what reasons or motives other than those described by *Bishop* as "unavailing" could be cited by the plaintiff in the current case to justify her appointment as administratrix. Her relationship to the decedent is not enough. Her relationship to the statutory beneficiary is not enough. Her expertise as a business woman is not enough. The understandable grief of the mother is not enough. Perhaps the mother's current drinking problem could justify her resignation and appointment of someone else, but the facts do not show why the other instate relatives were passed over in favor of the nonresident aunt. And most importantly, any conceivable reason cannot hide the total lack of duties expected of this out-of-state administratrix. Her only role is to lend her name to the wrongful death litigation.

The *Bishop* approach was severely criticized by the Fifth Circuit in recent case of *Bianca v. Parke-Davis Pharmaceutical Division of Warner-Lambert Co.*, 723 F.2d 392 (5th Cir. 1984). That case, like the current case, involved a wrongful death action to recover for the death of an eleven-year-old girl. The child's parents, understandably distraught, were, in the words of the court, "psychologically unable" to pursue the wrongful death claim and procured the appointment of the mother's sister, who resided in a nearby, but out-of-state town. The trial court dismissed the action because the administratrix had no stake in the outcome of the action and was appointed solely to bring the wrongful death action. The Fifth Circuit reversed, criticized *Bishop*'s *stake in the outcome* test, and held that the crucial factor in finding a violation of section 1359 is the improper *motive* of manufacturing diversity of citizenship. The court rejected the *stake* test in no uncertain terms:

> We conclude that the "substantial stake" test cannot be justified under the language of 1359. The statutory interdict against jurisdiction where a party "has been improperly or collusively made or joined *to invoke* the jurisdiction" of the federal courts (emphasis added) incontrovertably suggests to us that the motive underlying the naming of the administrator must guide the diversity inquiry. If an out-of-state administrator has not been selected with the purpose of manufacturing diversity, the administrator's lack of a stake in the outcome of the litigation cannot alone trigger 1359's jurisdictional bar.

Id. at 398.

The court explained its previous decisions to clear up any misconception that *stake in the outcome* was the key factor in a section 1359 analysis. The court pointed out that some previous cases involved fact situations where the parties did not admit that the motive prompting the out-of-state appointment was the maufacture of diversity jurisdiction. In such cases, the court pointed out, district courts should look to a variety of factors to determine factually whether section 1359 had been violated. Those factors included:

> "the relationship of the representative to the party represented;
> the scope of the representative's powers and duties; any special
> capacity or experience which the representative may possess
> with respect to the purpose of his appointment; whether there
> exists a nondiverse individual who might more normally be
> expected to represent the interests at stake; whether those
> seeking the appointment of the representative express any
> particular reasons for selecting an out-of-state person; and
> whether, apart from the appointment of an out-of-state repre-
> sentative, the suit is one wholly local in nature."

Id. at 395, *quoting Green V. Hale*, 433 F.2d 324, 325 (5th Cir. 1970).

Thus, according to *Bianca*, the key is *motive*, which must be an *impure motive*, a motive to manufacture diversity to invoke the jurisdiction of the federal court. Whereas in *Bishop, pure motives* may show the necessary *stake* to satisfy the statute, in *Bianca* the *stake* may show the absence of *impure motives* to satisfy the statute. These factors, without direct evidence of improper motive, may be used by the district court to find a violation of the statute.

In the current case, if the Fourth Circuit should decide to retreat from its *stake* test and use the *motive* test of *Bianca*, the district court still should dismiss the case as a violation of section 1359. Assuming we can obtain no direct evidence of motive to gain access to federal court, the factors listed above tend to favor dismissal. Though the parties are related, the "scope of powers and duties" is limited to passing along any recovery to the sole statutory beneficiary. Because the decedent's estate has already been administered, the administratrix' expertise as a business woman is totally unnecessary. Also, the nondiverse uncle or his wife, who reside in High Point, could serve as administrator or administratrix. Finally, the suit is a North Carolinian affair. The accident happened in North Carolina. The parties reside in North Carolina. The witnesses are North Carolinians. The recovery will be distributed in North Carolina. The state of Virginia is involved only because the parties appointed a Virginian in the first place.

Regardless of which test applies in the current case, other factors the courts consider seem to weigh in on the side of dismissal. All the courts since *McSparran* have stressed the policy of diversity of citizenship jurisdiction in analyzing the thrust and purpose of section 1359. *McSparran* itself, in holding that section 1359 was violated, noted that "one of the reasons underlying diversity jurisdiction, the prevention of discrimination against out-of-state litigants, is completely absent." *McSparran v. Weist*, 402 F.2d at 876. *Bishop* echoed this view by saying:

> To permit the appointment of a nominal non-resident fiduciary to create federal diversity jurisdiction would clearly "run counter to the general policy of viewing the federal courts as tribunals of limited jurisdiction whose subject matter jurisdiction principles should be applied with restraint," and, through its artificial creation of diversity, would represent an "improper manufacture of jurisdiction" in obvious violation of the purposes of Section 1359. [Citations omitted.]

Bishop v. Hendricks, 495 F.2d at 292-93.

Certainly in the present case, it would be irrational to be concerned about local bias, appoint a nonresident who might bear the brunt of local bias, and then usher her into federal court in order to protect her from that local bias. If protection from local bias is the worry, then suing in state court with an instate administrator as plaintiff is the perfect solution.

As another factor, many cases have considered the impact of appointing a relative of the beneficiaries. Though family relationship can play some role in determining the validity of the appointment under section 1359, the factor alone is not dispositive. In *Bishop*, for example, the administrator was related to the decedent by marriage. According to the court, however, "mere kinship" was not enough. *Bishop v. Hendricks*, 495 F.2d at 293. "[T]he fact that the beneficiaries . . . are related to the out-of-state administrator . . . will not justify diversity based on the administrator's citizenship." *Id.* at 295. In wrongful death actions, of course, those who stand to gain from any tort recovery typically are family members. At least one court has stated that such a family member appointed to serve as administrator will be "immune from challenge" under section 1359. *Hackney v. Newman Memorial Hospital, Inc.*, 621 F.2d 1069, 1071 (10th Cir. 1980). *Hackney*, of course, can be explained as merely supporting the *stake in the outcome* standard of *Bishop*, rather than establishing family membership as the significant factor in a section 1359 analysis. If family membership alone would justify an out-of-state appointment, then section 1359 could be easily thwarted, for it is the rare American family that lacks some out-of-state relative.

The new rule of *McSparran* does not preclude the appointment of any nonresident administrator or guardian to bring otherwise local cases in federal court. *McSparran* itself left the door open for such appointments by declaring that section 1359 "does not ban the appointment of nonresident fiduciaries . . . ." *McSparran v. Weist*, 402 F.2d at 874-75. The Third Circuit, just two years after the *McSparran* decision, confronted a case where the appointment of a nonresident did not offend the collusive joinder provisions of section 1359. In *Joyce v. Siegel*, 429 F.2d 128 (3d Cir. 1970), decedent, a resident of Pennsylvania, was killed in an automobile accident. A year earlier, decedent's wife, named as executrix in decedent's will, had predeceased him. His father-in-law, named as alternate executor, was ill and died a short time after decedent's death. Decedent's mother was ill and distressed over the accidental death of decedent's father a short time before decedent's death. Other instate family members were engaged in battles over the custody of decedent's three children. To serve as administrator and to administer decedent's $50,000 estate, decedent's out-of-state uncle was chosen. As plaintiff, he instituted a diversity action against an instate defendant. The Third Circuit upheld the appointment as supported by *legitimate considerations*:

> His residence and citizenship outside of Pennsylvania was the reason for his selection, but this was because it freed him from close involvement in the family's personal problems, and his selection for this reason and because he was experienced in financial affairs was quite different from an effort to create artificial diversity. In these circumstances the plaintiff was entitled to select the federal courts for the decision of the claim against defendant, and the action should therefore go forward in the district court where it was brought.

Id. at 130.

When the district court considers all these factors and analyzes the situation in the current case, it should be persuaded to dismiss this action as a violation of section 1359. Certainly if the *stake* test of *Bishop* continues in the Fourth Circuit, the case should be dismissed. The assets of the decedent have already been distributed to the sole statutory beneficiary—the mother. Nothing remains for the administratrix to do. She has no stake in this proceeding. She has nothing to gain from its successful completion. She can only lend her name to the proceedings and her citizenship to the complaint to support an allegation of diversity.

Furthermore, even if the *motive* test of *Bianca* should prevail or make inroads on the *stake* test, the court still should dismiss the suit. Though additional investigation might fail to uncover direct evidence of the *impure motive* of manufacturing diversity jurisdiction, the factors mentioned in *Bianca*, which can show improper motive, seem to weigh heavily in the defendant's favor. Next, though the current administratrix is the sister of the statutory beneficiary, *Bishop* made it abundantly clear that a familial relationship is not enough. And unlike *Hackney*, the family member here is not a statutory beneficiary who stands to collect part of the proceeds of any wrongful death recovery. Finally, the turmoil of the mother's drinking problem and understandable grief does not come close to approaching the level of turmoil experienced by the family in *Joyce*. Even if it did, the administrator in *Joyce* had substantial duties to perform in administering a $50,000 estate. Here, the estate has been administered. All that remains is picking a plaintiff to bring a wrongful death case. That duty alone is clearly not the kind contemplated by the courts. Indeed, that duty alone should show the *impropriety* of the current appointment. For these reasons, the case should be dismissed.

The End

Nunc est bibendum, nunc pede libero
Pulsanda tellus.

Now for drinks, now for some dancing with a good beat.

—Horace

Absolute, as clause substitute, 109

Abstract Words, avoiding, 135

Action Verb, transitive or intransitive, 118

Active Voice, defined and discussed, 117-29; formation, 122; grammatical analysis of style, 5, 7

Adjective Appositive, as clause substitute, 108

Adjective Clause, clause-cutting, 106-10; defined, 90

Adjective, as clause substitute, 107; device of modification, 136; prepositional phrase, 74; verb used as, 52

Adverb Clause, clause-cutting, 106-10; defined, 98-99

Adverb, as clause substitute, 107; device of modification, 136; nouny expressions of, 53-54; prepositional phrase, 74; relationship to intransitive verbs, 12, 14; split infinitives, 30-31

Antecedent, pronoun agreement with, 141-43

Application of Law to Facts, 192-93

Appositive, adjective, as clause substitute, 108; art of subordination, 24-26; noun clause used as, 92; noun function, 91; noun, as clause substitute, 108

Auxiliary Verb, nouny expressions of, 53-55; use in verb conjugation, 28-29; use of *to be*, 65

Bad Writing, grammatical analysis of style, 4

Because, beginning a sentence, 111-12

Bianca v. Parke-Davis Pharmaceutical Division of Warner-Lambert Co., 156; text of opinion, 213-30

Bishop v. Hendricks, 156; text of opinion, 220-26

Black, Justice Hugo, example of good writing, 5-6, 15, 34

Boolean Logic, rules of tabulation, 37

Brackets, use in quotation, 188-89

Brief Answer, in Memorandum of Law, 165

Caption, format of Memorandum of Law, 158

Cardozo, Justice Benjamin, example of good writing, 27

Case, possessive case used to modify gerund, 104; *who* vs. *whom*, 97-98

Case Discussion, in Memorandum of Law, 181-84

Choppiness, subordination as cure, 24-25

Citing & Typing the Law, rules on quotation, 187-89

Clause, defined, 25, 86-87; dependent, 86-87; independent, 86; noun clause as object of preposition, 75; noun clause starters, 89

Cognitive Verb, retaining *that*, 110

Comma, restrictive and non-restrictive clauses, 96

Commager, Henry Steele, *The American Mind*, 67

Complex Verb, gaps, 28-29

Compound Preposition, compost of language, 73-81; criticized by Fowler, 76; defined, 75-76; grammatical analysis of style, 5; list of compound prepositions, 78-79; nouny expressions, 55

Conclusion, in Memorandum of Law, 165-66

Concrete Words, preferring, 135

Conjugated Verb, defined, 49; examples, 28-29; relationship to the problem of gaps, 28-29; use in sentences, 13-15

Conjugation, active voice, 121; passive voice, 121-22

Conjunction, rule of parallelism, 33

Content, in legal writing, 166-95

Coordinating Conjunction, defined, 33; distinguished from subordinating conjunction, 87

Correlative Conjunction, defined, 33; distinguished from subordinating conjunction, 87

Dangling Participle, defined, 51

Demonstrative Pronouns, as transitional devices, 191-92

Denounification, the cure to wordiness, 47, 53; *to be* and nouny expressions, 66

Dependent Clause, conjugated verb, 49; defined, 86; three myths, 111-13; use of verb, 13

Derivative Adjective, defined, relationship to nouniness, 47

Derivative Noun, converting to verbs, 53; defined, relationship to nouniness, 47

Direct Object, active voice, 118; noun clause used as, 92; noun function, 90; use in sentences, 14

Discussion of Authority, in Memorandum of Law, 166-95

Easterbrook, Judge Frank, use of verbs, 56-57

Ellipsis Signal, 188-89

Expletive, construction of *to be*, 68

Format, of Memorandum of Law, 158-59; sample, 159

Fowler, Henry, *Modern English Usage*, xxi; compound prepositions, 76; long words, 134; nouniness, 47-48; nouny abstractions, 135; split infinitives, 31

Future Perfect Tense, function of verbs, 49

Future Tense, function of verbs, 49

Gaps, examples, 27-32

Gault, In re, example of paragraphing, 177

Gender, pronoun agreement with antecedent, 141-43

Gerund, as noun clause-cutting device, 102-103; as object of preposition, 75; functions of verbs, 50; with compound preposition, 78

Go, go like talk, 62-64

Grammar, analysis of style, 7

Grammatical Sentence, defined, 44; distinguished from typographical sentence, 44

Grandmother's House Syndrome, inverting sentences, 24

Groped-for Verb, used in nouny constructions, 46-47

Hackney v. Newman Memorial Hospital, Inc., 156; text of opinion, 211-13

Harvard Bluebook, rules on quotation, 186-87

He/she, nonsexist writing, 141-44

Health Care Financing Administration, workshop by the author, 62

Helping Verb, use in verb conjugation, 28-29

Him/her, nonsexist writing, 141-44

His/hermaphrodism, nonsexist writing, 141-44

Impact, as transitive verb, 120

Indented Quotations, 186-87

Independent Clause, conjugated verb, 49; defined, 86; use of verb, 13

Indirect Object, noun clause used as, 92; noun function, 90

Infinitive Phrase, as clause substitute, 107-108; defined, 33; functions of verbs, 50; in parallel form, 35; in passive voice, 124; split infinitive rule, 30-31

Internal Revenue Service, training program developed by the author, 3-4

Intransitive Verb, active vs. passive voice, 118-20; defined, 12

Introduction, function in legal writing, 174-76

Inversion, changing order of sentence, 23-24

Joyce v. Siegel, 156; text of opinion, 208-10

Law Review Articles, in Memorandum of Law, 184-85

Legal Comparisons, 193-94

Legislative Presentation, paraphrasing and quoting, 179-81; within Introduction, 175

Like, go like talk, 62-64

Linking Verb, use in sentences, 13

Long Words, avoiding, 133-35; grammatical analysis of style, 5

Long-Winded Sentence Syndrome, sentence length, 16

Lowercase, in tabulated list, 36

Main Verb, defined as conjugated verb, 13, 49; examples, 28-29

McSparren v. Weist, 156; text of opinion, 199-208

Memorandum of Law, format, 158-59; purpose, 157-58

Message, one per sentence, 16-21

Modification, device to prevent wordiness, 136-37

Monosyllabic Words, grammatical analysis of style, 5, 6

Nelson, Willie, use of verbs, 55

Nevada v. Hall, example of paragraphing, 178

No, avoiding negative expressions, 137

Nonrestrictive Clause, defined, 93-98

Nonrestrictive Phrase, punctuation, 108

Not, avoiding negative expressions, 137

Not-Too-Many-Thoughts-Per-Sentence Rule, 16-21; gaps, 26

Noun Appositive, as clause substitute, 109

Noun Clause, clause-cutting, 100-105; defined, 90-93

Noun, clauses used as, 92; eight grammatical functions, 90-91; prepositional phrase, 74; used as modifier, 137

Nouniness, defined, 44-45

Number, pronoun agreement with antecedent, 141-43

Object Complement, noun clause used as, 92; noun function, 91

Object of Preposition, in parallel form, 35; noun clause used as, 89; noun function, 45-46, 91

Object of Verbal Phrase, noun clause used as, 92; noun function, 91

Object, of infinitive phrase, 50; of present participial phrase, 50-51; of preposition, 73; of transitive verb, problem of gaps, 29-30

Objective Case, of pronouns, 97-98

One, as subject of sentence, use of passive voice to avoid, 126

Organizational Devices, case-by-case approach, 170-71; definitional approach, 123-24; in Memorandum of Law, 168-74; historical approach, 169-70; issue-by-issue approach, 171-73; theory-by-theory approach, 173; type-of-law approach, 168-69; yes-no approach, 170

Paragraphing, 176-79

Parallel Construction, grammatical analysis of style, 6; rule of grammar and style, 32-35

Passive Voice, clause cut to phrase, 107-108; defined and discussed, 117-28; criticized, 124-26; formation, 122-24; grammatical analysis of style, 5, 6, 8; use of *to be*, 65

Past Participial Phrase, as clause substitute, 107-108; functions of verbs, 51-52

Past Participle, role in passive voice, 122-24

Past Perfect Tense, function of verbs, 49

Past Tense, function of verbs, 49; main or conjugated verb, 49

Perfect Tenses, use of past participles, 51-52

Phrase, defined, 25; present participial, 26, 50-51; past participial, 51-52

Polysyllabic Words, grammatical analysis of style, 5

Possessive Case, pronoun modifying gerund, 104

Predicate Adjective, defined, 13-15; function of *to be*, 64-65

Predicate Nominative, defined, 13-15; function of *to be*, 64

Predicate Verb, conjugated verb, 49; use in sentences, 13-15; examples, 28-29

Preposition, compound, 73-80; defined, 73; list of simple prepositions, 79-80; defined, 45; ending a sentence or clause, 97; subordinating conjunction used as, 88

Prepositional Phrase, as clause substitute, 107; defined, 73; in parallel form, 35; noun function, 45-46; uses, 74-75

Present Participial Phrase, art of subordination, 26; as clause substitute, 107-108; defined, 29; functions of verbs, 50-51; in passive voice, 124

Present Perfect Tense, function of verbs, 49

Present Tense, function of verbs, 49; main or conjugated verb, 49

Progressive Tense, examples, 28-29; clause cut to phrase,

107-108; function of verbs, 49; use of *to be*, 65

Punctuation, restrictive and nonrestrictive clauses, 96; restrictive and nonrestrictive phrases, 108

Question Presented, in Memorandum of Law, 164-65

Quotation, 185-89; introduction, 185; length, 186; traps to avoid, 186

Reaching the Final Result, 194-96

Real Estate Classified Ad Syndrome, inverting sentences, 24

Regulatory Presentation, paraphrasing and quoting, 179-81

Relative Pronoun, adjective clause starter, 88-89

Restrictive Clause, defined, 93-98

Restrictive Phrase, punctuation, 108

Secondary Authority, law review articles and treatises, 184-85

Securities & Exchange Commission, workshop by the author, 61

Sentence Structure, four structures, 14, 21-22, 25; length, 6, 15-16; main message rule, 21-23; too many thoughts, 16-21

(S)he, nonsexist writing, 141-44

Short Words, preferring, 133-35

Since, meaning *because*, 112

Split Infinitive, the no-split rule, 30-31

Statement of Facts, in Memorandum of Law, 160-61; sample fact pattern, 161-64

Strunk & White, *The Elements of Style*, xxi; long words, 134; passive voice, 124; *the fact that*, 91

Subject Complement, defined, 13-15; function of *to be*, 64; noun clause used as, 92; noun function, 91

Subject, function in active or passive voice, 121; inversion, 23-24; noun clause used as, 92; noun function, 91; of sentence, 13

Subject-Predicate Rule, main message, 21-23

Subject-Verb Gap, defined, 27-28

Subjective Case, of pronouns, 97

Subordinating Conjunction, defined, 33; use with adverb clause, 98; use with dependent clause, 87-88

Subordination, cure for choppiness, 24-25

Tabulation, to present complex information, 36-39

Tense, main or conjugated verb, 49; to show time, 27; verb conjugation in active voice, 122; verb conjugation in passive voice, 123

That and *Which*, confused, 93-98

That, gaps in clause, 31-32; grammatical analysis of style, 6; omitted in clause, 110-11; relative pronoun used with adjective clause, 93-98; to modify generic person, 98

Their, plural, genderless pronoun, 141-44

Them, plural, genderless pronoun, 141-44

They, plural, genderless pronoun, 141-44

Thomas Payne Syndrome, subordinating main message, 22

To Be, as auxiliary verb, 28-29; in noun clause, 105; inversion, 24; meaning, 64-65; proper use, 61-69; role in passive voice, 122-24; use in sentences, 13

Topic Sentence, 176-79

Transition, sticking paragraphs and sentences together, 190-92

Transitive Verb, active vs. passive voice, 118-20; defined, 12; gap between verb and object, 29-30

Treatises, in Memorandum of Law, 184-85

Truncated Adverb Clause, as clause substitute, 109-10

Typographical Sentence, defined, 44; distinguished from grammatical sentence, 44

Verb Conjugation, relationship to the problem of gaps, 27

Verb, groped-for verb, used in nouny constructions, 46-47; transitive vs. intransitive, 118-20; use in clause, 86

Verbal, functions of verbs, 49-52

Verbal Phrase, as clause substitute, 107-108

Voice, active and passive, 117-28

Walpole, Jane, *The Writer's Grammar Guide*, 44

Which and *That*, confused, 93-98

Which, grammatical analysis of style, 6; relative pronoun used with adjective clause, 93-98

While, meaning *although*, 113

Who, relative pronoun starting clause, 91-92; relative pronoun used with adjective clause, 93-98

Whom, relative pronoun starting clause, 97; relative pronoun used with adjective clause, 93-98

Whose, relative pronoun starting clause, 98; relative pronoun used with adjective clause, 93-98

Wordiness, modification as cure, 136-37; nouniness as cause, 47-48

Wydick, Richard, *Plain English for Lawyers*, 52